Letters to Edward Gibbon, Esq. ... By George Travis, ... The second edition, corrected, and considerably enlarged.

George Travis

Letters to Edward Gibbon, Esq. ... By George Travis, ... The second edition, corrected, and considerably enlarged.

Travis, George

ESTCID: T130532

Reproduction from Huntington Library

The Appendix and Index are each separately signed and paginated.

London : printed, and sold, by C.F. and J. Rivington, 1785.

vi,[2],376;61,[1];ivp. ; 8°

Eighteenth Century
Collections Online
Print Editions

Gale ECCO Print Editions

Relive history with *Eighteenth Century Collections Online*, now available in print for the independent historian and collector. This series includes the most significant English-language and foreign-language works printed in Great Britain during the eighteenth century, and is organized in seven different subject areas including literature and language; medicine, science, and technology; and religion and philosophy. The collection also includes thousands of important works from the Americas.

The eighteenth century has been called "The Age of Enlightenment." It was a period of rapid advance in print culture and publishing, in world exploration, and in the rapid growth of science and technology – all of which had a profound impact on the political and cultural landscape. At the end of the century the American Revolution, French Revolution and Industrial Revolution, perhaps three of the most significant events in modern history, set in motion developments that eventually dominated world political, economic, and social life.

In a groundbreaking effort, Gale initiated a revolution of its own: digitization of epic proportions to preserve these invaluable works in the largest online archive of its kind. Contributions from major world libraries constitute over 175,000 original printed works. Scanned images of the actual pages, rather than transcriptions, recreate the works *as they first appeared.*

Now for the first time, these high-quality digital scans of original works are available via print-on-demand, making them readily accessible to libraries, students, independent scholars, and readers of all ages.

For our initial release we have created seven robust collections to form one the world's most comprehensive catalogs of 18th century works.

Initial Gale ECCO Print Editions collections include:

History and Geography
Rich in titles on English life and social history, this collection spans the world as it was known to eighteenth-century historians and explorers. Titles include a wealth of travel accounts and diaries, histories of nations from throughout the world, and maps and charts of a world that was still being discovered. Students of the War of American Independence will find fascinating accounts from the British side of conflict.

Social Science
Delve into what it was like to live during the eighteenth century by reading the first-hand accounts of everyday people, including city dwellers and farmers, businessmen and bankers, artisans and merchants, artists and their patrons, politicians and their constituents. Original texts make the American, French, and Industrial revolutions vividly contemporary.

Medicine, Science and Technology
Medical theory and practice of the 1700s developed rapidly, as is evidenced by the extensive collection, which includes descriptions of diseases, their conditions, and treatments. Books on science and technology, agriculture, military technology, natural philosophy, even cookbooks, are all contained here.

Literature and Language
Western literary study flows out of eighteenth-century works by Alexander Pope, Daniel Defoe, Henry Fielding, Frances Burney, Denis Diderot, Johann Gottfried Herder, Johann Wolfgang von Goethe, and others. Experience the birth of the modern novel, or compare the development of language using dictionaries and grammar discourses.

Religion and Philosophy
The Age of Enlightenment profoundly enriched religious and philosophical understanding and continues to influence present-day thinking. Works collected here include masterpieces by David Hume, Immanuel Kant, and Jean-Jacques Rousseau, as well as religious sermons and moral debates on the issues of the day, such as the slave trade. The Age of Reason saw conflict between Protestantism and Catholicism transformed into one between faith and logic -- a debate that continues in the twenty-first century.

Law and Reference
This collection reveals the history of English common law and Empire law in a vastly changing world of British expansion. Dominating the legal field is the *Commentaries of the Law of England* by Sir William Blackstone, which first appeared in 1765. Reference works such as almanacs and catalogues continue to educate us by revealing the day-to-day workings of society.

Fine Arts
The eighteenth-century fascination with Greek and Roman antiquity followed the systematic excavation of the ruins at Pompeii and Herculaneum in southern Italy; and after 1750 a neoclassical style dominated all artistic fields. The titles here trace developments in mostly English-language works on painting, sculpture, architecture, music, theater, and other disciplines. Instructional works on musical instruments, catalogs of art objects, comic operas, and more are also included.

The BiblioLife Network

This project was made possible in part by the BiblioLife Network (BLN), a project aimed at addressing some of the huge challenges facing book preservationists around the world. The BLN includes libraries, library networks, archives, subject matter experts, online communities and library service providers. We believe every book ever published should be available as a high-quality print reproduction; printed on-demand anywhere in the world. This insures the ongoing accessibility of the content and helps generate sustainable revenue for the libraries and organizations that work to preserve these important materials.

The following book is in the "public domain" and represents an authentic reproduction of the text as printed by the original publisher. While we have attempted to accurately maintain the integrity of the original work, there are sometimes problems with the original work or the micro-film from which the books were digitized. This can result in minor errors in reproduction. Possible imperfections include missing and blurred pages, poor pictures, markings and other reproduction issues beyond our control. Because this work is culturally important, we have made it available as part of our commitment to protecting, preserving, and promoting the world's literature.

GUIDE TO FOLD-OUTS MAPS and OVERSIZED IMAGES

The book you are reading was digitized from microfilm captured over the past thirty to forty years. Years after the creation of the original microfilm, the book was converted to digital files and made available in an online database.

In an online database, page images do not need to conform to the size restrictions found in a printed book. When converting these images back into a printed bound book, the page sizes are standardized in ways that maintain the detail of the original. For large images, such as fold-out maps, the original page image is split into two or more pages

Guidelines used to determine how to split the page image follows:

• Some images are split vertically; large images require vertical and horizontal splits.
• For horizontal splits, the content is split left to right.
• For vertical splits, the content is split from top to bottom.
• For both vertical and horizontal splits, the image is processed from top left to bottom right.

LETTERS

TO

EDWARD GIBBON, Esq.

AUTHOR OF THE HISTORY

OF THE

DECLINE, AND FALL,

OF THE ROMAN EMPIRE.

By GEORGE TRAVIS, A.M.

PREBENDARY OF CHESTER, AND VICAR OF EASTHAM.

THE SECOND EDITION,
CORRECTED, AND CONSIDERABLY ENLARGED.

LONDON:
PRINTED, AND SOLD, BY C. F. AND J. RIVINGTON,
ST PAUL'S CHURCH-YARD.
MDCCLXXXV.

ADVERTISEMENT.

AS the prefent edition of thefe LETTERS de-
viates, in many refpects, from the former;
it will be thought neceffary, perhaps, that fome
account fhould here be given of fome, at leaft, of
thofe deviations.

1. The LETTERS are, now, FIVE, in number;
and they are all addreffed to Mr. GIBBON, who
was the occafion of them all.

The *firft* of them is introductory to the general
fubject : which is—A VINDICATION OF THE AU-
THENTICITY OF THE VERSE, 1. JOHN, v. 7 (*a*)

The *fecond* contains all the POSITIVE evidence,
which the author has adduced *directly* in proof of
that authenticity. Many other proofs are urged
thereto, *indirectly*, as it were, or *collaterally*, in the
three fubfequent letters. (*b*)

The *third* ftates, and replies to, the objections,
which

(*a*) Pages 1—16.
(*b*) —— 17—57.

which Dr. BENSON has brought against the authenticity of this contested passage (c)

The *fourth* is employed in considering the objections of Sir ISAAC NEWTON, M. GRIESBACH, and Mr. BOWYER. (d)

The *fifth* (e) attends to the THREE, principal, objections, which are, or may be, alledged against this disputed text: and sums up the whole argument, applying it particularly to Mr. *Gibbon*.

In the three Letters, last mentioned, many allegations, against this verse, are occasionally answered, which have been brought by M. SIMON, EMLYN, MICHAELIS, WETSTEIN, LA CROZE, and LE LONG.

2. Two mistakes, contained in the former edition of these Letters, are now rectified. The former respected the *first* publication of *Valla*'s Commentary by ERASMUS; which happened in A D. 1505, and not in A. D. 1526, as erroneously stated in that edition. The latter related to some portions of Scripture; which it was then said that BEDE had not noted in his Commentary.

But,

(c) Pages 59—221.
(d) ——— 222—314.
(e) ——— 315—376.

But, fortunately, thefe errors do not, properly, belong to the author of this Treatife. He confided the examination of the ONLY edition of *Valla*'s Commentary in 1505, which is, perhaps, to be found in ENGLAND, (if not in EUROPE) and which is in the *Bodleian* Repofitory, to the care of one who was difinterested in this enquiry, and competent to that examination. And he pofitively and repeatedly, but (it appeared at length) miftakenly, affirmed, that ERASMUS was NOT the editor of that publication! The other miftake arofe in the fame manner. It was impoffible to rectify thefe mif ftatements in the former edition, becaufe it was publifhed long before they were difcovered.

It is moft fortunate, however, that thefe involuntary errors do NOT, at all, affect the great queftion, difcuffed in thefe Letters. The original infertion of them was an unintentional offence in the author. Their expulfion has not enfeebled, or impaired, his argument.

To thofe who have honored the former edition of thefe LETTERS with their approbation, the author will venture to fubmit the prefent with fome confidence as being his unworthy of their protection To thofe, who have (in any manner, known to the author of thefe pages) mingled their indulgence with reprehenfion,—he begs to prefent his

his thankful acknowledgments for BOTH. The one may have been honorable to him; the other has been advantageous. They will find that he has, in general, not rejected their strictures, but hath profited by them, wheresoever they were just. (f)

TRUTH is the sole aim, object, and end, of the writer of the following pages. If he shall seem, in any part of those pages, to have animadverted, with some severity, upon Mr. GIBBON, or upon Dr BENSON, such animadversions will, he trusts, be, at least, pardoned, when the nature of the offence shall be considered, which excited them. When men, but too evidently, postpone the love of truth to the desire of victory, and sacrifice the faithfulness of facts to their own predilections,—such conduct becomes more than a common transgression and, therefore, not only calls for, but justifies, a more than common severity of reprehension

MAY 2, 1785.

(f) One stricture, in particular, by a late writer, respecting a quotation from *Tertullian*, is of so different a description, that, when read, it is also *answered*.

TO THE RIGHT REVEREND

B E I L B Y,

LORD BISHOP OF CHESTER,

THE FOLLOWING LETTERS ARE

MOST HUMBLY

INSCRIBED, AND DEDICATED:

AS SOME TESTIMONY, HOWEVER SMALL,

OF REVERENCE FOR HIS VIRTUES;

AND

AS SOME TOKEN, HOWEVER INSIGNIFICANT,

OF GRATITUDE FOR HIS FAVORS,

BY

THE AUTHOR.

LETTER I.

SIR,

I SHALL make no apology to you, for the following addrefs. It is caufed by certain affertions, which are contained in a work, lately given by you, to the public, in the truth, or falfehood, whereof the public is materially concerned.

The affertions, here meant, are found in the following note to the third volume of your " Hiftory of the Decline, and Fall, of the *Roman* Empire."

" The three witneffes" (1 *John*, v. 7.) " have been eftablifhed in our *Greek* Tefta- " ments, by the prudence of *Erafmus*; the " honeft bigotry of the *Complutenfian* Edi- " tors: the typographical fraud, or error, " of *Robert Stephens*, in the placing a crot- " chet; and the deliberate falfehood, or

B   " ftrange

" ftrange mifapprehenfion, of *Theodore*
" *Beza.*" (*a*)

The verfe of St. *John*, here alluded to,
ftands thus in our common Teftaments—

  " *For there are Three that bear record in*
  " *Heaven; the Father, the Word, and*
  " *the Holy Ghoft: and thefe Three are*
  " *One.*"

As the charges, which you have thus
brought againft the *Complutenfian* Editors,
againft *Robert Stephens,* and *Theodore Beza,*
(*Erafmus* being rather praifed, than cenfured, by you, for a reafon which may hereafter appear) feem expreffed in terms purpofely obfcure,—it appears neceffary, in the
firft place, briefly, to enquire, whether they
have done any thing to deferve thefe feveral
accufations;

(*a*) There is a deficiency in this fentence which ought
to be fupplied. St *John* fpeaks, in two fucceffive verfes
of the chapter in queftion, of *fix* Witneffes *three* in
heaven, and *three* on earth. Mr. *Gibbon* has no quarrel
with the three Witneffes on earth. His Note is levelled
againft the *three, heavenly, Witneffes,* only. It feemed neceffary to ftate this diftinction here, and to keep it conftantly in view in the following Differtation.

accufations; making, however, fome previous mention of *Erafmus.*

I. *Erafmus* publifhed his *firft* edition of the
Greek Teftament at *Bafil,* A. D. 1516, in lefs
than a century after the invention of the art
of printing. It was the firft *Greek* Teftament which the world had, then, feen iffue
from the prefs. He publifhed a fecond edition of the fame work, at the fame place, in
A. D. 1519. In thefe two editions this
verfe (1 *John,* v. 7.) was not inferted; which
omiffion *firft* caft the imputation of impofture
upon it. Being publicly reprehended, for
this omiffion, by our countryman *Edward
Ley,* and by *Lopez Stunica* (or *Aftuniga,* as it is
fometimes written) a learned *Spaniard, Erafmus* afterwards, in A. D. 1522, publifhed
his third edition, in which he reftored this
text of the *three* (heavenly) *Witneffes* · de-
claring, as his apology for having left it out
of his two former editions, that he had not
found it in five *Greek* MSS, which he had
then confulted; but that he had now replaced
(" *repofuimus*") the verfe, becaufe he found

that it did exist in an ancient, *Greek*, MS in *England*. (*b*)

II. The famous *Polyglott* of the Old, and New, Testament was printed in *Spain*, at *Complutum*, (or *Alcala de Henares*) under the patronage of Cardinal *Ximenes*, A. D. 1514; but it was not published until several years afterwards. It was the result of the joint labors of many (*c*) learned men, who were selected, by the Cardinal, for that purpose, and furnished with all the *Greek* MSS, and other aids, which his great political, as well as personal, influence could procure. In this work the " *Complutenfian* Editors" have inferted the text of 1 *John*, v. 7. which infertion, it feems, deferves no better an appellation, from Mr. *Gibbon*, than that of " *honeft bigotry*."

III. In A. D. 1546, *Robert Stephens* publifhed his valuable edition of the *Greek* Teftament. That this work might be as perfect

---

{ (*b*) Appendix, No. XX.
  (*c*) The number of thefe learned men, was *forty-two :* —and they were employed in this great work, not lefs (as is commonly believed) than *fifteen* years. *Alftedii* Encyclop. Book xxxii, Chap. 7. *Gomez*, in Vita *Ximenis*.

fect as poffible, gieat induftiy was ufed to collect fuch *Greek* MSS, as had efcaped the enquiiies of the editors of *Complutum*. And thofe endeavours were attended with fuch fuccefs, that *Robert Stephens*, in the profecution of that work, " *collated (d) his* Greek *text with fixteen very ancient, written, copies.*" This edition of A. D. 1546, and a fubfequent one in A. D. 1549, not being piinted in a volume large enough to admit of marginal remarks, and notations of different readings, contained only the plain *Greek* text of the New Teftament. And in both thefe editions ftands this teftimony of the *three* (heavenly) *Witneffes*. In A. D. 1550, *Robert Stephens* gave a thiid edition to the world, on a laiger fcale: in which he diftinguifhed the diffeient *Greek* MSS, which he had collated, by *Greek* letteis (β, γ, &c.) and the vaiious readings by an *obelus*, and *femi-parenthefis*, or ciotchet; which, wherever infeited, were meant to denote, that, from the word, before which the *obelus* was placed, to the ftation where the *femi-parenthefis* was found, in the *Greek* text, the whole of that

B 3   verfe,

(d) Sce his Preface, Appendix, No. XII.

verſe, or verſes, word, or words, was wanting in the particular MSS cited in the margin. In this third edition, *Robert Stephens*
has thus marked, in a great variety of inſtances, ſometimes a ſingle word alone, and
ſometimes ſeveral words following each
other. As he found in ſeveral of (for it
ſeems to have exiſted in them all) his own
Greek MSS, and in the *Complutenſian* Bible,
this *ſeventh* verſe *entire*; ſo in ſome others
he remarked the particular words (εν τω ερανω)
" *in Heaven*," to be wanting. At the head
of theſe three words, therefore, *Robert Stephens* placed an *obelus*, in his edition of A. D.
1550, and a *ſemi-parentheſis* at the end of
them. thereby denoting, to the reader, that
thoſe *three words* were wanting in the particular MSS, referred to in the margin.
And this, Sir, you call " *the typographical
fraud, or error, of* Robert Stephens."

IV. *Theodore Beza* (whoſe erudition, and
piety, did honor to the age in which he lived) was born at *Vezelai*, in, or about A. D.
1519, and died in A. D. 1605. He publiſhed

ed an edition of the New Teſtament, with annotations, at *Geneva*, in A. D. 1551. He was urged to this work by *Robert Stephens*, who, on *Beza*'s compliance with his ſolicitations, permitted to him the free uſe of all his *Greek* MSS. In his notes on this paſſage of St. *John*, he ſays (*e*) " This verſe does not " occur in the *Syriac* verſion," &c. " but " is found in the *Engliſh* MS, in the *Complutenſian* edition, and in ſome ancient " MSS of *Stephens*. In the *Engliſh* MS, the " words Father, Word, and Spirit, are " written without their articles; but they " are read with their articles in *our* (*f*) " MSS. The *Engliſh* MS has, ſimply, the " word Spirit, without adding to it the " epithet Holy; in *ours* they are joined, and " we read Holy Spirit. As to the words, " *in Heaven*, they are wanting in *ſeven* an- " cient MSS." And he further uſes theſe remarkable expreſſions (which, indeed, Sir, ſeems to have drawn down the plenitude of

your

(*e*) Appendix, No. XI.
(*f*) *Beza*, throughout his annotations, calls the MSS of *Stephens* " *noſtri codices*,"—*our* MSS.
The notes, juſt referred to, ſupply, in a very ſmall compaſs, *two* inſtances of this appellation.

your anger upon him)—" *I am entirely*
" *satisfied that we ought to retain this verse.*"

This is the plain truth, briefly stated, of
the proceedings of *Erasmus, Robert Stephens,
Theodore Beza,* and the editors of *Complutum,*
relative to the verse in question. To this
short statement permit me to add the following observations.

I. You seem, Sir, not to be more happy
in your *indirect commendation* of *Erasmus,* in
this matter, than we shall, hereafter, find
you to have been in your *direct censures* of the
other editors. In whatever light we view
the conduct of *Erasmus,* it betrays, at least,
great weakness. If he was really possessed
of *five* ancient MSS, in which this verse had
no place, and had thought it his duty to ex-
pel it, accordingly, from his two former editions, he ought not to have restored it, in his
third edition, upon the authority of *a single*
MS only. It seems impossible to account for
the behaviour of *Erasmus,* in this matter,
taking the whole of it into contemplation at
once, but upon one of these suppositions :

Either

Either he *could not produce* the five MSS, in which he had alledged the verse to be omitted; or he had *other* authorities, much superior to the testimony of a single MSS, for re-placing the verse, which he was not, however, ingenuous enough to acknowledge. And this conclusion will not, perhaps, seem altogether unwarrantable, when the testimonies which I mean to produce, in my next letter, in favor of the originality of this verse, shall have been fully weighed; and when it is further considered, that *Erasmus* was secretly inclined (*g*) to *Arianism:* a circumstance, which rendered him, by no means, *an indifferent* editor of this *fifth* chapter of St. *John.* Upon the face of his own Apology, then, the conduct of *Erasmus,* in this instance, was *mean.* Upon the supposition of his having kept back from the world his *true* motives of action, it was *grosly disingenuous,* and unworthy. And yet for a proceeding, which must fall under one of these inevitable alternatives, you, Sir, it seems, cannot find a more severe stricture, than, " *the pru-*
                                        dence

_____

(*g*) Int. al.—*Chamb.* Cyclopæd. (by *Rees*) Tit. " *Arianism.*"

dence of Erafmus !" If *Erafmus* had not poffeffed the *merit* of cafting the *firft*, (*b*) public, imputation of impofture on this verfe,
which others have fince been induftrious to
prove,—his fubfequent *recantation*, his " *repofuimus*," would hardly have met with fo
mild a rebuke from Mr. *Gibbon*.

II. The admiffion of the text, in queftion,
into the feveral additions of *Robert Stephens*'s,
Greek Teftament, was not owing to a " *typographical error*" of that editor. You, Sir,
I prefume, would fay, that *Robert Stephens*
meant to have placed his *obelus*, and crotchet,
fo as to have denoted the whole of the verfe
1 *John*, v. 7, (inftead of the three words, ε)
τω εξανω) to have been wanting in *feven* of his
MSS; and that his not doing fo was a miftake.
Without requiring your authority for fo arbitrary an affumption, we may fatisfy our-
felves from the beft authority poffible, the
internal evidence of the volume itfelf, that
the

(*b*) " Præfatio *Hieronymi* Interpretes quofdam ob *omif-*
" *fionem* ejus" [this Verfe] " culpat, *infertio.* vero, ejus
" NON, ante *Erafm* ætatem, *ut fraudis plena, damnata*
" *eft*." (*Wolfius*, Curæ Philologicæ, Edit. *Hamb*. Vol.
v, pa. 306.)

the whole of such a suppofition muft be groundlefs. To this edition, of A. D. 1550, Robert Stephens has annexed a lift of *Errata*, or " typographical errors," wherein he has been fo affiduoufly correct, as anxioufly to point out to the reader *one comma forgotten*, and *another mifplaced*, in that laborious volume: but there is no reference, in the *Errata*, to this verfe of St. *John*. If an argument, like this, could want fupport, it might be further remarked, that *John Crifpin* (an advocate of the parliament of *Paris*, who had retired to *Geneva*, for the fake of the free exercife of the reformed religion) publifhed a new edition of the *Greek* Teftament, at *Geneva*, in A. D. 1553; wherein the *obelus*, and *crotchet*, retain the fame place, in regard to this verfe, that they poffeffed in the edition of *Robert Stephens*: which is a proof that *Stephens*, who was then *a fellow citizen with Crifpin*, never found out (what you, Sir, it feems, have now found out for him) any " *typographical error in the placing his crotchet*." Nor,

III. Was this text inferted in *Beza's Greek* Teftament

Teſtament through the " *ſtrange miſapprehen-*
ſion," or through any miſapprehenſion at all,
of *Theodore Beza.* The debate between *Eraſ-*
mus, *Ley,* and *Stunica,* had awakened the
attention of Chriſtians, in general, to this
ſubject, upwards of *twenty* years before *The-*
odore Beza began his commentary. As a
principal member of the reformed church,
as a man famed for erudition, and integrity,
the eyes of all *Europe* were fixed on *Beza's*
expected publication. Indeed, he ſeems to
have felt himſelf called to the taſk : and accordingly his own words, before quoted in
this letter, ſhew that he gave the matter a
full conſideration ; that he contraſted the
Syriac verſion, &c. with his own authorities, and compared them together ſo atten-
tively, as even to note in which of them a
ſingle article, or epithet, was wanting ; that
he had, in ſhort, fully weighed the reaſons
on both ſides, and found thoſe for the authenticity of the text ſo greatly to preponderate, as to enable him to ſpeak his ſerious
conviction in the moſt deciſive terms.—" *I*
am entirely ſatisfied that we ought to retain this
verſe." Such motives for caution, and ſuch

marks

marks of diligence, in such a man, leave no room for the idea of *misapprehension*.

Thus acquitted of " error, and misapprehension," it remains for you, Sir, to shew, how you can substantiate the other parts of your charge against *Robert Stephens*, and *Theodore Beza*,—namely, of " *fraud*" and " *deliberate falsehood*." It will become one who wishes to live to posterity as a historian, to consider well, how he can justify himself, either in literary candor, or Christian charity, for accusing men so evidently conscientious,—men, whose characters have hitherto been not unsullied only, but illustrious,—of the complicated crime of a deliberate falsification of Scripture !

IV. Nor, are the *Complutensian* editors, as it seems, justly chargeable with *bigotry*, (either *honest*, or *dishonest*) for the part which they took in this transaction. They were assembled to collate the MSS of the original language of the Scriptures, and to perpetuate their contents to posterity by means unknown to former ages. And what was the

conduct,

conduct, which they pursued, as far as we, at this distance of time, are enabled to trace it out ? It appears, in general, from their Preface (*i*) that these Editors had been favored with several *Greek* MSS, from the *Vatican*, at *Rome*, for the use of their Edition. It appears, in particular, from the testimony of *Stunica* himself, (*k*) that they had procured another, most valuable, *Greek* MS from the Isle of *Rhodes* (which, from that circumstance, is usually stiled the *Codex Rhodiensis*) for their assistance in this undertaking. Possessed of such treasures, it cannot be supposed, with reason, that these Editors would neglect them. Led by such guides, it is not to be presumed, without the most clear and unequivocal proof, that they would wilfully refuse to follow them. They did no more, then, in this transaction, as it seems from this general view of the subject, than insert, in their *Polyglott*, a verse which, we have reason to conclude, (*l*) was found in all these MSS, thus consulted by them.

(*i*) Appendix, No. XIVI .
(*k*) Contra *Erasmum*, passim.
(*l*) The objections to this conclusion will be considered hereafter.

them. And are you, then, Sir, ferioufly offended, that thefe Editors, as far as their conduct can thus be traced out, did not abufe the confidence repofed in them? Are **they** *bigots*, becaufe they would not falfify the text, which they were convened to afcertain? *Bigotry* may be defined to be *a perverfe adherence to any opinion of any kind, without giving to the evidence, on the contrary part, an open hearing, and a candid judgment.* Surely, then, it is *bigotry* in Mr. *Gibbon*, (leaving him at liberty to chufe his own epithet for it) to exprefs what might, by any mode of inference, be conftrued into a wifh, **that** thefe editors had, in *favor of the opinion to which he adheres,* mutilated thofe **records,** which they were urged, by every principle that ought to govern the human mind, **to** deliver down, to future ages, unabridged, and unperverted. I would not, Sir, willingly remind you of the reproaches of your learned opponents, (*m*) refpecting the quotations, and authorities by which **you** attempted to fuppoit the pofitions, affumed in **the** *two* well-known *chapters* of the firft

volume

' (*m*) Dr. *Watfon*, Dr. *Chelfum*, Mr. *Davis*, and others.

volume of your history. I should still more unwillingly permit myself to draw any inference, either from those instances, or from your present indignation against the editors of *Complutum*, as to the probable manner in which you would have proceeded, had you been the sole editor there. But, I trust, I may be allowed to say, that if these editors had acted as you more than seem to wish they had done, they would, for ought that appears to the contrary, have merited the appellation of *dishonest bigots*—would have proved themselves unworthy betrayers of their trust, and unfaithful stewards of the oracles of GOD !

I now beg leave, Sir, to submit the question to yourself, how far these three Editors have deserved the charges of *error*, and *misapprehension*, on the one hand, or of *bigotry*, *fraud*, and *deliberate falsehood*, on the other, which you have thus brought against them. And I request your permission to establish, in a future letter, the authenticity of the text in dispute, by proofs, all of them, antecedent to the days of *Robert Stephens, Theodore Beza*, or the Editors of *Complutum*.

I am, Sir, &c.

LETTER II.

SIR,

IN my former letter, I truft, it is proved, that the charge, which you have brought againft *Theodore Beza*, *Robert Stephens*, and the *Complutenfian* Editors, relative to the Verfe 1 *John*, v. 7, is not warranted by fact, and cannot be fupported in argument. I mean now to proceed, as was at firft propofed, to eftablifh the authenticity of the Verfe itfelf, by teftimonies of different kinds, all antecedent, in point of time, to the days of any of the Editors here mentioned; (*a*) by

C   proofs,

(*a*) The teftimony of *F. Amelotte*, inferted here in the former Edition of thefe Letters, is now omitted, becaufe many learned, and worthy, men have expreffed doubts of his veracity. His accufation, and defence, are ftated at large, by *Emlyn*, on the one hand, and by *Martin* on the other, and alfo in the *Journal Britanique* for A. D. 1752, and 1753. [I am indebted for this laft reference to Mr. *Maty*'s NEW REVIEW for Auguft 1784, p 74] The deductions from the whole of this accufation, and defence, feem to be greatly in favor of *Amelotte*. But I wifh not to bring forward any witneffes, of any kind, againft whom any objections may be made, which are even only apparently reafonable; becaufe this Text does not feem to ftand in need of any precarious fupport.

proofs, commencing with the age of *Erasmus;* and ascending, from thence, to that of the Apostles. And

First,—*From the writings of individuals.*

1. *Laurentius Valla,* an *Italian* nobleman, of great erudition, was the first person (as M. *Simon* (*b*) confesses) who set himself to correct the *Greek* MSS of the New Testament. He lived nearly a century before *Erasmus.* (*c*) By assiduous, and long continued, enquiries he got into his hands seven *Greek* MSS; a number very considerable, if we reflect, that, through the universal ignorance of those ages, the *Greek* language was then, become

come

<hr/>

(*b*) *Hist. des Versions,* C. xii. *Du Pin. Hody,* De Bibliorum Textibus originalibus, Edit *Oxon* A. D. 1705, p. 441, 2. The learned Dr. *Mill* seems to have fallen into several mistakes, in his *Prolegomena,* respecting the MSS of *Valla.* See *Bengelius* (Introd. in Crisin) p. 437.

(*c*) *Erasmus* has, himself, paid a deserved tribute of praise to *Valla*'s Annotations. In one part of his Epistle to *Fischer* he says, " *Laurentius,*—collatis aliquot *vetustis,* " *atque emendatis, Græcorum exemplaribus,* quædam anno- " tavit in Novo Testamento." In another place he says, " Si quibus non vacat totam *Græcorum* linguam " perdiscere, ii tamen *Vallæ* studio non mediocriter adju- " vabuntur, qui mira sagacitate Novum omne Testa- " mentum excussit." (Appendix, No. XV.)

come almoſt a dead letter, and its MSS were periſhing with it. This paſſage of St. *John* was found in all theſe MSS; and is commented upon by *Valla*, in his Notes upon this Epiſtle (*d*).

2. In the Commentary upon the Scriptuies, written by *Nicholas de Lyra*, this Verſe of St. *John* is found, in the place which it it now poſſeſſes, accompanied by the learned author's Annotations, without the ſmalleſt, expreſſed, ſuſpicion of its authenticity (*e*). He held the profeſſorſhip of Divinity, at *Paris*, with great reputation, in the *fourteenth* century.

3. About a century before this laſt-mentioned time, appeared the Commentary of St. *Thomas* (as he is commonly called) on this Epiſtle; in which this Verſe is not only admitted, but commented upon, without any infinuations of interpolation. He has, alſo, frequently quoted it in his great work,

C 2 " *Summa*

(*d*) " Opera *L. Vallæ*, Edit. *Baſil.* A. D. 1543, p. 892

(*e*) Edit. *Antverpiæ*, A. D. 1634.

" *Summa totius Theologiæ*;" which, for many centuries after its publication, was the admiration of all *Europe* (*f*).

4. This Verſe is found in the *Rationale of Divine Offices*, compoſed by the celebrated *Durandus* (*g*) Biſhop of *Mende*, in *Languedoc*, in the *thirteenth* century.

5. *Lombard*, who was Biſhop of *Paris*, (*h*) in the *twelfth* century, expreſsly cites this Verſe in the firſt book of his *Sentences*. His words may be thus tranſlated: " The " Father, and the Son, are one, not by con- " fuſion of Perſons, but by unity of nature, " as St. *John* teaches in his canonical epiſ- " tle, ſaying, *There are Three which bear* " *record in Heaven, the Father, the Word,* " *and the Holy Ghoſt, and theſe Three are* " *One*."

6. This

(*f*) Part 1, Qu. 30. Art. 2, Qu. 31, Art. 1, 2, Qu. 39, Art. 2, 3, and 6, and Qu. 41, Art. 6

(*g*) *Rationale Div. Offic* Edit. *Ludg.* A. D. 1551, Lib. vi, chap. 97, p. 238. *Moret*, Tom. 1. p. 388, Edit. A. D. 1724

(*h*) Lib. 1. p. 10—Edit. *Paris*. A. D. 1738.

6. This Verſe is quoted, in the ſame century, by *Rupert*, Abbot of *Duyts*, in *Germany*, in his Treatiſe on the " *Glorification of the Trinity* (*i*)."

7. In the *eleventh* century lived St. *Bernard*, whoſe Sermons are yet extant. This Verſe is inſiſted upon, by him, in ſeveral of theſe diſcourſes, particularly in one upon the *Octave* of Eaſter, and in the *Sixteenth* of his *Parvi Sermones*.

8. In, or about this age, *Radulphus Ardens, Hugo Victorinus*, and *Scotus*, with other authors, whoſe works have ſurvived to the preſent times, referred to the Verſe in queſtion (*k*). It would be tedious to particulariſe all the citations made, in this century, of this paſſage of St. *John*.

9. The *Gloſſa Ordinaria*, the work of *Walafrid Strabo*, was compoſed in the *ninth* century.

C 3

(*i*) *Ruperti* Opera, Edit. A. D. 1602, Vol. ii, p. 26, *et alias ſparſim.*

(*k*) *Dorſchei* (Calov. Bibl.) Diſſertatio de Spir. Aqua, and Sanguine, p. 11. *Calov.* de Puritate Fontium, § 131, p. 479.

tury. This performance has been diftinguifhed by the higheft approbation of the
learned, in every age fince its appearance in
the world. Even M. *Simon* confeffes, that
" *no comment on the Scriptures is of equal au-*
" *thority with this expofition.*" In this woik,
the text, in queftion, is not only found in the
Epiftle of St. *John*, but is commented upon,
in the Notes, with admirable force, and per-
fpicuity.

In his Preface to this valuable Commentary, *Walafrid Strabo* lays down the following rules, as means whereby to difcover, and
correct, any errors that might fubfift in the
tranfcripts of his times, either of the Old, or
of the New Teftament. " Let it be noted,"
(fays he, fpeaking to his readers) " that
" where any errors are difcoveied in the
" Tranfcripts of the Old Teftament, we
" muft have recouife to the *Hebrew* Origi-
" nal, becaufe the Old Teftament was ori-
" ginally written in the *Hebrew* tongue.
" But where any fuch errors fhall be difco-
" vered in our Tranfcripts of the New Tef-
" tament, we muft LOOK BACK TO THE
GREEK

" GREEK MSS, becaufe the New Teftament
" was originally written in the *Greek* lan-
" guage, except the Gofpel of St. *Matthew*,
" and the Epiftle of St. *Paul* to the *He-*
" *brews.*" (*l*)

If, Sir, it fhall be allowed, that this celebrated Commentator followed, in his own
pratice, the rules which he has thus prefcribed to others, (which will hardly be
doubted) the *Greek* MSS, which directed him
to infert this Verfe in his Text, and Commentary, muft, in all probability, have been
more ancient than any now known to exift.
He flourifhed about A. D. 840. Some, at
leaft, of the *Greek* MSS, which were ufed
by him, cannot well be fuppofed to have
been lefs than 300, or 400, years old; the
latter of which dates carries them up to
A. D. 440. But the MOST ANCIENT *Greek*

C 4　　　　　　MS,

(*l*) " Nota, quod ubicunque in libris *Veteris* Tefta-
" menti mendofitas reperitur. currendum eft ad volu-
" mina *Hebræorum*, quia vetus Teftamentum primo in
" lingua *Hebraica* fcriptum eft. Si verò in libris *Novi*
" Teftamenti, revertendum eft ad volumina *Græcorum*;
" quia Novum Teftamentum primo in lingua *Græca*
" fcriptum eft, præter Evangelium *Matthæi*, et Epiftc-
" lam *Pauli* ad *Hebræos.*"

MS, which is *now* known to exift, is the *Alexandrian*; for which, however, *Wetftein*, who feems to have confidered the queftion with great attention, claims no higher an antiquity than the clofe of the *fifth* century, or about A. D. 490. (*m*) If this mode of reafoning, then, be not (and it feems that it is not) fallacious, the text, and Commentary, of *Walafrid Strabo* ftand upon the foundation of *Greek* MSS, which are more ancient, in point of time, and therefore, which ought to be more refpected, in point of teftimony, than any poffeffed by the prefent age.

10. In the middle of the *eighth* century *Ambrofe Anfbert*, Abbot of St. *Vincent*'s, in *Italy*, wrote a comment upon the *Apocalypfe*; wherein this verfe of St. *John* is applied, in explanation (*n*) of the fifth Verfe of the firft Chapter of the *Revelations*.

In his Comment upon this Verfe of the *Apocalypfe*, he fays, " Although the expref-
" fion of *faithful Witnefs*, found therein,
refers,

(*m*) See, alfo, *Mill*. Proleg. 1338.
(*n*) Biblioth. Max. Patrum, Edit. *Ludg.* A. D. 1677,
Vol. xiii. p. 415.

" refers, *directly*, to *Jesus Christ* alone,—yet
" it equally characterises the Father, the
" Son, and the Holy Ghost; according to
" these words of St. *John*, *There are three*
" *which bear record in Heaven, the Father,*
" *the Word, and the Holy Ghost, and these*
" *three are one.*"

11. In the same century lived *Elipandus*,
Archbishop of *Toledo*, in *Spain*, who maintained that *Jesus Christ* had no existence, antecedent to his coming into the world, and
that he was the Son of God by *adoption*, only, and not by any *co-essentiality* in
nature. These opinions of *Elipandus* were
strenuously opposed by *Etherius*, Bishop of
Uxame, a Suffragan to *Elipandus*, and by *Beatus*, a Priest in the *Asturias*. In the Treatise which they published against *Elipandus*,
on this subject, they quoted several passages
of this Epistle of St. *John*; (o) and *this* verse
in particular, which speaks of the *three Witnesses in Heaven*, the Father, the Son, and
the Holy Ghost.

12. *Cassiodorius*

(o) *Du Pin, Lond.* Ed. Vol. vi, p. 121—4—Bibl.
Max. Patrum, Vol. xiii. p. 360.

12. *Cassiodorius* lived in *Italy*, in the middle of the *sixth* century. Among other works, he wrote a Commentary on the Epistles, &c. of the New Testament, which he entitled *Complexiones*. This work had lain long in obscurity, in the great library at *Verona*, where it would, probably, have still remained unnoticed, and unknown, had not the late, very learned, *Maffeius* found it there, in some of his various researches, and caused it to be printed, at *Florence*, in A. D. 1721. In his Annotations on this chapter *Cassiodorius* uses these words : " Three mysteries bear wit-
" ness in earth, the Water, the Blood, and
" the Spirit, which are, we read, fulfilled in
" the passion of our Lord ; and *in Heaven, the*
" *Father, and the Son, and the Holy Spirit,*
" *and these three are one GOD (p)."*

The testimony of this writer is of the greatest weight, because it appears from his own work, as well as from the testimonies of *Bengelius,* and *Wolfius,* (q) that he was
exceedingly

(p) Appendix, No. X
(q) *Bengelius,* Edit, *Tubingæ,* A. D. 1734, p. 755,
Hody, De Bibl Text. Orig. p. 399. *Wolfii,* Cur. Phi-
lolog. (Index, Tit. *Cassiodorius,* and particularly Vol. v

exceedingly attentive to the true readings of ſuch works as he commented upon, particularly the Scriptures; and becauſe he lived antecedently to the reviſal of the New Teſtament, by *Alcuinus* and otheis, under *Charlemagne,* which will be mentioned hereafter.

13. In the beginning of the *ſixth* century flouriſhed *Fulgentius,* Biſhop of *Ruſpe,* in *Africa.* In that age the tenets of *Arius* were eſpouſed by, at leaſt, two *African* kings, *Thraſimond,* and *Huneric. Fulgentius* oppoſed the *Arians* (although ſupported at that time by the former (*r*) of theſe kings) with zeal, and fortitude. And in his works we find this verſe, among other paſſages of Scripture, expreſsly cited, and inſiſted upon, as being concluſive againſt the tenets of *Arius :* “ The bleſſed Apoſtle St. *John*” (ſays he) “ teſtifies, that *there are three which bear re-* “ *cord in Heaven, the Father, the Word, and* “ *the Spirit, and theſe Three are One.* Which
“ alſo

p. 297, and 306.) Alſo *Simon,* Hiſt Crit. des Verſions, C. viii.

(*r*) *Du Pin,*—Art. *Fulgentius,* Edit. *Lond.* A. D. 1693, Vol. iv, p. 14.

" also the moſt Holy Martyr, *Cyprian*, de-
" clares in his Epiſtle *De Unitate Eccleſiæ* ;
" wherein, to demonſtrate that there ought
" to be an unity in the Church, as there is
" in the Godhead, he has brought the FOL-
" LOWING PROOFS, directly, from SCRIP-
" TURE; the Lord *(Jeſus)* ſays, *I, and my Fa-*
" *ther, are One* ; and *again it is written* of the
" *Father, Son, and Holy Spirit, And theſe*
" *Three are One (ſ).*"

Fulgentius, alſo, quotes this Verſe in his
Treatiſe on the Trinity, dedicated to *Felix.*
" I, and my Father, ſays St. *John*, are One
" [*unum ſumus*] ; " thereby teaching us to
" apply the word *unum* to their nature, *ſumus*
" to their perſons. So in the following words,
" *There are Three which bear witneſs in Hea-*
" *ven, the Father, the Word, and the Spirit* ;
" *and theſe three are one. (t)*

14. In one of the laſt editions (*u*) of the
works

(ſ) Reſponſio contra *Arianos*,—Bibl. Max. Patrum,
Vol. ıx, p 41. (Appendix, No. IX.)
(t) Bibl. Max. Patr. Vol. ıx, p. 160.
(u) Biblioth. Max. Patrum, Vol. ıx. p. 276 and 287.

works of this Bishop, two Tracts are inserted under his name; although some respectable Critics, of modern times, have rather
wished to ascribe them to some other Writer
of that age. They are addressed to two
Arian Controversialists, then living, *Pinta*
and *Fabian*, in opposition to the tenets which
they maintained. In the former of these
Tracts the Verse in question is thus quoted.
" In the Epistle of St. *John*,—*There are*
" *Three in Heaven which bear record, the Fa-*
" *ther, the Word, and the Spirit ; and these*
" *three are one."*

The title of the latter Tract is—" *The*
" *Trinity in persons, and the Unity in essence*"
[of the Godhead] " *proved from Holy Scrip-*
" *ture."* The title of this Tract, or Frag-
ment, is striking ; and the manner, in which
this Verse of St. *John* is cited therein, is as
remarkable as the title (*v*). " *The Apostle,*
" St. John, *has expressly said, in speaking of*
" *the Father, the Son, and the Holy Ghost,—*
" *And these three are one."*

It

(*v*) This Treatise is affirmed, by *Du Pin*, to be the
work of *Fulgentius.* Vol. iv, *Lond.* Edit, p. 18.

It feems to be of little moment, in this difquifition, whether we conclude thefe Tracts, or Fragments, to have been the work of *Fulgentius*, or of fome contemporary Writer. They, prove, under either fuppofition, (in corroboration of other authorities here adduced) both thofe points, by which the prefent queftion is affected; namely, that this verfe *was quoted in the* Arian *contro-verfy*,—and was there *appealed to*, as indubitably *proceeding from the pen of St.* John.

15. A few years before *Fulgentius*, lived *Vigilius*, who was Bifhop of *Tapfum*, fituated in the fame province, and kingdom, with *Ruffe*. He thus urges the teftimony of this Verfe, in oppofition to the errors of *Arius*, in the *firft* book of his *Treatife on the Trinity*. " The names of the Perfons in the God- " head" (fays he) " are evidently fet forth " by St. *John*, the Apoftle, who fays in his " Epiftle, *There are three which bear record* " *in Heaven, the Father, the Word, and the* " *Spirit*, and in *Chrift Jefus they are one* (w)."

Again,—

' (w) Bibl. Max Patrum, Vol viii, p 775.—" *Unum*; non tamen *unus* eft, *quia non eft in his una perfona*," are the words of the original. (Appendix, No. VII.)

Again,—" To what purpofe is it" (fays he, in his *feventh* Book, addreffing himfelf to the *Arians*) " that ye read in *John*, the " Evangelift, *Thefe Three are One*, if ye ftill " perfift that there are different natures in " their perfons ? I afk, in what manner are " the *Three One*, if the nature of their di- " vinity is different in each ?" (*x*)

In the *tenth* Book he repeats the argu- ment, herein before cited from the *firft* Book, with little variation.

And, laftly, in his conteft with *Varima- dus*, the *Arian*, he ufes thefe expreffions : " *John*, the Evangelift, in his Epiftle to the " *Parthians*, fays,—There are Three, which " bear witnefs in Earth, the Water, the " Blood, and the Flefh [*et tres in nobis funt*] ; " and *there are Three, which bear witnefs in* " *Heaven, the Father, the Word, and the Spirit* " [et hi tres unum funt], *and thefe three are* " *one.* (*y*)

16. A

(*x*) Appendix, No. VII.
(*y*) Magna Bibl. Veter. Patr. Vol. ii, p 623—Edit. *Col. Agripp.* A. D. 1618. (Appendix, No. VIII.)

16. A little before the days of *Vigilius*, flourifhed in the Weft, the good *Eucherius*. He was confecrated Bifhop of *Lyons* (z) about A. D. 434. There was not a Bifhop, in the weftern world, more revered for learning, and piety. Permit a quotation from his works (a): " As to the Trinity" (fays he) " we read in the Epiftle of St. *John, There* " *are Three which bear record in Heaven, the* " *Father, the Word, and the Holy Spirit. And* " *there are Three which bear witnefs in Earth,* " *the Spirit, and the Water, and the Blood.*"

17. When the pious *Jerome* (who died (b) A. D. 420) had compleated that great work, of correcting the *Latin* verfion of the Old, and fettling the text of the New, Teftament, which he undertook at the re-queft of Pope *Damafus*, he clofed the ar-duous tafk with a folemn proteftation, (c) that, in revifing the New Teftament, he had adhered entirely to the *Greek* MSS : " *Novum*

(z) *Du Pin*, Art. *Eucherius*

(a) Formulæ, C. XI, Sect. 3 —Bibl. Max. Patrum, Vol. vi, p. 838. (Appendix, No. VI.)

(b) *Moreri*, Art. *Jerome*.

(c) Catal Ecclef. Scriptor. ad finem. (*Hieronymi* Opera, per *Erafmum*, Vol i, Edit. *Parifiis*, A. D. 1546.)

"*Novum Teſtamentum fidei Græcæ reddidi.*"
And in *Jerome*'s Teſtament this verſe of St.
John is read, without any doubt of its au-
thenticity.

18. Nor is the inſertion of this verſe, in
his Teſtament, in obedience to his *Greek*
MSS, the only teſtimony which *Jerome*
hath given to its authenticity. He has alſo
quoted it in the ſolemn confeſſions of his
Faith, which are inſcribed, reſpectively, to
Pope *Damaſus*, before mentioned, and to
Cyrillus, then Biſhop of *Jeruſalem*.

" And as, in oppoſition to *Arius*, we
" affirm that the *Trinity* is of one and the
" ſame eſſence, and confeſs, in three perſons,
" one God: ſo, ſhunning the hereſy of
" *Sabellius*, we diſtinguiſh thoſe three per-
" ſons by their ſeveral properties. The Fa-
" ther is always the Father; the Son is al-
" ways the Son; and the Holy Ghoſt is
" always the Holy Ghoſt. In eſſence,
" therefore, THESE" [three] " ARE ONE"
" [*unum ſunt*]. They are diſtinct in perſon,
" only, and in names."

And

And again, in the explanation of his faith to *Cyrillus*—" *To us, therefore, there is one* " *Father ;—one Son, who is very God; and* " *one Holy Ghost, who is very God:* AND " THESE THREE ARE ONE." The words of *Jerome* are, " *Et hi tres unum funt,"* which are also a literal quotation from this Verse of St. *John.* (*d*)

19. *Augustine* was contemporary with *Jerome,* and corresponded with him on many Biblical subjects. In his Commentary upon the first Epistle of St. *John,* and upon this very Chapter of that Epistle, *Augustine* uses these expressions. " And why is Christ the " end of the commandment ? Because Christ " is God; and the end of the command- " ment is Love ; and God is Love. For the " the Father, and the Son, and the Holy " Ghost" [UNUM SUNT] " are one."

Again, in his Treatise against *Maximinus,* the *Arian,* he expresses himself in these re- markable terms. " For there are three per- " fons" [in the Godhead] " the Father, the " Son,

(*d*) Appendix, No. XXII.

" Son, and the Holy Ghoſt: AND THESE
" THREE (becauſe they are of the ſame ef-
" fence) ARE ONE". [*Hi tres unum ſunt.*]
" And *they are* compleatly *one,* [*unum ſunt*]
" there being no diverſity either in their na-
" tures, or in their wills. THESE THREE,
" therefore, *who* ARE ONE" [*hi tres qui unum
ſunt*] " through the ineffable unity of the
" Godhead, in which they are incompre-
" henſibly joined together, *are one God.*" (e)

The ſtriking reiteration, in theſe paſſages,
of the ſame expreſſions,—*Unum ſunt,*—*Hi
tres unum ſunt,*—*Unum ſunt,* and *Hi tres qui
unum ſunt,*—ſeems to beſpeak their derivation from the Verſe, now in debate, too
clearly to require any comment.

20. In the expoſition of the Faith, written to *Cyrillus,* by *Marcus Celedenſis,* an *African,* the writer thus expreſſes himſelf: " To
" us there is one Father, and one Son, who
" is truly GOD, and one Holy Spirit, who
" is alſo truly GOD; *and theſe Three are*

" *One*

(e) Appendix, No. XXII.

" *One* (*f*) :"——the precise words of the verse in question.

21. *Phœbadius* was Bishop of *Agen*, in *France*, in the *fourth* century. He thus cites this Verse, in his Book against the *Arians:* " The Lord says, I will ask of my Father, " and he shall give you another comforter. " Thus is the Spirit different from the Son, " as the Son is from the Father. Thus the " Spirit is the Third Person, as the Son is " the Second, yet they all constitute but " one GOD, because *these Three are One.*" Quia *tres unum sunt* (*g*) are the words of *Phœbadius*, which are also a literal quotation from St. *John.*

Jerome gives the most honorable testimony to this author, in his *Catalogue of Ecclesiastical Writers.* " *Phœbadius*," (says he) " Bishop of *Agen*, in *France*, published a " Book against the *Arians*. It is said that " he has been the author of *other* works " also,—but *those I have not yet read.* He is " alive

" alive at this day, in a very advanced age
" (*h*)."

22. *Cyprian* was made Bifhop of *Carthage*,
(*i*) A. D. 248. In his treatife *De Unitate
Ecclefiæ*, written againft *Novatus*, he ufes
thefe words : " Our Lord declares ; *I and
" my Father are One*; and *again it is writ-
" ten* of the Father, the Son, and the Holy
" Spirit,—And *thefe Three are One*." *Et
hi tres unum funt* (*k*) are the exact words of
this Holy Martyr. Here *Cyprian*, therefore, manifeftly makes two quotations from
the Scriptures ; the former from the Gofpel
(*l*) of St. *John*, the latter from 1 *John*, v.
7, the Verfe in queftion. " *It is written*,"
fays he ; but in what part of Scripture is it
fo written, in thofe particular terms, fave in
1 *John*, v. 7? In that Verfe, alone, through-

D 3   out

(*h*) Catal Eccl Scriptor p. 125. (Appendix, No.
V) In *Erafmus*'s edit. his name is written *Sæbadius*.

(*i*) Annales *Cyprianici*, Edit *Oxon*. A. D. 1682, p. 9.
Jerome's character of *Cyprian* is given in his ufual, ner-
vous, manner. " *Cyprianus Afer*,—Hujus ingenii fuper-
" fluum eft indicem texere, cum Sole clariora funt ejus
opera." [Catal. Scriptor. Eccl. p. 125]

(*k*) *Cypriani* Opera, Edit. *Oxon*. *De Unitate Ecclefiæ*,
p. 109 (Appendix, No. III.)

(*l*) Chap. x, V. 30.

out the whole of thofe facred pages, is the precife phrafe, *Et hi tres unum funt*, applied to the Trinity of perfons in the Godhead. This quotation, then, was made, and was meant to be made, (*m*) from this Verfe of the Epiftle of St. *John.*

In his Epiftle to *Jubaianus, Cyprian* again urges this teftimony of the three (heavenly) Witneffes, by a reference to the fame Verfe, " Cùm *hi tres unum funt* (*n*)."

23. *Tertullian* was born about the time of St. *John*'s death, if fome Chronologifts may be (*o*) credited. But other computations, which indeed feem to be much more accurate, place his birth about A. D. 140. In

either

(*m*) See the words of *Fulgentius*, No. 13, before quoted, whofe teftimony renders all argument on this head fuperfluous.

(*n*) *Cypriani* Opera, (inter Epiftolas) p. 203. (Appendix, No IV.)

(*o*) *Eufebius*, in his *Chronica*, p. 165, fays that St. *John* was alive in A. D. 101. And *Tertullian* died (in A. D. 196, according to Dr. *Blair*'s Chronology, but according to Dr. *Playfair*, which, indeed, feems to be the more accurate account) about A D. 234, in a very advanced age " *Fertur vixiffe ufque ad decrepitam ætatem*" are the words of *Jerome*, who was born in A. D. 331, or little-more than a century after the death of *Tertullian*. (*Catal. Scriptor. Eccl.* Art. *Tertullianus*.)

either cafe, it will be no incredible thing to suppofe, that *Tertullian* had converfed with Chriftians of his own times, who had actually fat under St. *John*'s miniftration of the Gofpel. In thofe days arofe, in *Afia*, the heretic *Praxeas*, who maintained that there was no plurality of perfons in the Godhead, but that the Father fuffered on the crofs. Againft the opinions of this man *Tertullian* wrote a treatife, in the *twenty-fifth* chapter of which he thus alledges this paffage of St. *John* : " The connection of the Father in " the Son, and of the Son in the Holy Spi- " rit, makes an unity of thefe three, one with " another, *which Three are One.*" The *Latin* is, Qui *tres unum funt* (*p*), a literal quotation of the Verfe in queftion. And the teftimony of *Tertullian* feems to carry irrefiftible conviction with it, to every unprejudiced mind, not only from its proximity to the age of the Apoftles, but becaufe he teftifies, that, in thofe times, *their authentic Epiftles were actually read to the Churches* (*q*), not through

---

(*p*) Lib. adv. Praxeam Cap xxv, ad init. (Appendix, No. II.)

(*q*) " Percurre ecclefias Apoftolicas, apud quas ipfe " adhuc cathedræ Apoftolorum fuis locis præfident, apud

through the medium of the *Latin*, or of any
other tranflation, but in the *original Greek*;
to which originals *Tertullian*, himfelf, directly appeals in the *eleventh* chapter of his
Monogamia. " *Sciamus planè* " (fays he,
fpeaking of fome erroneous opinions which
were then attempted to be proved by Scripture) " *non fic effe in authentico Græco*."

I have now, Sir, gone through the teftimonies of many individuals to the authenticity of this Verfe, all of whom wrote antecedently to the days of *Erafmus*. Others
might be adduced; but it feems, at prefent,
unneceffary to call for their affiftance.

To

" quas *ipfæ authenticæ literæ eorum recitantur*, fonantes
" vocem, et repræfentantes faciem uniufcujufque " (*Tertullianus*, de præfcriptionibus adverfus Hæreticos, Edit.
Fran. A D. 1597, p. 211.)
    It appears, moft clearly, from the Epiftle of *Ignatius*
(Cap. 8.) to the *Philadelphians*, that, in his times, the
original MSS of the Apoftles were extant, and were held
in great veneration   He died early in the *fecond* century.
And *Peter*, Bifhop of *Alexandria*, in the *fourth* century,
refers to the original of St *John*'s Gofpel, which, he
fays, was then preferved, with even a religious refpect,
at *Ephefus*. *Michaelis* feems to doubt (*Introd. Lect*. Edit.
Lond. A. D. 1761, Sect. 12.) as to the truth of this
latter teftimony; but without much reafon. For, furely,
it feems far from being improbable, that a MS of fuch
importance, and kept with fuch peculiar care, fhould
fubfift a little more than *two hundred* years.

To the evidence thus furnished *by Individuals*, I now beg leave to subjoin---THE TESTIMONY OF COUNCILS, AND OTHER COLLECTIVE BODIES OF MEN,---in support of the originality of the Verse in question.

1. The Council of *Lateran* was held at *Rome*, under *Innocent III*, A. D. 1215. Of all the assemblies, of this kind, which the Christian world ever saw, this was the most numerous. It was composed of more than 400 (*r*) bishops, of about 800 abbots, and priors, and of an equal number of deputies from prelates, colleges, and chapters, who could not attend in person. Among others, the *Greek* patriarchs of *Constantinople*, and *Jerusalem*, were present; and the several patriarchs of *Antioch*, and *Alexandria*, sent, each, a bishop, and a deacon, as their representatives. The chief purpose of convening this council, was, for the examination of certain opinions of the famous *Italian*, Father *Joachim*, founder of the congregation of *Flora*. These opinions were accused of *Arianism*, and were unanimously condemned

by

(*r*) *Du Pin*, Bibl. Ecclef. vol. X. P. 103.

by the council : in whofe act, or decretal, containing the reafons of fuch condemnation, we find the Verfe now in queftion, among other paffages of Scripture, thus particularly fet forth (s). It is read in the Canonical Epiftle of *John*, that " *there are* " *Three which bear Witnefs in Heaven, the* " *Father, the Word, and the Holy Spirit, and* " *thefe Three are One.*"

It may be permitted to me, perhaps, juft to remark, that the univerfal deference yielded to the known learning, and integrity, of the members of this council, caufed its decrees, in matters even of a fecular nature, to be received as law, not only in *England*, (t) (where they ftill continue fo) but through the reft of the *Chriftian* world.

2. About the clofe of the *eighth* century, the Emperor *Charlemagne* called together the learned of that age, and placed *Alcuinus*, an *Englifhman*, of great erudition, at their head ;

(s) Collection of Councils, by *Labbe*, and *Coffart*, Edit. *Paris* A. D. 1671, vol XI, pa. 144.
(t) *Bacon's* Abridgment, vol. V title *Tithes*. *Burn's* Ecclef. Law, vol. III, (8vo. edit.) p 381.

head (*u*) ; inſtructing them to ievife the MSS of the Bible then in uſe, to fettle the text, and to rectify the errors which had crept into it, through the haſte, or the ignorance, of tianſciibers. To effect this great purpoſe, he furniſhed theſe commiſſioners with every MS, that could be piocuied throughout his veiy extenſive dominions. In their *Correcto-iium*, the iefult of their united libors, which was prefented in public, to the Emperor, by *Alcuinus*, the *teſtimony of the thiee* (heavenly) *Witneſſes* is iead, without the ſmalleſt impeachment of its authenticity. This very volume Caidinal *Baionius* affiims to have been extant, at *Rome*, in his life-time (*a*), in the libiaiy of the Albey of *Vaux-Celles*; and he ſtiles it " *a treaſuie of ineſtimable value.*"

It cannot be ſuppoſed, that theſe Divines, thus aſſembled under the auſpices of a learned prince, would attempt to fettle the text of the New Teſtament, without ieferring to the

the *Greek* Original, by which alone that text could be afcertained ; or that they would, in that arduous inveftigation, collate MSS only of a modern date, juft wet, as it were, from the pen of the copyift. Candor requires us to admit, that their refearches muft have extended many centuries upwards,—in all probability even to the age of the Apoftles.

3. In A. D. 484, an affembly of *African* Bifhops was convened at *Carthage*, by King *Huneric*, the *Vandal*, and the *Arian*. The ftyle of the edict, iffued by *Huneric*, on this occafion, feems worthy of notice. He therein requires the Bifhops, of his dominions, to attend the council thus convened, there " to " defend, *by the Scriptures*, the confubftan- " tiality of the Son with the Father," againft certain *Arian* opponents. At the time appointed nearly *four hundred* bifhops attended this council, from the various provinces of *Africa*, and from the ifles of the *Mediterranean* Sea ; at the head of whom ftood the venerable *Eugenius*, bifhop of *Carthage*. The *public profeffions* of *Huneric* promifed a fair, and candid, difcuffion of the divinity of *Jefus Chrift* ;

Chrift; but it foon appeared that his *private intentions* were, to compel, by force, the vindicators of that belief to fubmit to the tenets of *Arianifm.* For when *Eugenius*, with his *Anti-Arian* prelates, entered the room of confultation, (y) they found *Cyrila*, their chief antagonift, feated on a kind of throne, furrounded by armed men; who quickly, inftead of confuting the arguments of their opponents, offered violence to their perfons. Convinced, by this application of force, that no deference would be paid to reafon, *Eugenius*, and his prelates, withdrew from the council-room; but not without leaving behind them a proteft, in which (among other paffages of Scripture) this Verfe of St. *John* is thus efpecially infifted upon, in vindication of the belief to which they adhered.——
" That it may appear more clear than the
" light, that the divinity of the Father, the
" Son, and the Holy Spirit, is one, fee it
" proved by the Evangelift St. *John*, who
" writes

(y) *Victor Vitenfis*, who was then an *African* bifhop, and *prefent at this council*, has left us a circumftantial account of the whole tranfaction. Vide Biblioth Max. Patrum, vol. VIII, p. 686 *Grynæ.* Coll Patr. Orthod. (Edit. *Bafil.* A. D. 1569) p. 799, and Appendix, No. V.

" writes thus : *There are Three which bear* " *record in Heaven, the Father, the Word,* " *and the Holy Spirit, and these Three are One.*" *Hi tres unum sunt* are the very words thus quoted by these bishops, as we have before seen them cited by *Cyprian, Tertullian,* and others, in the same literal order.

This remarkable fact appears to be, alone, amply decisive as to the originality of the Verse in question. The *manner,* in which it happened, seems to carry irresistible conviction with it. It was not *a thing done in a corner*, a transaction of solitude, or obscurity. It passed in the metropolis of the kingdom, in the court of the reigning prince, in the face of opponents exasperated by controversy, and proud of royal support, and in the presence of the whole, congregated, *African* church. Nor is the *time*, when this transaction happened, less powerfully convincing than its *manner*. Not much more than *three* centuries had elapsed, from the death of St. *John*, when this solemn appeal was thus made to the authority of this Verse. Had the Verse been *forged* by *Eugenius*, and

his

his bishops, all Christian *Africa* would have exclaimed, at once, against them. Had it even been considered as of *doubtful original*, their adversaries, the *Arians*, thus publicly attacked by this protest, would have loudly challenged the authenticity of the Verse, and have refused to be, in any respect, concluded by its evidence. But nothing of this kind intervened. *Cyrila*, and his associates, received its testimony in sullen silence ; and, by that silence, admitted it to have proceeded from the pen of St. *John*.

To the authority of these councils, and of the revision of *Charlemagne*, let me now subjoin the most sacred sanction, which any collective body of Christians can give to the truth of a passage of Scripture, namely, the admission of it into the public rituals, or service-books, of their churches. For,

4. This Verse of St *John* was inserted in the ancient service-books of the *Latin* Church. It was read in them, as part of the office for Trinity Sunday, and (as it now is in the church of *England)* for the *octave* of Easter.

It

It appears from the *Rationale* of *Durandus*, mentioned in my former letter (z), that this passage also formed a part of the office for the ministration of baptism, in those ancient liturgies, pursuant to the regulations of the *Ordo Romanus*, or " *The Roman order of Of-* " *fices to be used throughout the year.*" The *precise* time of the establishment of this ritual, in the *Latin* churches, is not clearly known: its antiquity has, in some degree, thrown a veil over it. But that it was, in those churches, the established directory of public worship, and consequently, that this Verse was received, by them, as part of the inspired writings, long before the revisal of the Scriptures in the reign of *Charlemagne*, (already stated in this letter) we are certified from authority (a) which will not be disputed

5. This Verse of St. *John* is found in the *Confession of Faith* of the *Greek* church. The words of this confession where it refers to the passage in question, are these: " The " Father,

(z) Page 20.
(a) For the antiquity of the *Ordo Romanus*, see *Usher's* works—*Cave*, Appendix ad Hist. Lit.—and *Selden*, de Sy-nedris, vol. II, p. 1250.

" Father, the Son, and the Holy Spirit, are
" all of the fame effence; as St. *John* tefti-
" fies—*There are Three who bear record in
Heaven, the Father, the Word, and the Holy
Spirit, and thefe Three are One.*" (b) The
time, when this public confeffion of faith
was firft compiled by the *Greek* church, does
not, now, appear. But the arguments, which
were urged on another occafion, and for another purpofe, by one of the moft zealous an-
tagonifts (c) of this Verfe, might be here applied to prove, that this confeffion was drawn
up in an age *very remote* from our own times.
Its *exact* date, however, like that of the
proof laft alledged from the *Latin* church,
is loft in its great antiquity.

(.. This Verfe is alfo found in the liturgy,
or public fervice-books, of the *Greek* church.
Among thefe one in particular, entitled

E   Απος̔ολο☙

(b) " Αλλα μεν &c —Deus autem eft natura verus,
" et æternus, et omnium conditor, vifibilium, et invifi-
" bilium. talis etiam eft Filius, et Spiritus fanctus.
" funt etiam ejufdem inter fe effentiæ, juxta doctrinam
" *Joannis* Evangeliftæ, qui dicit,—*Tres funt qui teftimo-
" nium perhibent in cælo, Pater, Sermo, et Spiritus fanctus
" et hi tres unum funt.*" Dr *Thomas Smith*'s Mifcellanea,
p. 155, Edit. *Lond* A. D. 1686
(c) M. *Simon*, Hift. Crit. du Texte, &c. C. ix.

Αποϛολο☉ (*a*) (the Apoſtle) bears a diſtin-
guiſhed place, being a collection of the *Epiſtles*
of the Teſtament, taken ſeparately from the
Goſpels: ſelect parts of which are appointed,
like thoſe which ſtand in the Communion-
ſervice of the Church of *England*, to be read,
in ſucceſſion, in the proper offices for particular days. Among other portions of
Scripture, this Verſe of St. *John* is directed,
by the *Greek* rituals, to be read in its courſe,
in the *thirty-fifth* week of the year. As to
the antiquity of this Αποϛολο☉, we have the
moſt poſitive proofs (*e*) that it was uſed in
the *Greek* church, in the *fifth* century. How
long it might have been eſtabliſhed there *before* that æra, is known only to *Him*, " *in*
" *whoſe ſight a thouſand years are but as yeſter-*
" *day.*"

If there can be, at this time, an *unerring*
method

(*d*) *Smith*'s Miſcellanea, p **155**. " *In illa* COLLEC-
" TIONE EPISTOLARUM *Novi Teſtamenti*," &c. Alſo
Martin's La Verite, p. ii. C. v.
(*e*) *Cave*, Vol. ii. Diſſ. 2, Edit. *Oxon*, A. D. **1743**, p. 23.
Selden de Synedriis, Vol. ii, p. **1250**, &c.
Fabricius, Biblioth. *Græc.* Vol. v. Diſſ. **1**, p. 34, Edit.
Hamb. A. D. **1712**.
Cotelerius, Eccl. *Græc* Monum. Tom. iii, p. 222—351,
Edit. *Paris*. A. D. **1656**.

method of demonſtrating, that any particular paſſage of Scriptuie was conſidered, by
the primitive Chriſtian church, as authentic, as bearing upon it the ſeal of divine in-
ſpiration, it muſt be by ſhewing ſuch paſſage
placed in its public creeds, or confeſſions of
faith, and appointed to be read in the ſolemni-
ties of its religious woiſhip. By the former,
the Church ſpeaks to men ; by the latter, it
intercedes with God : and in both with ſin-
cerity, becauſe all human principles of action concur to forbid even an attempt to de-
ceive, in either. Of both theſe pre-eminent
ſanctions the Verſe in queſtion can, fortunately, avail itſelf. It can plead *both* of
them in its favor. While numberleſs other
teſtimonials of its originality have, without
doubt, periſhed by neglect, or by accident ;
have been deſtroyed by the hoſtile invaſions of
rude, and unlettered, barbarians, or have
been crumbled into duſt under the deleteri-
ous hand of time, in the long lapſe of *ſeven-
teen hundred years :* theſe have, happily, eſcaped all thoſe perils, and have ſurvived to
the preſent age. And when we can trace
(as we are enabled to do in the inſtance now
before us) ſuch confeſſions, and liturgies,

E 2   back

back into ages fo remote as the *fourth*, or *fifth*, century after *Chrift*, without being able *even there* to difcover the *actual time* of their eftablifhment in the Chriftian Church;—we are then, by all the rules of right reafoning, well warranted to conclude, that fuch creeds, or confeffions of faith, fuch rituals, and formularies of devotion, muft have been nearly coeval with Chriftianity itfelf.

But the infertion of this Verfe in the *Confeffion of Faith* of the *Greek* Church, and in the public Liturgies of both the *Greek*, and *Latin*, Churches, joined to the authority of the *Councils*, and of the *Revifion* of *Charlemagne*, —which have been juft ftated,—are not the only teftimonies, (however ftrong, and convincing they may feem) which have been given, by collective bodies of Chriftians, to the authenticity of this verfe. Let it be here, finally, obferved, that the New Teftaments, which were anciently read in the Churches of *far the greateft number* of thofe nations, who made an early profeffion of the Chriftian faith, either in the *original Greek*, or in the ancient Verfions of that original
ginal

ginal into the language of thofe nations, (*f*)
furnifh the moft poweiful pioofs of the truth
of this difputed paffage of St. *John*. For

7. The ancient Veifion, or Tranflation,
of the New Teftament into the *Armenian*
language, hath always contained (*g*) this
verfe. It is affiimed, by the moft refpectable opponent of the authenticity of
this difputed paffage, that this Verfion hath
been ufed, by the *Aimenian* nations, at leaft
ever fince the age of *Chryfoftom*; who (*h*)
died in A. D. 407. The ieal date of this ancient Veifion, however, cannot, peihaps, be
caiiied higher than A. D. 432. But, even
in this cafe, the *original* MS, or MSS,
fiom which this Verfion muft thus have
been made, in the *fifth* century, cannot,

E 3   reafon-

(*f*) The *Syiiac*, and the *Coptic*, Verfions, with their
Tranfcripts, are the only exceptions to this general propofition And thofe veifions weie adopted by a very
few nations, indeed, when compared with the *Latid*,
Gieek, and *Aimenian*, Chriftians, who comprifed *three*
parts out of *four*, at leaft, of the then Chriftian world.
(See the objections of Dr *Benfon*, xlv to xlix, inclufive,
hereaftei ftated, and the anfwers made to thofe objections)
(*g*) See objection xlix, of Dr. *Benfon*, herein after
ftited
(*h*) See objection xxviii, of the late Sir *Ifaac Newton*,
herein alfo after ftated.

reafonably, be fuppofed to have had a much latei date than the age of the Apoftles.

8. The απορολος, which hath been already mentioned, was a tranfcript, oi *Collection of the Epiftles of the New Teftament*, in the *original Greek*. It was read publicly in the *Greek* Churches, as early as, peihaps much earlier than, the *fifth* century; and it hath been juft pioved always to have contained the Verfe, in queftion.

9. The Veifion, or Tianflation, of the New Teftament, by *Jerome*, f.om the *original Greek* into the *Latin* tongue, was made (*i*) in, or about, A. D. 384.—It hath been already obferved, that this difputed paffage hath conftantly ftood in this Verfion.

10. Noi hath the verfe, in queftion, been thus found in the *Aimenian* Veifion, in the *Greek* απορολος, and in the *Latin* Tianflation of *Jerome*, only. The *moft ancient* of all the Veifions of the Books of the New Teftament, from the languages

(*i*) See page 33, and objection xix of Dr. *Benfon*; alfo *Michaelis*, Sect. 65.

languages in which they were originally written, is the *Old Italic*, or *Itala Vetus*. This Version was made in the *first* (*k*) century, and therefore WHILST ST. JOHN WAS YET ALIVE; and was used by all the *Latin* Churches of *Europe*, *Asia*, (*l*) and *Africa*, for many centuries after his death. And thus the origin of the Verse in question, is, at length, carried up, not by inferences, or implications, alone, however fair, and obvious, but by PLAIN, AND POSITIVE, EVIDENCE, to the age of St. JOHN himself. For this *most valuable*, as well as *most ancient*, Version hath (*m*) constantly exhibited the Verse, 1. *John*, v. 7.

E 4   I have

(*k*) The words of *Michaelis*, on this subject, which are the more to be relied upon, because they are the words of a very learned adversary, are, that " *The Old Latin*" (or *Itala Vetus*) " *is the most ancient, and best, of all European Versions*,"—that it is " *of uncommon antiquity*,"—and that " *no man of learning denies that this Version was done in the* FIRST *century, except only* Dr *Mill*, " *who argues from this, that, in the first century,* MOST " *of the Christians, at* Rome, *understood* Greek. *But how* " *will he prove*," (continues *Michaelis*) " *that there were* " *not many of those Christians*," (particularly in the *remoter Provinces*, and among the *lower* classes of mankind) " *who* " *understood no more than their mother tongue*" (Sects. 61 to 63.)

(*l*) The *Christians* near *Jerusalem*, and in many parts of *Syria*, were of the *Latin* church.

(*m*) See objection xlv of Dr. *Benson*, where, it is trusted, this point is proved at large.

I have now, Sir, gone through all the positive testimony, which I proposed, *directly*, to adduce in support of the authenticity of the Verse in question. But the subject is too important to be thus dismissed. The OBJECTIONS, which have been brought against the originality of this Verse, remain yet to be discussed; and demand from me, what they shall certainly receive, an attentive, and serious, investigation. In this proposed disquisition, many other proofs of the authenticity of this Verse are intended to be urged *indirectly*, and by implication. Such proofs, when produced, will not, it is trusted, lose any thing of their real weight, by the accidental circumstance of the *place*, in which they may be found. It is even possible, that a speculative mind may experience a peculiar satisfaction, in selecting them, hereafter, from those stations, where the necessity of answering those objections, and a desire of avoiding repetitions, compel them now to stand; and in adapting them to other situations, where, if no such necessity had existed, they might, perhaps, with more propriety, have been arranged. And it seems,

moreover,

moreover, that I should be deficient to my own future views, as well as unjust to the evidence which has been already stated, if I did not subjoin, to an examination of those objections, a few observations, which force themselves upon the mind, on an attentive contemplation of the whole subject. For these purposes you will perhaps, Sir, permit me to intrude yet more upon your leisure, at some future opportunity.

I am, Sir,

&c. &c.

LETTER III.

SIR,

I HAVE taken the liberty, herein, as well as in the preceding letters, of addreffing myfelf, directly, to you, inftead of ufing, as my means of approach, any fictitious name, or any artificial addrefs. I have, in fo doing, fubmitted to the juftice of the rule, which you have prefcribed to your opponents, in your *Vindication*; (*a*) namely, that the author of a work, " who boldly gives his " name, and his labours, to the world, im- " pofes on his adverfaries the fair and ho- " nourable obligation of encountering him " in open day-light, and of fupporting the " weight of their affertions by the credit of " their names." And yet, the rule applies only *in part*, on the *prefent* occafion. The *credit of a name*, little known to the world, will not *fupport the weight* of many *affertions*.

But

(*a*) A Vindication of fome paffages in the 15th and 16th Chapters of the Hiftory, &c.—by Mr. *Gibbon*, Edit. 2, p. 153.

But I am not, however, much difcomforted in this refpect, becaufe I purpofe to *load* it with very few . one found argument, one folid inference, being of more worth than a whole *Chapter* of affertions.

I will now, therefore, proceed to examine, as was before propofed, the moft material objections, which have been urged againft the originality of this Verfe; and will beg leave to fuperadd, to fuch examination, fome reflections, which feem to arife from an attentive confideration of the whole fubject.

In this difquifition it may, perhaps, be the moft fatisfactory method to ftate the objections of the chief opponents of this Verfe fingly, and to fubjoin to each its diftinct, and feparate, reply. Of thefe *Sandius*, (*b*) *M. Simon*, (*c*) and Mr. *Emlyn*, (*d*) among its more early opponents; and Dr. *Benfon*,
(*e*) Sir

(*b*) Nucl. Eccl Hift. and Appendix, p. 376, &c — Interpr. Paradox.

(*c*) Hift. Crit. du Texte &c. Differt. fur les MSS &c. Hift. des Verfions &c.

(*d*) Full Enquiry &c. See *Emlyn*'s Works, 2 Vols. *Lond.* Edit A. D. 1746.

(*e*) Sir *Iſaac Newton*, (*f*) M. *Grieſbach*, (*g*) and Mr. *Bowyer*, (*h*) among its more modern adverſaries, ſeem to have been the moſt diffuſe, in the variety of their remarks, and the moſt determined in their oppoſition. But as the four laſt-mentioned writers have collected into one point of view, all, or nearly all, the objections that have, at any time, been urged againſt the originality of the Verſe in queſtion,—and as their works are more generally known than thoſe of *Sandius*, *Simon*, or *Emlyn*,—I will conſider them as ſpeaking the ſenſe of their fellow-advocates, and will ſtate their own objections in their own words.

And firſt, as to Dr. *Benſon*.—

   I. " *Three of the (i) latin fathers have* " *been referred to, as having borne teſti-* " *mony to this diſputed text; namely Ter-* " *tullian, Cyprian, and Jerome.*"

By

(*e*) Paraphraſe on the Catholic Epiſtles, Vol. ii, Edit. A. D. 1756.

(*f*) Hiſtory of two Texts (Vol. v. of *Newton's* Works, by Dr. Horſley)

(*g*) Nov. Teſtam. Græc. Vol. ii, p. 225 &c. (in the Notes) Edit. *Halæ*, A. D. 1777.

(*h*) Conjectures on the N. Teſt. Edit. *Lond.* A. D. 1782.

(*i*) Dr. *Benſon's* Paraphraſe, Vol. ii, p. 632.

Dr. Benson.   By this introductory obſervation, a candid
reader muſt, at firſt, preſume, that Dr. *Ben-*
ſon really meant to confine, to the age of *Je-*
rome, his obſervations on thoſe *Latin* Fathers, whoſe works might be made uſe of,
in argument, reſpecting this Verſe ; and not
to travel below the *fifth* century, for authorities *on either ſide of the queſtion.* Yet, under
this preſumption, Dr. *Benſon* ought, at leaſt,
to have made his enumeration of thoſe Fathers, who have borne teſtimony to this
Verſe, compleat, by adding to this Liſt, (*k*)
Marcus Celedenſis, Phæbadius, Eucherius, Au-
guſtine, and *Vigilius* ; who lived, and wrote,
in the ſame century with *Jerome,* and have,
as well as *Jerome,* given their teſtimony to
the truth of the Verſe in queſtion.   But Dr.
Benſon does not ſuffer his readers long to retain this firſt preſumption.   They ſee him,
it is true, in the progreſs of his Diſſertation,
poſitively refuſing to admit the teſtimony of
Victor Vitenſis, in FAVOR of this Verſe, who
lived

(*k*) See pages 30 to 36, of theſe letters.
It ſeems, however, that Dr *Benſon* could not be ignorant of the two Writers, here firſt named , for he has
referred to *Bengelius,* in p 620 of his paraphraſe, by
whom their teſtimony is particularly ſet forth.

lived in the fame century, and was, proba- Dr. BENSON.
bly, alive at the fame hour, with *Jerome*.
But they foon afterwards find him travelling
down, for authorities (*l*) which oppofe (or
rather for *omiffions* which SEEM to oppofe)
the authenticity of this Verfe, fo low as to
Bede, of the *eighth*, and to *Oecumenius*, of the
eleventh, century.

If, then, Sir, we follow Dr. *Benfon* to the
age of *Jerome*, only, the references to *Latin* Fathers, in favor of this Verfe, commencing with the age of the Apoftles, will
be, not to " *three*" only, but at leaft to *eight*,
viz. to *Tertullian*, *Cyprian*, MARCUS CE-
LEDENSIS, PHÆBADIUS, *Jerome*, AUGUS-
TINE, EUCHERIUS, and VIGILIUS. But
if we purfue him to the age of *Oecumenius*,
this Lift, already more than doubled, will
receive an almoft incredible increafe ; among
whom the following " Latin Fathers" feem
worthy of being efpecially *referred to*, namely, (*m*) *Fulgentius*, *Caffiodorius*, *Ambrofe Anfbert*, *Etherius*, and *Beatus*, *Walafrid Strabo*,
Radulphus

(*l*) Paraphrafe, p. 614.
(*m*) See pages 21 to 30, of the preceding letters.

Dr. Benson. *Radulphus Ardens, Hugo Victorinus, Scotus,* and St. *Bernard*: the four hundred *African* Bifhops, who attended the public difputation, propofed by *Huneric*;—and the Divines of the reign of *Charlemagne,* who, under the prefiding care of *Alcuinus,* revifed the Bible of that age. To whom muft be added, laftly, and above all, the common confent of the whole *Latin* Church, which, *before* the reign of *Charlemagne,* had given the moft folemn atteftation to the originality of this text, by inferting it in its public Rituals of divine worfhip. To this mighty *Phalanx,* and within this limit as to time, might be added a great number of other witneffes to the authenticity of this Verfe, as unexceptionable, in point of evidence, and as decided in their teftimony, as any of thofe whofe fuffrages have been already thus particularly collected, and fet forth.

II. " *It is plain he* [Tertullian] *has " not quoted the paffage*" [viz. becaufe he does not exprefsly declare his words to be a quotation]

This objection is ill-founded, and inconclufive.

conclufive. It has been the practice of wri- Dr. Benson.
ters, in all ages, to infert quotations from
well-known authors, without exprefsly de-
claring them *to be quotations*, or introducing
them *as quotations*, in any refpect. A few
inftances, of this kind, will be fufficient to
fhew the weaknefs of the argument, here
ufed by Dr. *Benfon*.

And firft from *Irenæus*, who lived in the
fecond Century after *Chrift*.

" Our bodies, being [firft] nourifhed by
" the earth, [then] depofited in the earth,
" and [laftly] refolved into earth, fhall
" arife in his time ; the Son of God grant-
" ing them a refurrection to the glory of
" the Father : for the ftrength of God is
" made perfect in weaknefs." (*n*)

In like manner, from *Clemens Alexandrinus*, who lived in the fame age with *Irenæus*.

" But that which is holy, is dear to that
F " from

(*n*) *Irenæi* adverfus Hærefes, Lib. v, Cap. ii. Edit.
Oxon. A. D. 1702, p. 400.

Dr. Benson. " from whence it becomes holy; which is
" properly called light. for ye were (o)
" sometimes darkness, but now are ye light
" in the Lord."

Again, from *Origen*, who flourished in the
third Century.

" But let the faithful Christian, more
" wife, as well as more firm, follow reason,
" and the word of God; and from thence let
" him learn to distinguish between truth,
" and falsehood. even as they delivered
" them unto us, who, from the beginning,
" were eye-witnesses, and ministers of the
" word." (*p*)

Again, from *Cyril*, who was Archbishop
of *Alexandria*, in the *fifth* Century.

" As the Lord, and Saviour of all, who
" could have appeared in the form of the
" Father, and altogether equal to him, and
" could have exhibited his Majesty on the
" throne

(o) *Clementis Alexandrini* Pædag. Lib. 1, Cap. vi, p.
41, Edit. *Commel.* A. D. 1592.
(p) *Origenis* Opera, Hom. 1. Edit. *Parisiis*, A. D. 1619.

" throne of the divinity; thought it not Dr. BENSON.
" robbery to be equal with God, but made
" himfelf of no reputation, and took upon
" him the form of a Servant." (q)

The concluding words of all the preceding fentences are quotations from Scripture; the *firft* from 2. *Corinthians*, xii. 9; the *fecond*, from *Ephef.* v. 8; the *third* from *Luke* i. 2; and the laft from *Philipp.* ii. 6, 7;—although they are all thus introduced—like the example, now in debate, from *Tertullian*,—without any previous expreffions, denoting them to be quotations.

Inftances of a fimilar kind, will fcaicely be required from the *Latin* Fathers, as they abound in almoft every page of their writings. One example, however, may juft be produced (to which a thoufand others fhall be added, if required) from *Jerome*, in the *fourth* Century.

F 2 " As

(q) *Cyrillus* contra *Julianum*, Lib. vi. p. 195, Edit. *Lipfiæ*, A. D. 1696

The learned Reader needs not to be informed, that all the preceding quotations, as they ftand here, are tranflations from the *original* language of thefe *Greek* Fathers.

Dr. Benson. " As long as we are entangled in the af-
" fairs of the world, and our minds are en-
" groffed by our earthly poffeffions, it is im-
" poffible for us to give up our thoughts
" chearfully to God : For what fellowfhip
" hath righteoufnefs with unrighteoufnefs,
" and what communion hath light with dark-
" nefs ? what concord hath *Chrift* with Be-
" lial ? or what part hath he that believeth,
" with an (*r*) infidel ?

The laft words of the foregoing fentence
are cited, literally, from 2. *Cor.* vi. 14, 15 ;
although without any previous note of introduction, denoting them to be a quotation.

If more modern inftances fhall be required,
they are here fubjoined.

" The man, who proceeds in it with
" fteadinefs, and refolution, will, in a little
" time, find, that all her ways are pleafant-
" nefs, and all her paths are peace."
                    Addifon—Spect. No. 447.
                                   " To

(*r*) *Hieronymi* Epif. ad *Lucinium* · Edit. *Erafmi, Paris.*
A. D. 1546, Vol. 1, p. (71, as erroneoufly marked in
that Edition, but properly page) 66.

" To graft in his heart the principles of Dr. Benson.
" charity, which fome perfons ought not,
" by any means, wholly to renounce, be-
" caufe it coveieth a multitude of fins."

Dr. Swift.

The former of thefe quotations is from
Prov. iii. 17,—the latter from 1. Pet. iv. 8 ;
—and both without any previous expreffions
of citation.

But, Mr. Gibbon will, perhaps, be fatisfactorily convinced, that quotations of this
nature are not infrequent, among good writers even of the prefent times, by the following inftances.

" Here, too, we may fay of Longinus, his
" own example ftrengthens all his laws." (s)

" It never can become (t) a Chriftian to
" be afiaid of being afked a reafon of the
" faith that is in him ; or the Church of

F 3
" England

(s) Gibbon's Hift. of the Decline, &c. Vol. 1. (2d.
Edit.) Notes, p. 10.
(t) Dr. Watfon's Apology, Edit. 2d. ad init.

Dr. Benson. " *England* to abandon that moderation, by
" which she permits every Individual et
" sentire quæ velit, et quæ sentiat dicere."

The *Scriptural* quotation, contained in the
latter of these sentences, is from 1. *Pet.* iii,
15. I will not offend Mr. *Gibbon,* by pointing out the others.

It is so far, therefore, from being *plain*
that *Tertullian* has not quoted this verse,
because he has not expresly *stiled his words
a quotation* from St. *John*; that there must,
from a candid consideration of the passage,
under all its circumstances, be, necessarily,
deduced the very opposite inference. The
striking peculiarity of the words themselves,
the literal order in which they stand in *Tertullian,* and the constant practice of writers,
ancient and modern, compel, as well as justify, the conclusion; that these words, when
written by *Tertullian,* must have been a direct, *intentional,* citation of the verse in question.

Thus far, then, Sir, for the imbecility of
the

the objection, which fuppofes the words of Dr. Benson, *Tertullian not to be* a quotation, merely becaufe they are *not declared fo to be* by *Tertullian*. Let us, now, turn to the *Treatife against Praveas*, and compare *Tertullian* with himfelf. Perhaps we may obtain new light by the comparifon.

In the *twenty-fecond* Chapter of this Treatife, *Tertullian* quotes the words of *Jefus Chrift*, as recorded by St. *John* in his Gofpel. " *Jefus Chrift* fays, *I and the Father are one.* " His expreffion is UNUM *fumus* ," [We are " one *thing*, or *Being*] " not UNUS" [one *Perfon*.] " He ufes the word UNUM, in the " neuter voice; which does not belong to " a fingle perfon, but to an (*u*) unity of " perfons."

With thefe helps, previoufly acquired, let us proceed to the paffage itfelf, of the *twenty fifth* Chapter, now in debate.

" *Jefus Chrift*, fpeaking of the Holy Ghoft, " faid, *He fhall take of mine*, as he himfelt

F 4 " had

(*u*) Appendix, No. I.

Dr. BENSON. " had taken of the Father. Thus the con-
" nection of the Father with the Son, and of
" the Son with the Holy Ghoſt, cauſes *theſe*
" *three* to be united together, one with ano-
" ther : *which three are one* [*thing*, or *Being*]
" not one [*Perſon*] IN THE SAME MANNER
" AS IT IS SAID, *I, and my father are*
" *one*." (*v*)

Tertullian here, moſt obviouſly, looks back
to that former quotation, in the *twenty-
ſecond* Chapter, which has juſt been ſtated.
He had there proved the Divinity of *Jeſus
Chriſt*, by a quotation from St. *John*, which
ſhewed HIS unity with the Father. He
here proceeds to prove the Divinity of the
Holy Ghoſt, likewiſe, by another quotation
from the ſame St. *John*, which ſhews *a like
unity* of THREE Perſons in the God-head.
And, leſt his meaning ſhould be miſunder-
ſtood, he, fortunately, adds a Comment,
which ſeems to place the whole matter in
the cleareſt light : " *Which three are one* Be-
" ing, not one Perſon, IN THE SAME MAN-
" NER

(*v*) Appendix, No. II,

" NER AS IT IS SAID, *I and my Father are* Dr. BENSON.
" *one*,"---viz. in the former quotation.

  III. " *In his Book concerning the Unity*
" *of the Church, Cyprian is fuppofed to*
" *have quoted this paffage.*   *His words*
" *are,—Of the Father, Son, and Holy*
" *Spirit, it is written, Thefe three are*
" *one.*—(p. 633.)

It were much to be wifhed, that Dr. *Benfon* had been more candid in his extracts, and
more faithful in his quotations. The words,
above cited, are *a part*, only, of the expreffions of *Cyprian*, fome very material
words being unfairly paffed by, and omitted.
The whole fentence taken together, ftands
thus : (*w*) " Our Lord declares, *I, and my*
" *Father, are one.* And *again it is written*
" of the Father, Son, and Holy Spirit, *And*
" *thefe three are one.*"

Let this fentence be analyfed.—" *Our Lord
declares, I, and my Father, are one.*" Where
does he make that declaration ? In Scripture,
        becaufe

(*w*) Appendix, No. III.

Dr. BENSON. becaufe *that* contains the record of the words of our Lord, as well as of his actions, whilft on earth. And in what part of Scripture is that declaration made ? It is in the *thirtieth* Verfe, of the *tenth* Chapter, of the Gofpel of St. *John*; and the quotation is literal. Let us now proceed.—" *And again it is written, of the Father, Son, and Holy Spirit, And thefe three are one.*"—AGAIN *it is written!*—When an author thus fpeaks of a *fecond* act of any kind, he muft be confidered as referring to a *former* act, of a fimilar nature with, or fimilarly cir- cumftanced to, that which refers to it. And what, in the prefent cafe, was *this former act* ? It was a *direct citation*, by *Cyprian*, of a paffage in Scripture. What, then, was the *latter* act ?——The inference needs not to be mentioned. It follows too clofely to be miftaken, or evaded.

Thus the conclufion,—that *Cyprian* DID mean to " quote this paffage, in his Book " concerning the *Unity of the Church*,"— feems to be inevitable, when we take *the whole* of his words into contemplation, at once, and place them in the fame point of

view.

view. But if we even receive their tefti- Dr. Benson.
mony in the mutilated, curtailed, condition,
in which Dr. *Benfon* has *thought fit* to ftate
it, the fame inference feems fairly deducible fiom them. For, as the volume of the
facred Wiitings, is, *emphatically*, called, *the
Book:* fo the phrafe, *it is written*, when employed by writeis on facred fubjects, *emphatically*, and *abfolutely*, without any other particulars of defcription, denotes (in geneial,
at leaft) the expieffions, which follow, to be
quotations from Scripture. It might be tedious
to pioduce many examples from many books.
A few from that book alone, *which was
wiitten for our learning*, may be fufficient.

" For *it is written*, I will fmite the Shep-
heid, and the fheep fhall be fcatteied."—
[*Maik* xiv. 27]

" For *it is written*, thou fhalt not fpeak
evil of [or curfe] the ruler of thy people."
—[*Acts* xxiii. 5.]

" For *it is written*, vengeance is mine."—
[*Romans* xii. 19.]

" And

Dr. Benson. " And fo *it is written*, Adam was made
" [or became] a living foul."—[1. *Cor.* xv. 45.

In thefe inftances, *Zechariah*, xiii. 7,—
Exodus, xxii. 28,—*Deuteronomy*, xxxii. 35,
and *Genefis*, ii. 7,—are literally cited, although
without any other previous introduction,
than the phrafe here ufed by *Cyprian*, viz.
It is written. The objection, therefore, that
Cyprian can only be " *fuppofed* to have quoted
this paffage," becaufe he has not ufed introductory words, fufficiently ftrong (as is alledged) to imply a fucceeding quotation
from Scripture, comes fomewhat unfeafon-
ably, when it appears, that he has adopted
thofe very words, to introduce his quotation,
which are made ufe of by *Jefus Chrift*, and
by his Apoftle St. *Paul*, to preface theirs ;
—the identical expreffions employed, *in Scripture itfelf*, to denote *a quotation from Scripture.*

IV. " *The query is, whether Cyprian*
" *defigned to quote the feventh Verfe, or*
" *to give a myftical interpretation of the*
" *eighth verfe, namely, that by the water,*
" *the*

" the blood, and the spirit, we are to un- Dr. BENSON.
" derstand the father, the son, and the
" holy spirit."

There seems to be no query in the case.
Had *Cyprian* designed to give a *mystical interpretation*, only, he would not, (as hath been
just observed) after having *literally quoted*
one passage of Scripture, have instantly followed that quotation with the words,—
" And AGAIN *it is written*." The assertion
would have been utterly false, at the very
hour of its being made by *Cyprian*, had not
the *seventh* Verse existed at that time. The
words, " *And these three are one*," were *never*
WRITTEN, of the Trinity of persons in the
Godhead, in any part of Scripture, save in
I. *John*, v. 7 ; which is the verse in question.

Let it be further remarked, on this head,
that had *Cyprian* designed a *mystical interpretation*, only, he would not have written,
Scriptum est, ET *hi tres unum sunt* ; but,
Scriptum est hos tres unum esse: as he *does write*
in another place, where he only designs to
allude,

Dr. Benson. *allude*, not *quote*, " *Scriptum (x) est justum fide vivere.*" Taking the sentence in question, as a glofs, comment, or *interpretation* of *Cyprian*, the conjunction, *Et*, is a moft abfurd, and a moft ungrammatical, Expletive. But, *as a quotation*, it ftands perfectly right. " *It is written of the Father, Son, and Holy Spirit.*"—What is written of them? Thefe words, *Et hi tres unum funt,*—" *And* " *thefe three are one.*" The conjunction, *(Et)* thus viewed, is fo far from being inconfiftent with Grammar, and common fenfe, that it ftands, with peculiar propriety, in its fituation ; not only proving the claufe, at the head of which it fo ftands, *to be a quotation,* but marking out the bounds of that quotation moft precifely.

     V. " *The loofe manner, in which the* " *fathers fometimes quoted, might cre-* " *ate a fufpicion. But there is more, in* " *the prefent cafe, than this general fuf-* " *picion.*" [viz. That *Cyprian* did not mean to quote the *feventh,* but to give a myftical interpretation of the *eighth,*
                        Verfe

(x) De Mortalitate, p. 157, alluding to *Romans* i, 17.

Verse.] " For Eucherius, (de Quæst. Dr. Benson.
" difficil. in loca V. et N. T.) about the
" year, 434, having cited these words,
" There are three which bear testimony,
" the water, the blood, and the spirit;
" says, if it be asked, what is the meaning
" of these words? I answer, many think
" the Trinity is here meant."

If Dr. *Benson* did *not know* that *Eucherius*
has actually quoted this Verse, *(y)* in his
works, he has, in this objection, betrayed a
most *blameable ignorance* of his subject. If he
did know, and yet *suppressed*, the quotation, he
has proved himself guilty of a most *disingenuous concealment* of the truth. Let his
advocates take either alternative. Want
of knowledge renders him *unfit* for the office
of a Commentator. Want of integrity makes
him *unworthy* of it. They are disqualifica-
tions very different, indeed, in their nature;
but they, alike, reject him from sitting in
judgement on the authenticity of the Verse in
question.

Both

(y) Letter ii, p 32, art 16,—where the quotation,
here referred to, is stated in the words of *Eucherius*.

Dr. BENSON. Both alternatives are thus offered to the reader. But he will, perhaps, soon perceive on which of them he ought to fix. For Mr. *Emlyn,* an *Englishman,* and a Diffenter, (the moft ftrenuous opponent which this verfe ever had, except M. *Simon)* in the difpute, which arofe, in the beginning of the prefent Century, between him and Mr. *Martin,* Paftor of the *French* Church, at *Utrecht,* in *Holland,* refpecting the authenticity of this verfe, thus ingenuoufly confeffes the embarraffment, into which this teftimony of *Eucherius* had thrown him. " The " paffage Mr. *Martin* brings out of *Eucherius,* " (of which indeed I was not aware before) " will need more confideration; for though " it only concerns the *fifth Century,* in which " I did allow that poffibly *the words* might " become *Text* in fome books, yet it will " carry it half a Century higher than the " *Confeffion* of the *African* Bifhops in *Victor* " *Vitenfis* and, I confefs, if the paffage be " genuine, it is more to the purpofe than " any, yea than all, the other teftimonies, " before, or after, *Eucherius,* for fome hun- " dreds of years, becaufe here we find both " the

" the *seventh*, and *eighth verses together*, at Dr. BENSON.
" once to fhew us all the *fiv* witneffes; and
" theie was *Father*, *Word*, and *Spirit*, befide
" what was faid of the *Water*, *Blood*, and
" *Spirit*; whereas only *Father*, *Word*, and
" *Spirit*, might have been the fame things
" myftically interpreted, after the prevail-
" ing cuftom of that time. So that I can-
" not deny but Mi. *Martin* had fome ground
" to fay, *this is decifive*, i. e. as to its being
" acknowledged by *Eucherius*, in the fifth
" Century." (z)

Dr. *Benfon* could not be *ignorant* of this
quotation of the Veife, in queftion, thus
made by *Eucherius*, or of Mr. *Emlyn*'s
diftrefs on the fubject; wheiein, as his laft
poor iefuge, he is driven, (as we have juft
feen) to affect a *doubt of the paffage being genuine*. Foi Dr. *Benfon* had read, BEFORE *he
began his Differtation*, not only Mi. *Martin's*
Differtation on this text, which *contains this
quotation* fiom *Eucherius*; but Mr. *Emlyn*'s
reply to it. He confeffes BOTH, in the outfet

G   of

(z) *Emlyn*'s Anfwer to *Martin*'s Differt. *Lond.* Edit.
A. D. 1746, p. 193.

Dr. Benson. of his own (a) Differtation; although he was not then, perhaps, aware of the confequence After this confeffion, which condemns himfelf, the plea of IGNORANCE,—of *not having feen the quotation,*—can no longer avail him ; and, that being once taken away, there can be no doubt as to the charge, which muft be fubftituted in its place.

VI. " *Facundus, who flourifhed in the*
" *fifth century, and was of the fame African*
" *Church ; did not only, himfelf, interpret*
" *the words of the eighth verfe, in that*
" *myftical manner : but has acquainted us*
" *that Cyprian, the Martyr, did fo un-*
" *derftand them.*"

What *Facundus,* or *Cyprian, underftood,* or *interpreted,* concerning that Verfe, is immaterial to the prefent enquiry. The queftion is not about the *eighth,* but about the *feventh,* Verfe. And it feems clear that *Cyprian* read
the

(a) " I have read Dr. *Mill's Prolegomena,*" &c " But
" above all, I HAVE READ Mr. *Martin's Critical Differ-*
" *tation on this text,* Mr EMLYN'S FULL ENQUIRY,
" &c and the letters of M. *La Croze,* and F. *Le Long,*
,, publifhed by Mr. *Emlyn*" (Dr. *Benfon's* Paraphrafe,
2d Edit. p. 631, and 632.)

the seventh Verse, in his Teftament, not
only from the arguments, which have been
urged, on that head, in the preceding part of
this letter, but from the pofitive (b) teftimony of *Fulgentius*, who lived in the fame century, and was of the fame *African* Church,
with *Facundus*. Nor could *Facundus*, even
if it fhould be granted that he *has not quoted*
this verfe, (which is more than ought to be
granted, unlefs we were in poffeffion of all
his works) be ignorant of its exiftence in this
Epiftle of St. *John*. The public appeal to
the teftimony of this Verfe, which was
made in *the country of Facundus*, by nearly
four hundred Bifhops at once, in the famous
(c) Convention of *Huneric*;—made at *Carthage*, the *Metropolis* of that country;—
made in oppofition to the *Arians*, of that age
who were fupported by the reigning Prince
of that country;—made in the life-time, in
the manhood, of *Facundus*;—(for it happened but a few years before the advance-
ment of *Facundus* to the Bifhopric of *Her-
miane*)—all thefe circumftances render it

G 2 impoffible

(b) See pages 27, and 28 ; and alfo the anfwers to the
two next fucceeding objections.
(c) See Pages 44—47.

Dr. Benson. impoſſible to ſuppoſe, that this Verſe was not found in the Bible of *Facundus*, as well as in that of *Cyprian*; although he, perhaps, may not, like *Cyprian*, have particulariſed it by a direct quotation.

VII. " *Fulgentius, who was cotem-* " *porary with Facundus, has been thought* " *to repreſent Cyprian as quoting the* " *words from St. John.*"

Theſe, which follow, are the words of *Fulgentius*, where he ſpeaks of *Cyprian*, and this Verſe, conjointly. " The bleſſed A- " poſtle St. *John*, teſtifies, that there are " three which bear record in Heaven, the " Father, the Word, and the Spirit, and " theſe three are one. WHICH, alſo, the " moſt holy Martyr, *Cyprian*, declares in " his Epiſtle, *De Unitate Eccleſiæ* ; wherein, " to demonſtrate that there ought to be an " unity in the Church, as there is in the " Godhead, he has brought the FOLLOWING " PROOFS FROM SCRIPTURE. *The Lord ſays,* " *I and my Father are one* ; and AGAIN IT

" IS WRITTEN *of the Father, Son, and Holy* Dr Benson.
" *Spirit, And thefe three are one.*" (d)

Thus *Fulgentius* has not only " been
thought to reprefent," but has *directly, and
pofitively*, reprefented, " *Cyprian* as quoting"
the verfe in queftion.   And, not contented
with this, he has done more ;—he has *quoted
the Verfe*, himfelf, in the moft explicit, and
un-myftical, terms.

But this, it feems, cannot be ; becaufe *Ful-
gentius* ufes the word [confitetur] *confeffes*.
For, as Dr. *Benfon* further argues concerning
Fulgentius——

VIII. " *He fays* [*fo Cyprian confeffes*]
" *Confeffes, what ? That thefe very words
" were in the epiftle of St. John ? What
" a mighty matter was that ; to confefs
" what he found in the writings of an
G 3   " *Apoftl !*

(d) Refponfio contra *Arianos*, Bibl M... Patrum,
vol ix, p 41.   (Appendix, No. IX)
    It cannot be doubted, that *Fulgentius* read this verfe in
the *Greek* MSS, as well as in his own Bible, becaufe he
was much practifed, and eminently fkilled, in the *Greek*
language.   *Du Pin, Lond.* Edit. A. D. 1693, vol. iv. ;
13, 14.

Dr. Benson.

" *Apoſtle ! But to confeſs, or acknowledge,*
" *that by the Water, the Blood, and the*
" *Spirit, were meant the Father, the Son,*
" *and the Holy Spirit, was a very re-*
" *markable confeſſion. And what thoſe*
" *who held the ſame opinion, would be*
" *glad to find ſo eminent a father and*
" *martyr confeſſing,*"—(p. 634.)

If this piece of verbal Criticiſm, ſuch as it is, were juſt, it would prove nothing. But it is not juſt. The Verb, *Confiteor*, may be rendered, to *declare*, to *ſhew*, to *profeſs*, as well as to *confeſs* ; and is frequently uſed in theſe ſenſes by the beſt Writers. Without taking the trouble of referring, for examples, to the *Latin* Claſſics, at large, the Dictionary of *Ainſworth* will ſufficiently atteſt the truth of this conſtruction. And thus this poor cavil falls to the ground.

IX. " *Yes, (you will ſay) but inter-*
" *preting is one thing ; and ſaying, ſo it is*
" *written, is quite a different thing.*"

It has, I truſt, been already not only *ſaid,*
but

but PROVED, that " faying, *So it is written,*" Dr. BRYSON.
is, in ferious truth, " quite a different thing
from *interpreting* ;" and was meant fo to be,
by *Cyprian* himfelf, in the cafe now before
us. And the argument will, perhaps, ac-
quire additional ftrength, by fhewing that
Cyprian has, in *other* paffages of his works,
frequently quoted Scripture, without ufing
any other prefatory words, to introduce fuch
quotations, than the phrafe, [*It is written*]
which is now under confideration.

" Becaufe *it is written*, He who endureth
" to the end, fhall be faved." (*e*)--[*De ha-*
" *bitu Virginum,* p. 93.]

" Since *it is written*, All things are lawful,
" but all things are not (*f*) expedient."
" [*Ibid.* p. 96.]

" Since *it is written*, Remember from
" whence thou art fallen, and (*g*) repent."—
" [*De Lapfis,* p. 129.]

G 4

" As

(*e*) A literal quotation from *Matthew* x. 22.
(*f*) From 1 *Cor* vi. 12.
(*g*) From *Rev.* ii. 5.

Dr. Benson. "As *it is written*, A man's heart deviſeth
" his way, but the Lord directeth his ſteps."
(*b*)—[*De zelo*, p. 228.]

" As *it is written*, am I a God at hand,
" and not a God afar off? If a man ſhall
" hide himſelf in ſecret places, ſhall not I ſee
" him? Do not I fill heaven and (*i*) earth?
" —AND AGAIN: The eyes of the Lord
" are in every place, beholding the evil and
" the (*k*) good."—[*De Oratione Dominica*,
p. 140.]

" Since *it is written*, The Lord will not
" ſuffer the ſoul of the righteous (*l*) to fa-
" miſh. AND AGAIN: I have been young,
" and now am old; yet have I not ſeen the
" righteous forſaken, nor his ſeed begging
(*m*) bread."—[*Ibid.* p. 148.]

The number of theſe examples might, if
neceſſary, be much increaſed. The two laſt
are

(*b*) From *Prov* xvi. 9.
(*i*) From *Jerem.* xxiii. 23, 24.
(*k*) From *Prov.* xv. 3.
(*l*) From *Prov* x. 3.
(*m*) From *Pſalm* xxxvii. 25. (Bible Tranſlation.)

are peculiarly appofite; being inftances of Dr. BENSON, two fucceffive quotations, coupled together, by the very fame link [*And again*] which joins the two quotations in the paffage now under confideration.

> X. " *Cyprian has, in other inftances,* " *quoted Scripture more by his fenfe of it,* " *than by repeating the words of the text.* " *Thus inftead of, Lead us not into tempta-* " *tion, he quotes it, Suffer us not to be led* " *into temptation.   And, Rev.* xix. 10. " *Worfhip thou the Lord Jefus, inftead of* " *Worfhip thou God.—Which were not* " *different readings ; but Cyprians's own* " *interpretations."——*

There is good reafon to believe, that the former of thefe inftances did not fall from the pen of *Cyprian.* It certainly is not *the only,* and it feems not to be *the genuine,* reading of this paffage.   *Lead us not into tempta-tion,* are the words of the *Arundelian* MS, of thofe from *Pembroke* College, *Cambridge,* of thofe from *York,* from *Lincoln* College, *Ox-ford,* of one belonging to the famous *Voffius,*

and

Dr. Benson. and of two others from the *Bodleian* Library; and the sentence stands thus, also, in the Collations of the Monastery of *St. Victor*, at *Paris.*

As to the latter instance, from *Revelations* xix. 10, it is, most probably, a *different reading*, notwithstanding Dr. *Benson's* positive declaration to the contrary. The old *Italic* Version was the Bible of *Cyprian*, and the public Bible of the age in which he lived. The Version of *Jerome* was not made until nearly *two hundred* years after the death of *Cyprian*; and it was, at least (*n*) *four hundred* years after his death, before that Version took place of the *Italic*, in the public Churches, as well as in the Libraries of the learned: which, indeed, it has done so completely, that there is not a single MS of the old *Italic* Version now, certainly, *known* (*o*) to exist in the world.

What

(*n*) *M Simon*, Hist. Crit. des Versions, Cap vii—ix.
(*o*) *Michaelis* seems to wish the learned world to believe, that the text of the *Old Italic* is annexed to the *Bœrnerian*, and *Claromontane*, MSS and that *Martianay* has already published the Gospel of St. *Matthew*, and the Epistle of St *James*, from that Version. But his own expressions—" *A Latin Version, which is* THOUGHT *to*

What then, Sir, fhall hinder us from con- Dr. Benson,
cluding, that the Verſion, from whence
Cyprian (*p*) drew his quotations, was the
old *Italic,* and that it read the words now
in queſtion, as *Cyprian* has quoted them? It
has not been ſufficiently attended to, by Dr.
Benſon, and by other writers, of modern
times, who have, too haſtily, accuſed *Cyprian,* and other ancient *Latin* Fathers, of
quoting looſely, and of giving *interpretations,*
inſtead of citations; that thoſe fathers did
not quote from the preſent *Vulgate* of the
New Teſtament, or from any other *Exemplar* of it, which is now known to be extant; but from a Verſion, which is *now,*
probably, *loſt.*

XI. " *Why might not he*" [Cyprian]
" *give*

" *be the Italic*"—" *a very ancient Latin Verſion*"—" *which*
" *Martianay cauſed to be printed from two very ancient*
' *MSS*"—are the uncertain language of a perſon, wa-
vering, and diſtruſtful of his own concluſions. (*Introd.
Lect* Sect. 24, 26, and 61)

(*p*) Dr *Pearſon,* in his Edition of *Cyprian's* works,
has adopted this idea of a *different reading* in this paſſage.
" Legiſſe videtur *Cyprianus* non τω θεω προσκυνησον, ſed
" τω κυριω." (Note, p. 220) But, not recollecting
the circumſtances above-mentioned, he has not attempted
any explanation of this note; but has left it, as it now
ſtands in his Edition, a reſpectable, yet unſupported,
conjecture.

Dr. Benson.

" *give the fenfe*" [of the *eighth* verfe]
" *in his own words; and fay, Of the*
" *Father, Son, and Holy Spirit, it is*
" *written, Thefe three are one?*" (p.
635.)

Becaufe he would, in fuch a cafe, have
faid the thing which was not. IT IS NOT
WRITTEN, of the Father, Son, and Holy
Spirit, *Thefe three are one,* in any part of the
eighth Verfe of this chapter. To fuppofe
that *Cyprian* would have affirmed a thing to
be written, which *never was written,* is to
fuppofe that he would have been guilty of
uttering an intentional falfehood; a fuppofition altogether monftrous, and abominable !

XII. " *For my own part, I make no*
" *doubt but that was the fact.*"

INDEED !

XIII. " *The reafon, why Jerome has*
" *been appealed to, in this point, is, that*
" *there is, in feveral latin bibles, a pre-*
" *face to the catholic epiftles, which goes*
" *under his name.*"

This

This affertion is true, in part; but it does Dr. Benson, not contain the whole truth. The appeal to the teftimony of *Jerome,* in favor of this Verfe, is *not* founded on this preface *only;* but partly on this preface, and partly on his having been the Author of that Tranflation of the Bible, which is now called the *Vulgar Latin,* or the *Vulgate:*—in which Tranflation this Verfe has always had a place.

XIV. " *But feveral learned men, and* " *even fome, who plead for the genuine-* " *nefs of this text, have given up that* " *preface, as fpurious. Their reafons,* " *for rejecting it, are fuch as thefe,—*

" *It is not in* Jerome's *catalogue of* " *prefaces.*"

Jerome wrote, in the fourteenth year (*p*) of *Theodofius,* A. D. 392, a Catalogue of the works, which he had *then* compofed. He lived *twenty-eight* years longer, or until A. D. 420: in which latter part of his life he compofed, not only this preface to the *Catholic*

Dr. Benson. *tholic (or Canonical)* Epiſtles, but alſo ſeveral other ſimilar prefaces, and commentaries, particularly to the *greater* Prophets, as they are commonly called, (r) *Iſaiah, Ezekiel,* and *Jeremiah*; to the leſſer Prophets *Zechariah, Malachi, Hoſea, Joel, Amos,* and *Jonah*; to the Acts of the Apoſtles, alſo, as it ſeems, and to the Epiſtles of St. *Paul.*

It is true, then, that this preface is not inſerted in *Jerome*'s Catalogue: but it is not true, that it is, therefore, ſpurious. The preface has no place in the Catalogue, not becauſe it was NOT WRITTEN by *Jerome,* but becauſe it was written by him AFTER that Catalogue was compoſed.

XV. " *It*" [this preface] " *is often* " *found in latin MSS, without his*" [Jerome's] " *name.*"

It is found without his name, in ſome *Latin* MSS. But that omiſſion does not prove its ſpuriouſneſs. *Jerome*'s preface to the Books of the *Chronicles* is not mentioned as his

(r) *Hody,* De Bibl. Text. Orig p. 378.

his work, even in his own Apology; although Dr. Benson.
written by him long before the date of that
Apology. (s) His preface to the *Pſalms* is
" without his name" in ſeveral ancient MSS,
particularly in that of *Carcaſſonne* (t) : yet
that preface is confeſſedly his work. *Jerome's*
preface to the Book of *Eſdras* is, alſo, " with-
" out his name," in one of the moſt ancient
MSS in the Royal Library at *Paris*. Yet
this preface is now allowed, by all learned
men, to be the work of *Jerome*. Omiſſions,
of this kind, prove nothing,—but the negligence of haſty tranſcribers.

XVI. " *It*" [the preface] " *makes*
" *uſe of the words,* canonical epiſtles :
" *whereas* Jerome's *title for them was,*
" The Catholic Epiſtles."

Jerome has, himſelf, applied the epithet,
Canonical, to theſe Epiſtles, in other parts
of his works, as well as in the preface
now in queſtion (u). So hath *Auguſtine,*
(v) the

(s) *Idem,* p. 374.
(t) *Hieronymi* Opera, vol ii p 546.
(u) See Notes by *Eraſmus,* on *Jerome's* Treatiſe on
Ecclefiaſtical Writers vol. i, p 103, F and G. Edit.
Paris. A. D. 1546. *Eraſmus,* however, was offended with

DR. BENSON.

(v) the Contemporary, and Correspondent, of *Jerome*. And so hath *Vigilius*, who also lived in the same age. In his treatise against *Varimadus*, the *Arian*, he says—" It is written " in the CANONICAL Epistles, *My little* " *children, this is the last time:*" and the quotation is made from this very Epistle of St. *John*. And so hath *Junilius*, likewise, who lived in the sixth century, about one hundred years after the death of *Jerome*. *Junilius* stiles these Epistles *Canonical*, without explanation, or apology, as an appellation well-known, and long applied to them ; *Quæ (w) Apostolorum* CANONICÆ *nuncupantur,*"

the epithet , and, at first, vainly, attempted to substitute *Catholic* in its place but he soon submitted, and stiled them *Canonical*, himself, viz. " 2 *Joan.* CANONICA— 3. *Joan.* EJUSDEM. (Vol. II, p. 109) In another work he even allows, that *Jerome* stiled these Epistles *Canonical.* These are his words " De hac quoque secunda *Petri* " epistola, cujus esset, controversia erat. Id testatur " *Hieronymus*, in Catalogo scriptorum illustrium, his " quidem verbis Scripsit [Petrus] *duas epistolas, quæ* " CANONICÆ *nominantur*, quarum secunda a plerisque " ejus negatur, propter stili cum priore dissonantiam " (Annot *Erasmi* in Nov. Test A D. 1522, p 614)

(v) *De Civitate Dei*, Lib. xv cap. 23 " Scripsisse " quidem nonnulla divina *Enoch* illum septimum ab *Adam*, " negare non possumus, cum hoc in EPISTOLA CANONICA " *Judas* Apostolus dicat." (*August* Opera, Edit. *Parm*, A. D 1680, vol. vii, p 408)

(w) De Partibus Divinæ Legis, Cap. 6 —(Max. Bibl. Patrum, vol. x. p. 341, Edit. *Lugd.* A. D. 1677)

tur," are his words. *Caſſiodorius* applies the ~~Dr. Benson.~~
ſame epithet to them, in the firſt Book of his
Inſtitutes; who lived in the ſame age with
Junilius. Nor was this epithet of *Canonical*
applied to theſe Epiſtles, at that time, by
Jerome, Vigilius, Auguſtine, Caſſiodorius, and
Junilius, alone, but by the whole *Latin*
Church ; which is proved by the beſt teſtimony poſſible,—the acknowledgement of an
adverſary. " The *Greeks*" (ſays M. *Simon*)
" have ſtiled the ſeven Epiſtles, *Catholic* ;
" but the *Weſtern* Churches ſeem, (*x*) ES-
" PECIALLY, to have given to them the
" epithet of CANONICAL."

> XVII. " *That preface is prefixed to*
> " *ſome latin copies of the catholic epiſtles* ;
> " *in which the diſputed text is not in-*
> " *ſerted.*"

The ſame adverſary, whom we have already quoted in reply to the laſt, ſhall, ſingly, anſwer this, objection. " This is the
" fault of tranſcribers ;" (ſays M. *Simon,*
ſpeaking on this ſubject) " who, being only
H   " juſt

(*x*) Hiſt. Crit. du N. T. C. xvii, ad init,

Dr. Benson. " juft equal to the tafk of *copying* the MSS,
" did not confider the difagreement, which
" there was between the text of their
" copies, and this preface."

    XVIII. " *The preface is not found in*
" *fome of the beft and moft ancient MSS*
" *of Jerome's verfion.*"

If by the expreffion, " *fome*," it was here
meant to infinuate, that this preface is not
found in the greater part, or in the *generality*,
of the MSS of *Jerome's* verfion,—the in-
finuation is not founded in truth. Nor are
thofe MSS of *Jerome's* verfion, in which
this preface " is not found," either *the beft*,
or the *moft ancient*. The truth is, thofe
MSS of *Jerome's* verfion, which want this
preface, are few, and, in other refpects, very
incorrect; and (as hath been in part obferved before) no conclufion can be drawn,
to overturn the authenticity of this preface,
from fuch, or any fimilar, acts of negligence,
or omiffion, in ignorant, or hafty, tranfcribers.

    XIX. " *It*" [the preface] " *infinuates*
" *one falfehood—that all the greek copies*
                    " *of*

" *of the new teftament had this verfe.* Dr. Benson.
" *Whereas none of them had it. And*
" *Jerome, above all men, who was fo*
" *converfant in the greek copies of the*
" *new teftament, muft needs have known*
" *this to have been a direct falfehood.*"

It is really aftonifhing to fee fuch affertions advanced in direct oppofition to *Jerome's* own teftimony, and to the plain, and
obvious, truth of the cafe. This Verfe
ftands in *Jerome's* Teftament. *Jerome*
folemnly affures us, that he fettled the text
of that Teftament *by the* Greek *copies.* " No-
" *vum Teftamentum (y) fidei* Græcæ *reddidi.*"
Jerome, therefore, is fo far from knowing

H 2   that

(*y*) See the reference mentioned in page 33.
In his 28th Epiftle (to *Lucinius*) *Jerome* again makes
the fame declaration. " Septuaginta Interpretum edi-
" tionem et te habere non dubito, et ante annos plu-
" rimos diligentiffime emendatam, ftudiofis tradidi *No-
" vum* Græcæ *reddidi auctoritati.*" Edit. *Erafmi, Paris.*
A D. 1546, vol. 1 p (71, as erroneoufly marked in the
vol but really page) 66.
And again, " Sicut autem in Novo Teftamento, fi
" quando apud *Latinos* quæftio exoritur, et eft inter
" exemplaria varietas, *recurrimus ad fontem* Græci
" *fermonis, quo novum fcriptum eft inftrumentum* ita in
" Veteri Teftamento, fi quando inter *Græcos, Latinofque,*
" diverfitas eft, ad *Hebraicam* recurrimus veritatem."
(Hieron. *Sunæ* et *Fretelæ,* vol. III, p. 26.—)

Dr. Benson. that this Verfe was in none of the *Greek*
MSS, that he has, upon the authority of
thofe very MSS, inferted the Verfe in his
own Tranflation. This *Jerome*, " who,
" above all men, was fo converfant in the
" *Greek* Copies of the New Teftament,"
has tranfcribed this Verfe from thofe very
Copies !

  XX. " *Nor has any of the genuine*
" *works of the greek fathers once men-*
" *tioned it*"—[viz. the Verfe, 1. *John*,
v. 7.]

If this affertion were true, it would not
be conclufive againft the originality of this
pieface. But it is not true; as will appear
by the following inftances, taken from fuch
parts of the works of thofe Fathers, as have
furvived to the prefent times.

  1. *Euthymius Zygabenus* lived at *Conftan-*
tinople, in the *eleventh* century, in the reign
of *Alexis Comnenus*. In his works he thus
refers to this Verfe of St. *John*. " The
" term ONE denotes things, the effence, and
" nature, of which are the fame, and yet

" the perſons are different (a) ; as in this Dr. BENSON.
" inſtance, AND THREE ARE ONE."

2. A Dialogue, in the *Greek* language,
wherein *Athanaſius,* and *Arius,* are the real,
or aſſumed, interlocutors, which was written
about A. D. 336; thus expreſsly quotes
the Verſe in queſtion. " Is not that lively,
" and ſaving, Baptiſm, whereby we receive
" remiſſion of ſins, adminiſtered in the name
" of *the Father, the Son, and the Holy Ghoſt?*
" And St. *John* ſays, AND THESE THREE
" ARE ONE." (b) Whether this Dialogue was
written by *Athanaſius,* or not, has long been a
matter of debate among the learned. It is,
however, of greater moment, in the preſent
caſe, to aſcertain the time when, than the
perſon by whom, it was written. And this
circumſtance (the *time when* it was written)
ſeems to be clearly decided by the following
extract from the work itſelf. *Athanaſius,* to-

H 3 wards

(a) *Orthodoxæ Fidei Dogmatica Panoplia,* Part 1. Tit.
7, (Max. Biblioth. Patrum, vol. xix, p. 47 Edit. *Lugd.*
A. D. 1677.
The Council of *Lateran* was compoſed of GREEK,
as well as *Latin,* Fathers, and Biſhops, and this
Verſe is expreſsly appealed to in their *joint* Decretal.
(ſee p. 41 of this work.)
(b) *Athanaſii* Opera, Edit. *Paris.* A. D. 1698, vol.
II. p. 229.

Dr. Benson. wards the clofe of the debate, demands of *Arius*, " *Whether, by faying, the Emperor* " Conftantine *reigns by fea, and land, he there-* " *by affirmed that his Son,* Conftantius, *did* " *not reign there alfo.*" To which *Arius* replies, " *It is very dangerous to fay, that* " Conftantius DOES NOT *reign with* Con- " ftantine, *his Father.*" (*c*)

I need not obferve to Mr. *Gibbon*, that the *joint* reign of *Conftantine*, and *Conftantius*, ended with the death of the former, in the month of *May*, A. D. 337.

Laftly,---Among the works of *Athanafius*, (*a*) which are generally allowed to be genuine, is a Synopfis of this Epiftle of St. *John*. It is not the purpofe, or intent, of a *Synopfis* exprefsly to quote the work to which it refers ; but

(*c*) Ου μικρος κινδυνος &c. Non leve eft periculum dicere *Conftantinum* non IMPERARE [συμβασιλευει] cum *Conftantino* Patre fuo, èo quòd unà cum ipfo NUMERA- TUR. p. 215.

(*d*) *Du Pin*, Art *Athanafius, Lond.* Edit. vol. II, p. 34 *Hody,* (De Bibl. Text. originalibus, p. 309) fays the author of this *Synopfis*—" Qui, fi non fuit *Athanafius,* " vetuftiffimus tamen fuit " Dr. *Cave* fpeaks to the fame purpofe, Hift. Lit. *Lond.* Edit. A. D. 1688, p. 146.

but to give a compendious Summary of its Dr. Benson. scope, and subject. The verse in question, therefore, is not directly quoted in this Synopsis; but the author of it seems plainly to refer to this Verse, in these words: The Apostle (says he) " here teaches (e) *the Unity of the Son with the Father*·" for this unity is *not taught* in any part of that chapter, save in the *seventh* verse.

These instances, then, are flat contradictions to the assertions above stated. Had the works of the ancient *Greek* Fathers come down to us entire, the number of these instances would, without doubt, have been greatly increased.

XXI. " *It*" [the preface] " *asserts* " *two other direct and notorious false-* " *hoods,*"—viz. first, " *that the Latin* " *translators were unfaithful, in leaving* " *out the testimony of the father, the word,* " *and the spirit.*" p. 636.)
H 4   The

(e) " Και την ευοτητα δε τε υιου προς το πατερα δεικνυσι"—(*Athanas.* Opera, Edit *Paris* A. D. 1698, vol. ii. p. 190.)

Dr. Benson. The words of the Preface are, " In qua " etiam *ab infidelibus tranflatoribus* multum " erratum effe a fidei veritate comperimus." *Jerome* does not fay, that *the Latin Tranfla- tors*, collectively taken, were unfaithful; but that a great error had been fallen into *by unfaithful tranflators*, by fome, it might be even by a few, of them, refpecting this Verfe.

XXII. *The other " direct and notorious " falfehood," which this Preface afferts, " is—" That he, [Jerome] had reftored " this Verfe."*

The Preface afferts (*f*) no fuch thing !— Its words are—" The firft of thefe Epiftles " is one, of *James*; then two, of *Peter*; " three of *John*; and one, of *Jude*. WHICH, " if they had been faithfully tranflated into " the *Latin* language, AS THEY WERE " WRITTEN BY THESE APOSTLES, would " not have offered ambiguities to their " readers ;—nor would variations of the " text have thwarted each other; particu- " larly

(*f*) " See Appendix, No. XIII, where this preface is tranfcribed at length.

" larly in that paſſage of the firſt Epiſtle of Dr. Benson.
" St. *John*, where we find the unity of the
" Trinity ſet forth."

The obvious meaning of the Preface is—
that the exiſtence of this paſſage of St. *John*,
in ſome, and its non-exiſtence in others, of
thoſe Tranſlations, had cauſed certain *ambiguities*, and *variations of the text*, which are
here complained of. Had the Verſe been
omitted in *all* of them, no ſuch ambiguity
could have been offered to the reader, becauſe there would have been no variation to
cauſe, or produce, it. The Preface, therefore, does not ſuppoſe any *reſtoration* of the
Verſe by *Jerome*, becauſe it does not ſuppoſe
the Verſe ever to have been *loſt*. It goes no
further than, ſimply, to complain, that the
Verſe had been left out of certain Tranſlations · which we may even conclude to have
been few in number, in compariſon with the
reſt who retained the text, with as much
reaſon as any one can have to conjecture the
contrary.

XXIII. " *Auguſtine, who was inti-*
" *mate*

Dr. Benson.

" mate with Jerome, kept a correspondence
" with him, read his works, and more
" especially his Latin Version of the New
" Testament, has never once, in all his
" voluminous works, mentioned the dif-
" puted text.

It hath been already proved, (g) as it is
trusted, in direct contradiction to the preceding objection, that *Augustine* hath quoted
this disputed text. Nor is this quotation the
only testimony, which he hath given to its
authenticity. He has, moreover, expressed
the highest approbation of *Jerome's* Version
of the New Testament; which hath always
exhibited this verse. " *We heartily thank*
" *God*" (says *Augustine*, writing to *Jerome*)
" *for your* TRANSLATION *of the New Tes-*
" *tament; because there is scarcely any thing in*
" *it, which offends us,* (h) *when we compare*
" *it with the* ORIGINAL GREEK."

XXIV.

(g) Page 34.
(h) " *Proinde non parvas Deo gratias agimus de opere*
" *tuo, quod Evangelium ex Graeco* INTERPRETATUS ES
" *quia pene in omnibus nulla offensio est, cum Scripturam*
" *Graecam contulerimus.*" To which *Jerome* replies—
" *Si me, ut dicis, in* NOVI TESTAMENTI *emendatione*

XXIV. " *What may put the matter*" Dr. BENSON,
[the fpurioufnefs of the Preface] " *out*
" *of all difpute, is,* Jerome *himfelf, in*
" *his genuine, voluminous works, hath*
" *never quoted this difputed paffage.*"

If thefe premifes fhould be admitted, the
conclufion, drawn from them, does not, neceffarily, follow. *Jerome* may not have
quoted this difputed paffage in his other
works, and yet the preface may be genuine.
It is not for me, for Dr. *Benfon,* or even for
Mr. *Gibbon,* dogmatically to pronounce, that
an Author has not written a Preface, in
which a particular paffage of Scripture *is*
quoted, merely becaufe he has written other
works, in which that paffage is *not* quoted.

But the premifes, themfelves, are by no
means

" *fufcipis,*" &c.—(*Hieronymi* Opera, Ed. *Erafmi,* A. D.
1546, vol ii, p 111—114)
    Erafmus fpeaks of this intercourfe between *Auguftine,*
and *Jerome,* in the following terms.
    " Porro divus *Auguftinus,* quoniam ne *Græce* quidem
" ad plenum fciebat, non probat *Hieronymi* ftudium, qui
" *Novum Teftamentum ex* GRÆCORUM FONTIBUS, *vel*
" *verterit, vel emendarit* Quanquam hoc utcunque to-
" lerandum putat, propterea quod, COLLATIS CODICI-
" BUS, depiehendiffet *Hieronymianam in ea re* FIDEM."
(*Erafmi* Annot. in Nov. Teft. Edit. A. D. 1522, p 74.)

Dr. BENSON. means to be admitted. It hath already been proved, as it is trufted, that *Jerome* hath quoted this difputed paffage. *Erafmus*, indeed, enteitained, or affected to entertain, fome doubts of the authenticity of (*i*) thefe quotations. But, when ferioufly confideied, they do not (*k*) feem to have any ieal weight.

Jerome then, as it feems, hath, in the plain fenfe of the word, *quoted* this verfe. But,
in

(*i*) Pages 33—35.

(*k*) The words of *Erafmus*, refpecting the *Confeffions of Faith*, here referred to, are—"*Talia funt, ut* AMBIGI POSSIr, *utrum Hieronymi fint, necne.*" Their ftile, however, fhews them to be *Jerome's* which prefumption feems to be fully eftablifhed by the following confiderations.

1. *Jerome* frequently refers to *Tertullian*, and *Cyprian*, who have cited this Verfe in their writings. (Vide *Hieronymi* Opera, per *Erafmum*, A. D. 1546,—vol. i. pages 8 M, 36 E, 96 H, and 98 G. ;—vol. ii. p. 37, 49 M, and vol. iii, p 65 A · *et alibi paffim.*)

2 *Jerome* not only expreffes to *Marcus Celedenfis*, who was *Jerome's* friend, and correfpondent, the warmeft approbation of that *Expofition of the Faith*, (fee page 35 of this work) which *Marcus* had written to *Cyrillus*; but, at the fame time, pofitively declares that ONE of thefe *Confeffions*, which are now in debate, was his own compofition. " *De fide, autem, quòd dignatus es fcribere fanEto Cyrillo*, DEDI CONSCRIPIAM FIDEM " (Vol. ii, p. 104) And of this EXPOSITIO FIDEI cf *Marcus Celedenfis*, and and of his own CONSCRIPTA FIDES, here treated upon, *Jerome* further fpeaks, in thefe glowing terms. " *Qi*' " *fic non ciedit, alienus a Chiifto eft* "

in another fenfe, he hath done much more
than quote it, by inferting it in his Verfion
of the New Teftament; the moft laborious,
the moft important, of all his works. By
this infertion, indeed, *Jerome* may be faid,
moft truly, to have " *put the matter out of*
" *all difpute*;" but in a very different manner fiom the predeftinated fentence of Dr.
Benfon. The Preface of *Jerome* throws light
upon his Verfion; and his Verfion reflects
ftiength to the Preface: and in both, thus
mutually illuminating, and corroboiating,
each other, *Jerome* has fixed his own feal to
the authenticity of the Verfe, in queftion ;—
" *a feal, which will continue many days.*"

This, Sir, is the laft of the ELEVEN *proofs,*
(as he has thought proper to ftile them) which
are pioduced by Dr. *Benfon*, to fhew *the fpurioufnefs of this Preface.* They have been, I truft,
fairly weighed in the ballance, and found
wanting. Some of thefe *pretended proofs* are,
moft blameably, untrue. The reft, even
where not falfe, are yet, without a fingle
exception, vague, and inconclufive. They
are fo far from inducing a fober conviction

of

Dr. Benson. of the fpurioufnefs of this Pieface, that they do not, when combined together, amount even to a probability of it. Indeed, the af-peifions, which have been caft upon ths Pieface, are but the dieam of the prefent age. The moft difturbed imagination did not harbour any fuch *chimeras*, until the times of *Martianay*, and *Simon*. (*l*) Foimei ages would not have liftened to them foi a moment. Let piejudice, then, give way to moderation. Let candor pionounce her judgment; and let the Preface be, what it affiims itfelf to be, what even *Erafmus*, and (*m*) *Socinus*, confefs it to be, the work of *Jerome*.

We

(*l*) See *Cyprian*'s Works, Edit. *Oxon*. (Note on the Treatife, *De Unitate Ecclefiæ*) p 109.

Nicholas de Lyra, in the fourteenth, and *Walafi id Strabo*, in the ninth, Century, having occafion to fpeak of this Preface, exprefsly afcribe it to *Jerome*.

Erafmus admits it to have been the work of *Jerome*, in his Annotations upon this part of the New Teftament. " *Divus Hieronymus* PRÆLOQUENS IN EPISTOLAS CA-" NONICAS, *fufpicatur hunc locum fuiffe depravatum*," &c. Edit. *Bafil* A D 1522, p 616.

And Dr. *Cave*, alfo, places this Preface among the genuine works of *Jerome*. (*Hift. Lit.* Edit. *Lond.* A. D. 1688, p 223)

(*m*) *Smith*'s *Vindiciæ*, Edit *Lond* A D 1686, p. 136. See alfo *Calmet*—" *Mais Eraf*ne, *et apres lui* Socin, *M* " Le Clerc, &c *foutiennent que le Prologue, dont on vient* " *de parler, eft vraiment de Saint* Jerome." (Diff. Vol. III, Edit. *Paris.* A. D. 1720, p. 561.)

We may, Sir, I prefume, now quit this Dr. Benson. Preface, allowing it to have been written by *Jerome*, and proceed to the reft of Dr. *Benfon's* objections to the originality of the Verfe, 1. *John*, v. 7.

   XXV. " *As to what Victor Vitenfis*
 " *has faid, towards the conclufion of the*
 " *fifth century; or others in later ages,*
 " *it cannot be of much moment. And,*
 " *therefore, I fhall fay nothing to fuch late*
 " *teftimonies*"---(viz. in favor of the Verfe in queftion.)

This objection is fo extraordinary, that it feems to call for a very particular examination, in all its parts.

Firft, as to the OBJECTOR,---it feems, on a primary view, peculiarly ftrange, that Dr. *Benfon* fhould thus reject the evidence of *Victor Vitenfis*, who wrote (about A. D. 488, or) in the *fifth* century, as *late teftimony*; when he foon afterwards cites *Bede*, (*n*) of the *eighth*, and *Oecumenius*, of the *eleventh*, century.
           But

(*n*) Page 644.

Dr. BENSON. But this mode of selecting his evidence, strange as it seems, may, perhaps, be accounted for. The suffrage of *Victor Vitensis* SUPPORTS the authenticity of this verse. Those of *Bede,* and *Oecumenius* are, in some sense, ADVERSE to it. It seems but too plain, that these circumstances, alone, have prevailed with Dr. *Benson* to urge the latter testimony, and to reject the former.

This primary presumption seems, further, to become absolute certainty, when applied, comparatively, to the NATURE of the several testimonies, here rejected, or retained, by Dr. *Benson.* For, what is the nature of the proof, which is drawn from *Bede,* and *Oecumenius,* as to this verse? It amounts only to this,—*that* BEDE, *and* OECUMENIUS, *have* NOT *quoted this verse, in their works.* The whole of the evidence, then, which can be drawn from them, is barely *negative.* It is, only, *an omission in a Commentator ;* and, as such, affords *matter for conjecture,* merely, and no more.—But the evidence of *Victor Vitensis* is POSITIVE, clear, and pointed. He has related a plain history of plain facts.

He

He has given an unadorned account of what **Dr. Benson.**
he *faw* and *heard*, and *experienced*, when furrounded by the armed band of the defpotic
Huneric. His narrative was compofed, whilft
Arianifm fat triumphant on the throne, and
therefore muft be *circumfpect*. It was written in the face of exafperated enemies; (*o*)
and therefore muft be *accurate*. It was publifhed, whilft the parties, of whom it treated,
were living ; and therefore muft be *faithful*.
It recorded a tranfaction, known through all
the dominions of *Huneric*, and therefore muft
be *true*: becaufe the fmalleft deviation from
truth would have been followed by inftant
detection. This narrative of *Victor Vitenfis*,
then, is an argument in favor of this verfe,
which needs only to be read in order to
compel conviction. It is, in its *nature*, fu-
perior to all fophifms, and inexpugnable by
any cavils :——and yet, this is the teftimony,
which Dr. *Benfon* has thought fit (*p*) to put

I   afide,

(*o*) The account given by *Victor*, and here alluded to,
is ftated more at large in pages 44 to 47 of thefe letters.
See alfo Appendix, No. XIV and *Du Pin, Lond* Edit.
vol v p. 170.

(*p*) If Dr. *Benfon* would have given his *true reafon*, for
having " *nothing to fay to the teftimony*," of *Victor Vitenfis*,
it would, feemingly, have been, that he *knew not how to anfwer it.*

Dr. Benson. afide, as having nothing to do with, as being utterly unconcerned in, the decifion of the authenticity of the verfe, 1. *John*, v. 7!

Nor is this the only abfurdity, into which Dr. *Benfon* has here betrayed himfelf. His pretence, about the TIME, in which *Victor Vitenfis* lived, which he hath affigned as his reafon for rejecting *Victor's* teftimony, is as *futile*, as his real intentions, in rejecting it, feem to have been *blameable*. For in the outfet of his Differtation, he admits the teftimony of *Jerome*, in favor of this Verfe, as valid *in point of time*; for he fets himfelf ferioufly to do away its effect, if poffible, by laboring to prove (as we have already feen) that the Preface to the *Canonical* Epiftles is not the work of *Jerome*. Now *Jerome* lived in the fame Century with *Victor Vitenfis*; nay, it is poffible that they might both be alive at the fame hour for *Jerome* furvived until A. D. 420, and *Victor* was *a Bifhop* in (perhaps long before) A. D. 484, and was prefent, with *Eugenius*, and his Co-prelates, in that year, at the Council of *Carthage*. Dr. *Benfon*, therefore, allows the evidence of *Jerome*, *some*, in the beginning of the fifth Century, Dr. BENSON, to be early enough; and yet rejects that of *Victor*, and his Brethren, the Bishops of *Africa*, " towards the conclusion of that centu- " ry," as " *late testimony*,—as inadmissible *because* MODERN: for that is the only im- peachment which he ventures to cast upon it. But if the former be early enough, why is the latter too late? By what rule is a tes- timony of A. D. 414, for instance, to be ad- mitted, by a Critic of the *eighteenth* Century, by an author who writes nearly *one thousand three hundred years* afterwards, as *in time*, (the antiquity of the evidence being the sole point in question) and another, of A. D. 484, to be rejected, as *out of time*: nay, so much out of time, as to be out of all claim to no- tice,—so very " *late*," as that " nothing" *is* to be " said to it?" Will any one, who contends for the spuriousness of this Verse, —will Mr. *Gibbon*,—attempt to justify Dr. *Benson* in this rejection? If so, Sir, you will, perhaps, condescend to inform the world, what members, what fractional parts, of the *same* Century, (the *fifth*, for instance) are to constitute *ancient*, and what fractions, or

parts,

Dr. Benson. parts, thereof, *modern* teftimony. But you will not hazard the attempt.

XXVI. " *In fettling the text of the new*
" *teftament,* Robert Stephens *made ufe*
" *of fifteen ancient MSS.*" (p. 637.)

He made ufe of *fixteen,* befide the *Complutenfian* Bible, which was a printed book. His own words are (*q*) " *Teftamentum quâ (dic-*
" *tante Spiritu fanɛto) fcriptum fuit linguâ,*
" *cum vetuftiffimis* SEDECIM SCRIPTIS EX-
" EMPLARIBUS, *quantâ maximâ potuimus*
" *curâ, et diligentiâ, collatum excudimus.*"
Theodore Beza, who was permitted to collate thefe MSS for his own Verfions of the New Teftament, acknowledges himfelf indebted to the friendfhip of *Robert Stephens* for the ufe of *feventeen* (*r*) of his Copies; taking into the number the *Complutenfian* Bible, which *Robert Stephens* had ufed in his own Editions, and afterwards furnifhed to *Beza,* along with the *fixteen,* written, Copies.

XXVII.

(*q*) Preface to his Edition of A. D. 1550, printed at *Paris.* (Appendix, No. XII.)
(*r*) Preface to his Editions of A. D. 1582, and 1589.

XXVII. " *It is very certain that he* Dr. BENSON,
" [Robert Stephens] *did not scruple va-*
" *rying from his MSS, and has varied*
" *from them all, and from the* complu-
" tenfe *and* vulgate, *too, in feventy places,*
" *at leaft.*"

The plan, which *Robert Stephens* followed in his Edition of A. D. 1550, here alluded to, was,—to take all thofe fentences, or
words, to be original, in which all his authorities concurred, and to place them in the
text, generally, (*s*) without any marginal
notes, or references, whatfoever. But where
his authorities varied from each other, although by a fingle letter only, he adopted
that fentence, or word, alone, which feemed
to be the genuine reading of the paffage, inferting it in the body of the page, and noting, in the margin, the principal variations
of his other authorities.

If, then, the objection only means, that
Robert Stephens has fometimes varied from
I 3 fome

(*s*) *Robert Stephens*, in this work, took the laft Edition
of *Erafmus*, as the general foundation of his text; which
he has followed chiefly, but not fervilely,

Dr. Benson. some of his MSS, in preference to others; sometimes from all, or most, of them, in favor of the *Complutensian*, and the *Vulgate*; and at other times from *them* also, in obedience to his MSS, in proportion as any of these guides seemed to supply the most correct information;—it describes *Robert Stephens* as an assiduous investigator of truth, as an accurate, and judicious, Critic: a description, in which the whole literary world will concur. But if the objector meant to insinuate (and the plain construction of his words directly infers the insinuation) that *Robert Stephens* has, *in seventy*, or in any number of, places, varied from the whole tenor of his authorities, and interposed an arbitrary, unsupported, lection of his own, in contravention of them all,—the insinuation is illiberal; and, being unwarranted by any proof, ought to be rejected with disdain.

You will expect me, Sir, before I quit the objection now under consideration, to allow, that it was not originally urged by Dr. *Benson*, but copied by him from the writer

of

of the *Memoirs of the late Dr.* Waterland. Dr. BENSON.
That Dr. *Benson* was but a Copyist in this
objection, as well as in many others which
are urged in his Differtation, I do moft readily admit. But he has fo copied them, as
to make them his own. On feeing a charge
of this reproachful nature, brought againft a
man of fo fair a fame as *Robert Stephens,* one
who is acknowledged, even by Dr. *Benson,*
to be " a learned, worthy, man,"—a man
" of extenfive learning, indefatigable dili-
" gence, and zeal (*t*) to promote ufeful
" knowledge, and particularly that of the
" Scriptures," without the fhadow of a
proof to fupport the charge, beyond the
empty affirmation of the Affertor ;—a Commentator, without prejudice, without any
fecret partiality to either fide of the queftion,
would, at once, have challenged the imputation, and have refufed to admit it, againft
fo truly refpectable a character, without the
moft unequivocal demonftration of its truth.
He would have treated that Writer's " *feventy*
" *places,*" as the *Britifh* nation did his Majefty of *Spain*'s " *hundred injuries*" alledged

I 4 in

(*t*) Page 638.

Dr. BENSON. in a late memorable *Manifesto*. He would
have called for a specification of them; which
not being complied with, he would have
condemned the whole as a groundless allegation. But, instead of this, Dr *Benson* hastens
to admit the charge, and, to preserve the
appearance, at least, of candor, affects to
make this apology for it; viz. " As to his
" varying from his copies, it seems plain,
" from his Preface, that he had not an op-
" portunity to collate all the copies him-
" self." An apology, which, unfortunately, is as false, as it is frigid;—for the Preface (*u*) of *Robert Stephens*, so far from
making it " *plain*," does not even afford
foundation for a conjecture, that he did not
" collate all the copies himself." I think
myself justified, therefore, Sir, in asking,
whether a Commentator, without prejudice,
or partiality, would have acted like Dr. *Benson*? And I should rejoice in being able to
give any other solution of the question, than
that which the question, itself, pre-supposes,
and which the whole tenor of his Dissertation proves, to be the only true one.

XXVIII.

(*u*) See the Preface throughout. Appendix, No. XII.

XXVIII " *The sum of the matter is,* Dr. BENSON.
" *Robert Stephens was a learned, worthy,*
" *man. And, therefore, one would not*
" *willingly suspect, that he placed the lat-*
" *ter semi-circle wrong, on purpose. How-*
" *ever, in his famous Greek Testament,*
" 1550, *it is wrong placed.*"

Here is another instance of Dr. *Benson's*
keeping back a part of the truth, in order to
give the fairer color to his own predilections.
It is true, that *Robert Stephens* could only
place the semi-circles wrong, as to the Verse
in question, (provided he did place them
wrong at all, which is denied) *in his* Greek
Testament of A. D. 1550; because that was
the only Edition, in which he made use of
those semi-circles. But the whole truth is,
—that *Robert Stephens* has borne testimony
to the originality of this Verse, in *all* the
Editions of the *Greek* Testament, ever published by him; which are no less than four,
in number. In his Editions of A. D. 1546,
and 1549, in which the Semi-circles (or the
Obelus, and *Semi-parenthesis*) are *not used,* the
Verse is read entire, in the text, as well as

in

Dr Benson. in the Edition of A. D. 1550, in which they *are made use of.* To this third, succeeded a fourth, Edition, published by *Robert Stephens*, in A. D. 1551; wherein the Verse is still continued, still maintained in its place, without the least note of distrust, without the smallest impeachment of its authenticity.

These facts being premised, the whole question, as to this part of *Robert Stephens*'s conduct, will be reduced to this single *dilemma*. Either *Robert Stephens* placed the latter Semi-circle, as we now find it in his Edition of A. D. 1550, *on purpose*; or *by mistake.* Now he placed it there, *not by mistake*; because he had printed the Verse, *entire*, in his two former editions, and he expresly informs us that this Edition had been collated with the *same MSS,* from whence the foregoing Editions were made. *Not by mistake*; because he would, in that case, have cast out of his subsequent Edition, of A. D. 1551, a passage which he had intended to repudiate (for so the objection supposes) by the Semi-circle of the preceding year. *Not by mistake*; because a man, who

had

had been so painfully accurate in revising this work, as even to point out, in the *Errata* subjoined to it, the mis-placing of one *Comma*, in the body of the text, and the omission of another, cannot even be supposed to have suffered a whole Verse to have escaped his notice; a Verse, too, which on account of the then recent dispute between *Erasmus*, *Ley*, and *Stunica*, must have engaged his particular attention. *Not by mistake*; because the Verse, in question, is inserted in the New Testament of *John Crispin*, whose publication bears date three years subsequent to that of *Robert Stephens*, who was, at the time of his publication, the friend, and fellow-citizen, of *Robert Stephens*, and who must be concluded to have published with his privity, and assistance: for it is impossible to suppose, that *Crispin* would not in such an undertaking, constantly confer with such a neighbour, with such a friend, with such a man, as *Robert Stephens*. *Not by mistake*;—because the Verse is found in the New Testament of *Theodore Beza*, who, like *Crispin*, published whilst *Robert Stephens* was living, who mentions him frequently with

the

Dr. Benson. the moſt affectionate reſpect; who had in his poſſeſſion, by the peiſonal favoi of *Robert Stephens*, the identical MSS, uſed by him in this very Edition of A. D. 1550,— and (*x*) who ſolemnly declares, that this Verſe did actually exiſt in thoſe MSS.

If *Robert Stephens*, therefoie, did *not* place the

(*) " Hic Verſiculus—extat in *Complutenſi* Editione, " et in *nonnullis* Stephani *veteribus* libi is. *In cœlo*, deeſt " in *Septem* vetuſtis codicibus " (Appendix, No. XI.)

Mr. *Emlyn* endeavours to take away the weight of *Beza*'s teſtimony to this point, by alledging that he *nevei ſaw the MSS, themſelves*, of *Robert Stephens*, foi that *they* were not delivered to *Beza*, but only a Book, or Tranſcript, wherein *Robeit Stephens* had written down his *Collations* from them. But this objection may be repelled, in the preſent caſe, by the moſt unexceptionable teſtimony, which is that of Mr. *Emlyn* himſelf. For in the *ſecond* page after this allegation, Mr. *Emlyn* further affirms, that *Beza* detected a miſtake IN THOSE COLLATIONS, as to the fiiſt Chapter, of the *Apocalypſe*, in which *Robeit Stephens* had marked certain words to be wanting in two, only, ot his authorities, whereas (according to *Beza*'s account) thoſe words were wanting in the *reſt* ot *Stephens*'s MSS likewiſe. It would have been well worth Mr. *Emlyn*'s pains, when he gave this latter information to his readers, to have appriſed them, at tne ſame time, HOW *Beza* could, poſſibly, have detected a miſtake of this kind, in *Stephens*'s Book of *Collations*, unleſs *by reſoiting to the MSS themſelves* !

By Mr. *Emlyn*'s own argument, then, it clearly appears, that *Beza* DID poſſeſs the oiiginal MSS of *Robert Stephens*, becauſe he could not, but by the aid of *Robert Stephens*'s MSS, have detected any miſtake, of this nature, in his *Collations*. (See *Emlyn*'s reply, p. 214—9)

the latter Semi-circle in the fituation where Dr. Benson.
we now find it, *by miſtake,* (as he moſt af-
furedly did not) the confequence is inevitable :—He placed it there on purpose !—
And, unlefs we are now, at length, to fuppofe, that *Robert Stephens* firſt advanced an *intentional* falfehood in the face of the whole
Chriſtian world, as to the exiſtence of this
Verfe in his MSS, and that, afterwards,
Theodore Beza, who had thofe very MSS put
into his hands which enabled him to detect
the falfehood, did, inſtead of betraying, abet,
and fupport, him in it; unlefs we are now,
at length, to defpoil them both of thofe characters of learning, and worth, of probity,
and honor, with which their memories have
been fo long adorned, and confecrated, and
to conclude that they confpired to act, in
concert, the infamous (and, in the prefent
cafe, impious) part of cheats, and impoſtors:
Unlefs we are now become defperately determined to fpeak, and act, in contradiction
to the voice of all *Europe,* in defiance to the
teſtimony of ages, paſt, and prefent, as well
as in utter fubverfion of every principle of literary candor, and *Chriſtian* charity; we
muſt

Dr. Benson. muſt feel ourſelves, of neceſſity, compelled to acknowledge, that what *Robert Stephens* thus did *intentionally,* he alſo did *conſcientiouſly;* that he, and *Theodore Beza,* have a right to command our full aſſent, when they only affirm a plain fact, which lay within their own knowledge, and which, therefore, they were compleatly competent to aſcertain; that *Robert Stephens* did *not* place the latter Semi-circle wrong, either *by miſtake,* or *on purpoſe;*—and that when it is affected to teach us, either by Dr. *Benſon,* or by Mr. *Gibbon,* of the " *typographical fraud, or error, of* " Robert Stephens," in the preſent inſtance, at leaſt; or of the " *deliberate falſehood, or ſtrange miſapprehenſion of* Theodore Beza;" —ſuch teaching is in vain!

Theſe conſiderations ſeem to determine the whole debate, as to the MSS of *Robert Stephens.* Nothing can weigh againſt them, but the actual production of the MSS themſelves, accompanied by indubitable proof that they do not contain the Verſe in queſtion. And lo! the required *Deſideratum* ſtands before us!—For Dr. *Benſon* thus proceeds:

XXIX.

XXIX. " *And his*" [R. Stephens's] Dr. Benson.
" *MSS, are, upon the strictest examina-*
" *tion, found to want this disputed paf-*
" *sage.*"

As a decision of this point will materially
affect the whole question, respecting the originality of this Verse,––you will, Sir, pardon
me, perhaps, if I trespass somewhat longer
than usual upon your patience, in examining
the foundation of this assertion, and shewing
its falsehood at large.

In the course of the controversy (already
mentioned in (*y*) this letter) which arose,
in the beginning of the present century, between Mr. *Martin,* and Mr. *Emlyn,* as to the
originality of this Verse ; the propriety of
the *Obelus,* or Semi-circle, as placed in *Robert
Stephens*'s *Greek* Testament of A. D. 1550,
was warmly denied by Mr. *Emlyn,* and strenuously defended by his antagonist. During
the pendency, and indeed in the very height,
of this dispute, Father *Le Long,* a Priest of
the Oratory at *Paris,* published in the *Journal*

des

(*y*) Page 80.

Dr. Benson. *des Savans,* A. D. 1720, a letter, in which he affirms, that all the MSS, which had been used by *Robert Stephens,* in his Edition of A. D. 1550, (amounting, he says, to *fifteen* in number) were then in the Royal Library at *Paris* ; that *Robert Stephens* had borrowed them from King *Henry* the IId ; that they still bore the usual mark of the MSS of that Prince, namely, a Crown surmounted by a coronetted H ; that they were also marked with the *Greek* numerals, mentioned by *Robert Stephens* in his Preface ; that he (F. *Le Long*) had examined them several times ; and that, by comparing some of the marginal References of *Robert Stephens*'s Edition, with the MSS in the Library, upon which the corresponding *Greek* numerals were inscribed, he was perfectly satisfied of their identity. (z)

This is the testimony of F. *Le Long* ; which, *if it had been true,* might have merited the commendation, which Dr. *Benson* has been pleased to bestow upon it. But, unfortunately

(z) This Letter is printed in *Emlyn*'s Reply, vol. 2. of his works, *Lond.* Edit. 1746, p. 372.

tunately for this mif-placed *Eulogium*, the account, thus given by F. *Le Long*, is a total mif-apprehenfion, or mif-reprefentation, of the cafe. The truth of this affertion will inconteftibly appear, by comparing the foregoing account of F. *Le Long* with the defcription which *Robert Stephens* has given of his own MSS, and with the margins of (*a*) his own Edition of A. D. 1550, the book now in queftion.

For, in the firft place, the MSS, which *Robert Stephens* borrowed from the Royal Library, were not fifteen, but only *eight*, in number, as he exprefsly (*b*) declares in his Preface. Nor were thofe MSS borrowed from *Henry* 2, but from *Francis* 1, his predeceffor. For the firft of *Robert Stephens*'s four Editions of the *Greek* Teftament, for which thefe MSS were procured, and col-

K   - lated,

(*a*) The former Edition of thefe Letters referred, in this place, to *Martin*'s *La Verite*. On a fubfequent examination, I found his account of *R. Stephens*'s MSS tolerably accurate, as far as it proceeded, yet very inadequate and defective. I have, in this Edition, fupplied thefe deficiencies by an actual collation of all the references, contained in every page of that great work.

(*b*) " *Tertio, quarto, quinto, fexto, feptimo, octavo, decimo,* " *et quintodecimo, ea quæ ex bibliotheca Regis habuimus.*" (Appendix, No. XII.)

Dr. Benson. lated, and out of which they were ALL (c) compofed, and framed,—was publifhed before *Henry* 2 began his reign.

Nor laftly, does it all concord with the probability of the cafe, or with the known probity of *Robert Stephens*, that he, who had only borrowed *eight* MSS from the Royal Library, fhould return *fifteen* (b) thither, for no other purpofe, as it fhould feem, than to abufe the confidence of thofe friends, who had lent to him the other MSS, and to deprive them of their property.

Thefe circumftances would, alone, furnifh fufficient ground for a ftrong fufpicion, that the MSS of F. *Le Long* are *not* the MSS of R. Ste-

(b) *Mattaire*, in his life of *R. Stephens*, (Edit. *Lond* A. D 1709, p 67) affirms that he [*R. Stephens*] returned to the Royal Library, thofe MSS, which he had borrowed from thence. This plainly appears to be a miftake, in *Mattaire*, not only from *Beza*'s own words, (Appendix, No XI) but from the exprefs declaration of *R Stephens*, in his advertifement fubjoined to *Beza*'s Edition of A. D. 1556.

(c) " *Idem nunc iterum, et tertio, cum* IISDEM *collatum,* —*tibi offerimus* " (Appendix, No XII)

R Stephens, indeed, in his *Greek* Preface, fpeaks of thefe MSS in the following terms —τα εν τησγρατισε ημων βασιλεως Σοριας βιβλιοθηνης ληφθεντα αντιγραφα εςι.— But this is only an acknowledgement, that his MSS came from the Library *then* belonging to *Henry*, not that they were actually *borrowed* from him.

R. *Stephens.* But this fufpicion becomes Dr. BENSON.
certainty, when fortified by the following
obfervations, viz.

That there is no MS, in the Catalogue (*d*)
of F. *Le Long,* which contains the *Apoca-*
lypfe; whereas the *Apocalypfe* is found in no
lefs than *four,* namely, in the fifth, the
eleventh, fifteenth, and fixteenth, of the
MSS of *R. Stephens.*

That the MSS of F. *Le Long*'s Catalogue,
which refer to the Gofpels, are fewer by
three, than thofe which refer to the fame
Gofpels, in the Edition of *R. Stephens.*

That in the Lift of F. *Le Long* there are
only *feven* MSS which refer to the *Acts* of
the Apoftles; whereas *ten* MSS are cited
thereto in the margin of *R. Stephen*'s Edition.

That there are *three* fewer MSS, in the
Catalogue of F. *Le Long,* which refer to the
Epiftles to the *Romans,* and *Corinthians,* than
are found in the margin of the work of *R.*
Stephens. And laftly,

That

(*d*) (Appendix, No XIX.)

Dr. Benson. That in the Lift of F. *Le Long,* there is not a fingle MS, (*e*) which contains the words, *εν τη γη,* of the *eighth* verfe of the chapter in queftion. But thefe words were found in *all* the MSS of *R. Stephens.* (*f*)

Thus it is manifeft, that the MSS of F. *Le Long,* taken aggregately, or as a whole, have no parity, or agreement, with thofe of *R. Stephens*; and, therefore, cannot be the fame which *R. Stephens* ufed in his Edition of A. D. 1550. But this conclufion will become unanfwerably clear, when we proceed further to the examination of particular MSS. For

The MS, marked β, in the lift of F. *Le Long,*

(*e*) See *Le Long's* Letter, accompanying his Lift, *Emlyn,* p. 273—283

(*f*) Without having recourfe, in proof of this laft affertion, to the authority of *R. Stephens* himfelf, the note, which *Theodore Beza* has left upon this part of the eighth verfe is, beyond all queftion, decifive. " Thefe words" [fays he] " are not in the *Syriac* Verfion, nor in feveral " very ancient *Greek* copies, but *they are in our* Greek " *MSS,* and in the *Latin* Verfion." It has been, before, obferved, that this is the expreffion, " our MSS," whereby *Beza* conftantly diftinguifhes the MSS of *R. Stephens,* by whom they were lent to *Beza* for the ufe of this very Edition. (Appendix, No. XI.)

Long, contains the Gofpels, and the Acts of the Apoftles, only. But the MS of *R. Stephens*, which bore that mark, contains alfo the Epiftle to the *Romans* ; for it is cited by him, in the margin of his work, upon the tenth Verfe, of the third Chapter, of that Epiftle.

The MS, marked ε, in the Catalogue of F. *Le Long*, does not comprife the *Apocalypfe* : whereas the MS of *R. Stephens*, which was thus marked, certainly contained the *Apocalypfe*; becaufe he has particularly referred to this MS in *Rev.* iii: 18,—and xix: 14.—

The two MSS, marked ζ and η in the Lift of F. *Le Long*, do not contain the Acts of the Apoftles. But both the MSS, which *R. Stephens* diftinguifhed by the fame letters, contained the *Acts*; for the former is referred to, by him, in Chapter xvii: 5; and the latter in Chapters xxiv: 7, and 8; xxv: 14; xxvii: 1; and xxviii: 11.

The MS, marked with the letter ι, in the lift of F. *Le Long*, contains only the *Acts*,

and

Dr. Benson. and the *Epiftles*. But the MS, which is denoted by this letter, in the Edition of *R. Stephens*, comprifed alfo the Gofpels of St. *Luke*, and St. *John*. A various reading is quoted, by *R. Stephens*, from this MS, in St. *Luke*, v : 19, and another in St. *John*, ii: 17. Again,

The MS, marked ᵌα in F. *Le Long*'s Catalogue, comprehends, like the laft mentioned MS, no more than the *Acts*, and the *Epiftles*. But the MS of *R. Stephens*, which bore this mark, contained (befides the Acts, and the Epiftles) the Gofpels of St. *Matthew*, and St. *John*, together with the *Apocalypfe*. The citations of this MS, in the margin of *R. Stephens*'s Edition, which prove this affertion, are no lefs than *five*; namely, St. *Matthew*, x: 8, and 10; and xii: 32; St. *John*, ii: 17; and the *Apocalypfe*, xiii: 4. Again,

The MS, marked ᵌβ, in the lift of F. *Le Long*, comprifes the Gofpels, only. But the MS of *R. Stephens*, which was denoted by this mark, comprehended alfo the fiift Epiftle to the *Corinthians*; for he has referred

ferred to it in the margin of 1. *Corinthians*, Dr. BENSON.
xv : 44. Further,

The MS, marked $b\gamma$, in F. *Le Long*'s Catalogue, contains, like two former ones herein
before mentioned, no more than the *Acts,*
and the *Epistles.* (g) But in that of *R.*
Stephens, which carried this mark, was comprehended, also, the Gospels of St. *Matthew*
and St. *John.* Various readings are copied
by him, from thence, in the margins of St.
Matthew, xxvii : 64; and of St. *John,* ii, 17.

The MS, marked $b\delta$, among those of F. *Le*
Long, comprehends only the three Gospels
of St. *Matthew,* St. *Luke,* and St. *John.* But
the MS, denoted by these letters, in the Edition of *R. Stephens,* comprised likewise, the
Acts of the Apostles, and the second Epistle
of St. *Peter.* It is cited, by *R. Stephens,* in
the margins of *Acts,* xiii : 15; (h) and of
2. *Peter,* i: 4.

K 4   The

(g) It contains, in truth, only a part of the Epistles;
the third of St. *John,* and that of St. *Jude,* not being
comprised therein. (Appendix, No. XIX.)

(h) Dr. *Mill* affirms (Proleg 117.) that this MS contained no Chapter, but the *tenth,* or rather a part of the
tenth, of the *Acts* of the Apostles. Nothing is more

Dr. BENSON. The MS of F. *Le Long*, marked 16, contains no part of the New Teſtament, except ſeven of the Epiſtles of St. *Paul*. But the MS of *R Stephens*, which bore this mark, differed greatly from that of *Le Long*. Judging by *R. Stephens*'s references, it compriſed only *four* of thoſe Epiſtles. But beſide theſe four Epiſtles, it comprehended alſo the *Apocalypſe*. The references to this MS, in that part of his work, are too numerous to be here particulariſed: they abound in almoſt every page. Finally,

The MS of F. *Le Long*, which is marked 15, contains, only, the Goſpels of the two Evangeliſts, St. *Luke*, and St. *John*. But the MS of *R. Stephens*, which was thus marked, does not ſeem to have contained the Goſpel of St. *John*, at all; for there is no reference to this MS in the margin of *R. Stephens*'s Edition of this Goſpel.—But it certainly did further compriſe the ſecond

Epiſtle

certain than that he was miſtaken in this aſſertion. And indeed nothing *ſeems* more certain than that this, and many other groſs errors on the ſubject of *R. Stephens*'s MSS, have originated in an idea, that thoſe MSS are yet exiſting, whereas they are *all* (for any thing that appears to the contrary, at leaſt) undoubtedly *loſt*.

Epiftle to the *Corinthians*, the firft Epiftle to Dr. BENSON. *Timothy*, and the *Apocalypfe*; becaufe this MS is referred to, by *R. Stephens*, in the margin of his Edition of *all* thofe parts of the facred Canon.

And now, Sir, will you contend for Father *Le Long* (who cannot anfwer for himfelf) that you are " fatisfied of the iden- " tity of thefe MSS ?" Or will you fay, with Dr. *Benfon*, that thefe are the MSS of *Robert Stephens*, and that, " on the ftricteft exami- " nation, they are found to want this dif- " puted paffage ?" You will not venture to do either. The MSS, in queftion, have fcarcely any thing in common with each other. They do not agree even in the general refemblance. They differ in almoft every feparate feature. The MSS of Father *Le Long*, therefore, are not the MSS of *Robert Stephens*. They are a fpurious race, foftered, at leaft, if not be- gotten, by the difhoneft cunning of fome Librarian, or of fome other perfon equally difhoneft: who, neverthelefs, was not quite cunning enough, for he neglected to look in- to *Robert Stephens*'s Preface, elfe he would

not

Dr. Benson. not have made them into *fifteen*, only, but into *fixteen* Books ;—for fuch was the real number of *Robert Stephens*'s MSS. They are *Counterfeits* ; on whofe unrefifting Covers fome bufy impoftor has infcribed forged, and falfe, marks of *Robert Stephens*, from fome undue motive,—moft probably, in order to advance their reputation by his illuftrious name : but they are NOT the MSS *of Robert Stephens*.

 XXX. " *Yet it is infifted upon, that*
" *Erafmus fpeaks of a Britifh copy, which*
" *had the difputed text : and that upon*
" *the authority of that MS, he inferted it*
" *in his third and following editions;*
" *though he had left it out, in his firft*
" *and fecond editions.* But it does not ap-
" pear that *Erafmus* ever faw any fuch
" thing himfelf."

M. *Simon*, the great adverfary of this Verfe, acknowledges that *Erafmus* (*i*) DID fee the *Britifh* MS in *England*. And this account might have been prefumed to be the truth,
without

(*i*) Hift. Crit. du N. T. vol. iii, p. 205.

without much enquiry, becaufe it is the con- Dr. BENSON.

feffion of an enemy,—becaufe *Erafmus* fpent much time in this country,—and becaufe he has quoted this MS in many other parts of his works. But we need not leave any thing, even here, to prefumption. *Erafmus* declares, that he *collated this MS himfelf.* " *The MS* WHICH I COLLATED IN ENGLAND," (*k*) are his words, when difcourfing on this *Britifh* Copy. Indeed if no fuch proof as this could have been produced, the fame conclufion muft, in fact, have been adopted on this fubject. For to imagine that *Erafmus* would ever introduce to the world a MS which not only thwarted his own private predilections, but vitiated his two former Editions of the New Teftament, without being firft indubitably fatisfied of its exiftence,—is a fuppofition, which cannot be admitted for a moment; becaufe it violates every rule of probability, and is repugnant to common fenfe.

XXXI.

(*k*) " *In codice, urde* CONTULI *in Anglia, fuiffe fcriptum,*" &c.
" *Collationis negotium* PEREGRAM *in Anglia,*" &c.
Erafmi Opera, Ed. *Lugd.* A. D. 1706, vol. IX, p. 986.

Dr. Benson.

XXXI. " *It appears that he*" [Eraſ-
mus] " *had a bad opinion of it*"—
[the *Britiſh* MS] " *For he ſays, I ſuſpect*
" *that copy to have been corrected by ours*;
" *that is, from the* latin *copies.*"

The words of *Eraſmus* are—"*Quanquam e,*
hunc ſuſpicor ad Latinorum *codices fuiſſe caſti-*
gatum." The *evidence*, however, as far as
it can be now collected, is *directly adverſe* to
Eraſmus, in this matter. The *Latin* MSS,
univerſally, read *(Spiritus ſanctus)* the Holy
Spirit, in this Verſe : but the *Britiſh* MS of
Eraſmus read therein (πνευμα) *the Spirit*, only,
without the diſtinguiſhing epithet of (αγιον)
Holy. This difference, although of a ſingle
word alone, is too ſtrongly marked, to permit any ſuppoſition of one of theſe authorities having been corrected by the other.

But, even if no proof could have been
brought in oppoſition to it, ſurely, to advance
a charge of this kind, *unſupported by any evi-*
dence, or by any thing like evidence, (*l*) favour-
ed

(*l*) *Eraſmi* Opera, Edit *Lugdun.* A. D. 1706, vol.
X p 352. (Appendix, No. XX.)

ed more of pretence, than sincerity ; and was Dr. Benson, unworthy of a Writer much inferior to *Erasmus*. It is incumbent upon all authors, in all such cases, openly to relate their *suspicions,* (if they have any) and candidly to assign their reasons for entertaining them ; that the reader may judge, for himself, as to the degree of credit, which they ought to receive from him. It was especially incumbent upon *Erasmus* to have done thus, in the present instance, because he was then in the act of *retracting* that imputation of imposture, which his conduct had *first* caused to be thrown upon this Verse. At such an hour as that, for *Erasmus* to hint suspicions, without proof, and to hesitate dislikes, without explanation, gives his readers but too much reason to consider him, as determined to cast some imputation upon the MS, which had so mortified him ; although impotent of the means to do it with any effect.

Attempts of this nature often prejudice the cause, which they were meant to serve. The present may, at least, convince us of the reality of the existence of this MS, at
that

Dr. Benson. that time; and of its containing the Verse in question. Had there been the smallest room to doubt *either*, the sentence, just quoted from *Erasmus*, would have spoken a very different language.

> XXXII. "*And he*" [Erasmus] "*plain-*
> " *ly acknowledges, that what induced*
> " *him to insert the disputed text, was,* ne
> " sit ansa calumniandi, *that he might*
> " *not give a handle to any, to call him*
> " *an Arian, or suspect him of heresy.*"

I have, Sir, in a former *(m)* letter, given my sentiments, with some freedom, on the conduct of *Erasmus*, respecting this Verse. It was there observed, that it seemed " im-
" possible to account for the behaviour of
" *Erasmus*, in this matter, taking the whole
" of it into contemplation at once, but up-
" on one of these suppositions : Either he
" *could not produce* the five MSS, in which
" he had alledged the Verse to be omitted;
" or he had *other* authorities, much superior
" to the testimony of a *single* MS, for re-
" placing

***

(m) Pages 8 and 9.

" placing the Verſe, which he was not, Dr. BENSON.
" however, ingenuous enough to acknow-
" ledge." Now, how far it might have
been in his power to fulfil the former of theſe
alternatives, is not, perhaps, foɪ the preſent
age to determine. But this may, fortunately, be *now* determined; namely, that *Eraſ-*
mus " had *other* authorities, much ſupeɪior
" to the teſtimony of a ſingle MS, for re-
" placing the Veɪſe," and that he " was *not*
" ingenuous enough to acknowledge" them.
For, independent of the authoɪity of *Jerome,*
who declares his Tranſlation to have been
made according to the *Gɪeek* MSS, who ac-
cuſes certain *Latin* Tranſlators of unſaith-
ɪulneſs, for having left this Verſe out of
their copies; (for *Eraſmus* believed the preface, which contains this complaint, to be
the genuine work of *Jerome*)—independent
of, at leaſt, ſome part of the authorities,
which have been ſtated ɪn the pɪeceding
pages; (foɪ *Eraſmus* was a learned man, and
could not be ɪgnorant *(n)* of them all)—Independent

(*n*) *Eraſmus* was not ɪgnorant of them all, for he has
quoted the works of *Cyprian, Lyɪanus, Caſſiodoɪɪus, Wala-*
frɪd Strabo, and *Aquinas,* by whom this Verſe (as hath
bᴇen before proved) ɪs expreſsly cɪted as an authentic

Dr. Benson. dependent of thefe, *Erafmus* lay under an obligation, almoft peculiar to himfelf, arifing from the authority of the MSS of *Laurentius Valla*, to re-place the Verfe in queftion. He had, juft *eighteen* years before the publication of this Edition, of A. D. 1522, obtained poffeffion of the, then, unpublifhed, Commentary of *L. Valla*. The *Greek* MSS, on which it was founded, were no lefs than *feven (o)* in number; and this Verfe poffeffed its place in them all. In the exultation of his mind, arifing from this acquifition, *Erafmus* firft communicated *(p)* his difcovery to his learned

part of the facred Canon. (See his N. Teft. of A. D. 1522, paffim)

(*o*) Dr *Mill*, in his *Prolegomena*, fpeaks of *three* only " Comparatis *tribus* exemplaribus *Græcis*, ac totidem *La-* " *tinis.*" This is one of thofe miftakes which I ventured to lay to his charge, in a Note to page 18. He feems, alfo, to have fallen into another miftake, on this fubject, in confidering the Annotations of *Valla* as of little eftimation, for which he is warmly reproved by *Bengelius*. [*Introd. in Crifin* p 437)

L Valla certainly had seven *Greek* MSS, for, in his Annotations on the Gofpel of St. *John*, vii 29, 30, he pofitively affirms that his number was " *feptem* Græca " *exemplaria.*" And *Erafmus* confirms the affertion in his own Apology. (See *L Vallæ* Opera, *Bafil* Edit A. D. 1543, p 842,—and *Erafmi Græc.* Teft. *Bafil* Edit. A. D. 1516, Apol. p 3)

(*p*) Appendix, No. XV.

ed friend, and correspondent, *Fischer* ; and Dr. BENSON,
then, in the same year, A. D. 1505, pub-
lished this Commentary, or permitted it to
be published, from the press of *Jodocus
Badius*, at *Paris*. *Erasmus* had, therefore,
the authority of EIGHT *Greek* MSS, instead
of ONE (which alone he held forth) for
restoring the verse. For he had, in his
own Apology, in A. D. 1516, mentioned the
number of *Valla's (Greek)* MSS to be *seven*,
although he was, at that time, secretly medi-
tating the expulsion of this verse from the text
of St. *John*, in direct contradiction to them all.

Nor is this the only instance of disingenuousness, which is discoverable in the conduct
of *Erasmus*, respecting this verse. He omitted
it, as hath been before stated, in his Edition
of the New Testament of A. D. 1516. In
A. D. 1518, he published his Treatise, entitled *Ratio veræ Theologiæ*, which he dedicated to Cardinal *Chrysogom*: wherein he
cites, in serious argument, and as a legitimate
portion of Scripture, this (*q*) identical verse,
which, only two years before, he had ex-

L pelled

(*q*) Appendix, No. XXI.

Dr. Benson. pelled from the very text of the New Testament !——Nor is even this all. For in the next, succeeding, year, (A. D. 1519) he condemns the verse again, by leaving it out of his New Testament of that year. And yet he continued but a short time, even in that resolution :——for he restored the verse, finally, to its place, in his very next Edition of the New Testament, in A. D. 1522.

The facts, then, being thus clear, there seems but one consistent method of accounting for this incongruity of conduct in *Erasmus* ; which is, to suppose that he became a proselyte to *Arianism*, not before A. D. 1505, but in some part of the interval between that year, and A. D. 1516.—In A. D. 1505, then, not having then imbibed the tenets of *Arianism*, *Erasmus* gave to the world, in the commentary of *L. Valla*, the testimony of seven *Greek* MSS, in favor of the authenticity of this verse. In A. D. 1516, having suffered that leaven to enter into, and to ferment within, his mind, in a long interval of eleven years ; he expelled this verse from the text of his New Testament. But he ventured

on

on this expulfion, as it feems, under a fecret Dr. Benson,
fear of a fevere attack, on its account, from
the Chriftian world, in general; for which
the commentary of *L. Valla*, itfelf, would
furnifh no inconfiderable weapons: which
fear apparently induced him to provide fome
means of retreat, in cafe of neceffity, (fuch,
Sir, was *the* PRUDENCE *of Erafmus!*) by
bringing this verfe forward again, in A. D.
1518, in his *Ratio veræ Theologiæ.* In A.D.
1519, he hazarded a fecond expulfion: but,
ftill fearful, as it feems, of the argument deducible from *Valla*'s MSS, he gave up the whole
conteft, formally, and finally, but ftill in a
moft unchearful, and difingenuous, manner,
in A. D. 1522.

Thus, then, Sir, may the whole conduct
of *Erafmus*, in this matter, (which you have
attempted to dignify by the appellation of
prudence) be accounted for, at leaft, and explained.—that meannefs, which, upon the
face of his own apology, he was guilty of;
that departure from truth, which, when the
facts are fully confidered, he feems to be
juftly chargeable with; his hafty expulfion

of

Dr. BENSON. of the verfe, and his fullen re-admiffion of it; his confeffion of *one* MS only, in favor of this verfe, when he ought to have acknowledged *eight*; and his impotent attempt to depreciate even *that one*, by charging it with having been corrected by the *Latin* copies, although he did not attempt to produce a fingle inftance of fuch correction, in proof of the charge, fo alledged.

This conduct of *Erafmus* feems, in fome refpects, to have been the caufe, and in others the confequence, of his having been feduced, by pre-conceived prejudices, to affign an incompetent, and, apparently, an untrue, motive for his reftoration of this verfe, in A. D. 1522. And this conduct feems to juftify the cenfure, caft upon him by *Wetftein*, which is the more fevere, becaufe it falls from a friend, and fellow-advocate. " *It is an almoft intolerable thing*" (fays he) " *in Erafmus, that he will frequently try to fhelter himfelf* (r) *under* EXCUSES, *which are even*

" IDLE,

(r) " *Illud denique in* Erafmo *minime ferendum eft, quod fæpe excufationibus parum idoneis nec fatis honeftis uti, quàm erroris culpam fimpliciter fateri, maluerit.*" (*Wetftein,* Proleg p. 124)

" IDLE, *and* DISHONEST, *rather than make* Dr. BENSON,
" *an ingenuous confeſſion of a fault, or a*.
" *miſtake.*"

XXXIII. " *A MS has been referred*
" *to, which is now lodged in the Library,*
" *belonging to the Univerſity of Dublin.*
" *And Wetſtein reckons that MS to be*
" *what Eraſmus calls Codex Britannicus.*"

The *Dublin* MS is not the *Codex Britannicus* of *Eraſmus* ;—becauſe (as Dr. *Benſon* confeſſes in another (s) place) the latter reads πνευμα only, the former αγ.ον πνευμα, in the *ſeventh* Verſe :—and becauſe, in the *eighth* Verſe, the article οἱ is placed before μαρτυρουντες, in the MS of *Dublin* ; but the ſame article is not found, at all, in the *Codex Britannicus.* It is impoſſible that the ſame MS ſhould, in the ſame given paſſage, differ from itſelf ; or, in other words, be *the ſame,* and yet *not the ſame,* MS.

L 3 XXXIV.

(s) Note on page 640.
See Appendix, No. XX, where theſe Verſes are copied by *Eraſmus* himſelf,—as they ſtood in the *Codex Britannicus.*

Dr. Benson.

XXXIV. " *The learned author of The* " *Memoirs of the life and writings of* " *Dr. Waterland, (p. 79) gives this ac-* " *count of it.* *The Dublin MS now has* " *it [that is, the disputed text ;] written,* " *(as I am told, by one who has seen it)* " *in a different hand, (as all the Epistles* " *are) from the rest of the MS.*"

I have been favored, by the learned Dr. *Wilson*, of the University of *Dublin*, to whose care this MS is, at present, officially en-trusted, with the following account of it · which directly contradicts the affertion, thus brought from the writer of the Memoirs of Dr. *Waterland*.

" 1. The *Dublin* MS, as exactly as I can " form an opinion, is WRITTEN BY THE " SAME HAND. In the Gospel of St. " *Matthew* the letters are smaller, and the " lines more slender, than in the other parts " of the MS. In the rest of THE WHOLE " volume, the letters are uniformly larger, " but so *similar* as to indicate THE SAME " SCRIBE.

" SCRIBE.   It abounds in contractions. Dr. BESNON.
" There are NO RASURES.

" The Scribe, when he had immediate-
" ly diſcovered an erroneous letter, or ſylla-
" ble, drew a line acroſs the miſtake, and
" ſtraightway ſubjoined the word correctly
" written. When the error was not ob-
" ſerved, until the paragraph, or page, was
" concluded, the correction is exhibited in
" the margin; the faulty word croſſed,
" yet ſtill legible. But ſome of theſe cor-
" rections, thus noted in the margin, ſeem
" to have been made when the whole work
" was concluded; becauſe, in them, the
" ink is much blacker than in the text,
" having acquired, by ſtanding longer, a
" deeper tinge.

" It is written with accents, and ſpirits.
" The Acts are placed after the Epiſtles of
" St. *Paul*.

" 2. The CONTESTED VERSE is, indiſ-
" putably, WRITTEN BY THE SAME PER-
" SON, *who wrote the* REST OF THE PAGE,

L 4   " *and*

Dr. BENSON. " *and the* REST OF THE EPISTLE. This,
" on infpection, will appear felf-evident, and
" inconteftible.

" 3. As to the antiquity of the MS, I am
" incapable of giving a decided opinion,
" further than as follows. That it pre-
" ceded the æra of Printing feems very clear,
" from its having many readings not found
" in any edition prior to *Stephens*; there-
" fore not a tranfcript from any of them.
" But I do not think that it can be carried
" higher than a century, or two, at the ut-
" moft, before the invention of Printing.
" For it is certainly written on thick, po-
" lifhed, paper, which *Ycard* miftook for
" parchment. Now no paper records have
" been difcovered, anterior to the clofe of
" the *twelfth* century, as I find in the *Acta*
" *Leipfienfia*. It was, therefore, a tranfcript
" from fome MS now, perhaps, loft; and,
" on that account, claims the authority of
" an original. Whether corrected, and
" compleated, according to a *Latin* copy, is
" more than I know.——

" 4. The

" 4. The controverted paſſage ſtands thus. Dr. Benson,
" [In Martin's *La Verite*, Ed. *Utrecht*,
" A.D. 1721, p. 272, it is not accurately
" repreſented.]

7. Οτι τρεις εισιν οι μαρτυ
ρυντ' εν τω ουνω, πηρ, λογος και πνα αγιου·
και ουτοι οι τρεις εν εισι.

8. Και τρεις εισιν οι μαρτυ
ρυντ' εν τη γη, πνα, υδωρ, και αιμα· (*t*)

Before ſuch authority as this, the telling
of Dr. *Benſon*, who is told by the Author
of certain Memoirs, who is told by one who
has no name, that this text is *written in a
different hand from the reſt of the MS,*—va-
niſhes into nothing.

XXXV. " *It appears thence probable,*
" *that that part of the MS has been*
" *added ſince the time of Archbiſhop*
" *Uſher. In whoſe collations it*" [the
verſe in queſtion] " *is not found.*"

The

(*t*) The account of the *Dublin* MS, here ſtated, is more
particular than that which was ſet forth in the former
edition of this work, becauſe it is the reſult of the *whole*
of the communications, made to me, by Dr. *Wilſon*, as
well *before*, as *ſince*, the publication of the former edition
of theſe Letters.

Dr. Benson. The premifes, from whence the former part of this objection is drawn, having been juft difproved, the conclufion muft, of courfe, fall to the ground. And, as to the latter part of it,—the verfe, 1. *John*, v. 7, does not appear, it is true, in the Collations, which Archbifhop *Ufher* made of this MS ;—becaufe he did not live to carry thofe Collations beyond the firft Chapter of the Epiftle to the *Romans*.

This circumftance is evident from the *Prolegomena* (*u*) of Dr. *Mill*: which, however, Dr. *Benfon* has endeavoured to conceal from his readers. He did not chufe to communicate to them that part of Dr. *Mill*'s account of this MS, which fupported its reputation, and character; although he ufes all hafte (as will appear in the next fucceeding extract) to ftate thofe parts of the *Prolegomena*, at length, which tend to depreciate the

---

(*u*) *Milli* Proleg 1379, 1380 This circumftance is further affirmed by a Memorandum of Dean *Yeard*, prefixed to this MS. " The readings of this MS were " not gathered, but to the 22d of the Acts of the Holy " Apoftles, and thofe of the firft Chapter of the Epiftle " to the *Romans*." (See alfo *Wetftein*'s *Proleg.* p. 52, and *Emlyn*'s Reply, C. v. p. 269.)

the Verſe. But this, Sir, you will, perhaps Dr. Benson. denominate the *prudence* of Dr. *Benſon*. It will, at leaſt, rank, as a fit companion, with the " *prudence* of *Eraſmus* ;" of which you, ſome time ago, made ſuch honorable mention.

> XXXVI. " *Dr. Mill ſays, It is writ-*
> " *ten in a modern and careleſs hand; with*
> " *ſome things blotted out, and others inter-*
> " *polated.*"—(p. 640.)

It ſeems moſt probable, that Dr. *Mill*, and Mr. *Caſley*, had never ſeen this MS. Dean *Ycard*'s account, who HAD SEEN it formerly, and Dr. *Wilſon*'s deſcription, who has lately inſpected it, admit the blottings out, and interpolations, but explain them in a manner the moſt honorable to the Copyiſt. " The Writer" (ſays Dean *Ycard*)
" has not taken pains to make fair writing.
" He has often greatly neglected his hand;
" and, what is very diſagreeable to the eye,
" but is, neverthelſs, *the mark of integrity*
" *in a Tranſcriber*, is, that when, in copy-
" ing,

Dr. Benson, " ing, he perceived any word, or words, to
" have been omitted by him, he erafed thofe
" which he had written" [fubfequent to the
omiffion] " and re-placed them in the body
" of the work, after he had inferted there-
" in what he had before omitted." (w)

Blots, and interpolations, may be marks
of hafte in the Copyift; but they are not
certain proofs of inaccuracy in the MS itfelf.
It is morally impoffible, that the tranfcriber
of fo large a book as the New Teftament,
fhould travel through his tafk, without falling
into errors, without committing miftakes.
And if, upon revifion, he fhould decline to
blot, or to interpolate, left he fhould be faid
not to have " taken pains to make fair writ-
" ing," the outward fairnefs of his work
would ill atone for its internal errors, and
defects.

Thus far as to this charge, of blots, and
interpolations, in general. Let it be, finally,
remarked, as to this Verfe, in particular, that
it

(w) *Martin's La Verite*, Part II, C. 12. Dr. *Wilfon's*
account of thefe particulars hath been already ftated at
large in page 151.

it is *neither* BLOTTED, *nor* INTERPOLATED; Dr. BENSON, but is written in the body of the page, and in the fame fair, uniform, hand, with the 1eft of the MS.

  XXXVII. " *Mr. Cafley calls it a mo-*
" *dern MS, probably tranflated, or cor-*
" *rected, from the latin vulgate. Other*
" *learned men have obferved, that the*
" *form of the letters is the fame with that*
" *of our printed Greek Teftaments, with*
" *accents and fpirits. So that it may,*
" *poffibly, have been written, fince the in-*
" *vention of Printing."*——

Dr. *Benfon* ought to have ftated the cir-cumftances which make for the antiquity of this MS, as well as thofe which tend to pro-nounce it modern. But this, it feems, al-though greatly his duty, was no part of his defign.

Let it be here obferved, then, that the vowels *ι* and *υ* are written, throughout this MS, with double points placed over them : which method of pointing, by the teftimony

Dr. Benson. of (*x*) *Montfaucon*, the moſt competent of all men to decide a queſtion of this nature, ſhews a MS to be more than a thouſand years old. This is, at leaſt, a ſtrong preſumption in favor of the antiquity of this MS. But this diſpute will, perhaps, be the moſt ſatisfactorily decided, by referring to the deſcription of this MS, herein before ſtated (*y*) which, at leaſt, proves that it was written *before* (if not long before) " the in- " vention of Printing."

As to Mr. *Caſley*'s expreſſions, " PROBA- " BLY *tranſlated*, OR *corrected*," they are the very language of mere conjecture; and, as ſuch, deſerve little, or no, attention.

XXXVIII. " *I would have truth take* " *place, on which ſide ſoever it falls.*" [Note, p. 640.]

If

(*x*) *Pelæographia Græca.* Edit. *Paris.* A. D. 1708, lib. i p 33

(*y*) The words reſpecting the date of this MS, which were copied from it, in the former edition of theſe let- ters, are here omitted, becauſe they *may* be applied to the time when St Mark's Goſpel, itſelf, was *originally written* although that time really was, according to Dr. *Cave's* account, A D 56, and, according to Dr *Pearſon*, A D 60 I do not wiſh to urge any evidence in favor of this verſe, againſt which any objections may be brought, which can, in any degree, ſtand the teſt of examination.

If Dr. *Benson*, inftead of raking together every thing that hath been faid, however miftakenly, by *Mill*, and *Cafley*, in prejudice of the MS in queftion, and preffing that fide of the argument, *alone*, had thought fit, at the fame time, to have given to the world what *Martin*, and *Ycard*, had urged in favor of its antiquity, and authority ; his practice would have done as much honor to this declaration, as it now reflects difgrace upon it.

XXXIX. " *Again; we have been re-*
" *ferred to another MS, which is in the*
" *King of Pruffia's library, at Berlin.*
" *That MS has, indeed, the difputed*
" *text. But then it is acknowledged to*
" *be a late tranfcript from a printed Greek*
" *Teftament, and, particularly, from the*
" *Complutenfian edition ; which the ig-*
" *norant tranfcriber has followed fo clofely,*
" *as to copy exactly and without variation,*
" *even the very errors of the Printer.*"

This MS was purchafed, upwards of a century ago, at a high price, by *Frederic William the Great, Elector* of *Brandenburgh*,

and

Dr. Benson. and was believed to be very ancient, not only by the learned of that age in general, (as by the Librarian *Hendreichius*, by *Saubertus*, Profeſſor of Divinity at *Helmſtadt*, by *Tollius*, and by the great Orientaliſt, *Jablonſki*, at *Berlin*) but by the famous *Spanheim*. If the claim of this MS to antiquity were to be decided by authorities of this kind, it ſhould ſeem, that very reſpectable antagoniſts, and thoſe many in number, ſhould be oppoſed to names of ſuch eminence as theſe, to ſatisfy the world of its being a modern copy. And who are theſe many, and reſpectable antagoniſts? As to *number*, I know of none, but *one*; and as to the *reſpectableneſs* of that one, in this (z) inſtance, at leaſt, let the reader (if any reader ſhall have accompanied me thus far) condeſcend to afford me a few moments more of his patience, and then judge for himſelf.

ONE perſon, then, M. V. *La Croze*, a Librarian at *Berlin*, in the beginning of the preſent

fent

<hr />

(z) *Emlyn's* Reply, (Edit. as before) p. 229 —M. V. *La Croze* was, certainly, a very learned man. But his behaviour, in reſpect to this verſe, undoubtedly merits the moſt ſevere reprehenſion.

sent century, in a letter written A. D. 1720, Dr. BENSON, and published by Mr. *Emlyn*, in his contest with Mr. *Martin*, affirms this MS to be a late transcript from the *Complutensian* Edition. " I wonder," (says he) " that *our* " MS, a book of no authority, should be " alledged in confirmation of a dubious " reading, after I have already made it " manifest to *many* learned men, and to Mr. " *Martin* himself, that this book, although " sold by an artful impostor for an ancient " MS, and boasted of accordingly, is only " a late transcript from the *Complutensian* " Edition : and this" (he proceeds to say) " I PERCEIVED AT ONCE, when I former- " ly viewed this Library, as a stranger, and " before I had any intentions of settling at " *Berlin* ; and I made this declaration open- " ly to *Hendreichius*, now dead ; and ever " since this Library has been entrusted to " my care, I have candidly declared the " same to all persons, nor is Mr. *Martin* ig- " norant of it."—In another part of the same letter, the same *La Croze* says, " He " who has seen the *Complutensian* Edition, " has also seen our MS, without excepting

M " *even*

Dr. BENSON. " *even the very errors of the Printer, which*
" *the ignorant transcriber has followed so close-*
" *ly,* as to make it absolutely certain, that
" some illiterate copyist was employed by
" some learned cheat, in order to accomplish
" this imposture."

In another letter, much anterior in point
of date to this, which has just been abstract-
ed, the same *La Croze* says (with a for-
wardness, which indicates that he had, *even*
then, taken his side, and that the fate of the
Verse, in question, was, at that time, not
indifferent to him) among other things.—

" I read, YESTERDAY, (*a*) Dr. *Mill's*
" Differtation upon the paffage of St. *John;*
" and found there ALMOST all that I HAD
" THOUGHT upon the fame fubject.—ALL
" the ancient *Greek* and *Latin* MSS, in
" reckoning up the three" [THREE !] "Wit-
" neffes, mention only the Spirit, the Water,
" and the Blood. There is no account to
" be made of our *Greek* MS of the New-
" Teftament; it is a work, which, although
" *it*

(*a*) *Emlyn's* Reply, p. 286.—

" it has deceived many, I *never thought* a- Dr. Benson.
" bove eighty years old. In the year 1696,
" upon coming to *Berlin*, this MS was fhewn
" to me as being a thoufand years old : *After*
" *having examined it* A MOMENT, I maintain-
" ed that it was modern, and copied from
" the edition of the Bible of Cardinal *Xime-*
" *nes*. I convinced the late Mr. *Spanheim,*
" and the then Librarian, by comparing of
" paffages, the refemblance of characters,
" and other fenfible proofs. The paffage
" of the Three Witneffes is there word for
" word, as in the Bible of *Alcala*, AND IT
" COULD NOT BE THERE OTHERWISE.
" The ancient Fathers have (*b*) NEVER
" made ufe of fo remarkable a paffage.
" The Lectionary, entitled αποςολος, IN MY
" OPINION, is of no great authority in this
" cafe. I do not doubt its antiquity ; but
" thefe ecclefiaftical Books are more fubject
" to alterations than others."—

Such teftimony as this (to fay nothing of
that

(*b*) M. *La Croze*, it feems, had NEVER confulted any
of the authorities, ftated in the former part of thefe letters, which directly deftroy this affertion , or he would
NEVER have made it.

Dr Eesnon that air of affected felf-fufficiency, which appears in almoft every line, and is truly re-diculous) carries fufpicion upon the face of it There can be but fmall doubt of the then *Elector* having taken the opinions of the moft learned men of his Court, and Country, as to the antiquity of this MS, an-tecedently to his purchafe of it ; and of their having given their fentiments in its favor, after having tried it by the beft examination in their power. There can be no doubt of this MS being well known to *Hendreichius*, becaufe, as the *Electoral* Librarian, he had it under his care many years ; to *Saubertus*, becaufe he has fet forth nearly *two hundred* various readings from it, in his commentary on the Gofpel of St. *Matthew*, and he ftiles it " *Pervetuflus, (c) et admodùm pretiofus* ;"—to *Tollius*, becaufe he is cited, in relation to it, by Father *Le Long* ; to *Jablonfki*, becaufe he was confulted by *Kettner*, on the fubject, previoufly to his publication ; and to *Span-heim*, for *La Croze* affirms that he convinced *Spanheim* of its being an impofture. It is furely, then, on the very face of this account,

a

(*c*) *Prolegom* Edit. *Helmftadt*, A. D. 1672, p 41.

a moft ftrange, an almoft incredible, thing, Dr. Benson.
that *La Croze* fhould PERCEIVE AT ONCE,
at a fingle glance, as it were, and IN A MO-
MENT, what fo many learned men, upon a
long acquaintance with, and a clofe examination of, the MS, could not perceive at all.
Such a narration as this, having no fuppo1t
beyond the bare affirmation of the reporter,
would deferve little credit, even if no pofitive proof could be brought to deftroy it.

But, unfortunately for *La Croze*, his whole
charge is demonftrably falfe.—For,

1.—As to his affertion, that he had made
it manifeft to Mr. *Martin*, that the MS, in
queftion, was a late tranfcript from the *Complutenfian* Edition,—it turns out, by (*d*)Mr.

M 3

Martin's

(*d*) *Martin's* *La Verite*, Part 11, C. 7. *La Croze*, attempted, indeed, to apologife to *Weftein*, on this fubject,
by faying, that he had not defended himfelf, becaufe he
was unwilling to offend Mr *Martin*, or to treat him
harfhly. " *Hoc mihi fignificavit Cl La Croze, per epifto-*
" *lam, A D 1731, fe ad objectiones D Martini non refpon-*
" *diffe, quod fenem venerandum offendere, aut ipfi ægre fa-*
" *cere, noluiffet.*" (Proleg p. 59.) But this was a mere
pretence Whilft he thought himfelf able to fuppo1t
his own affumptions, he made no fcruple of treating Mr
Martin difrefpectfully enough He found himfelt *unwilling to offend this venerable old man*, precifely at the time
when he found himfelt *unable to anfwer his arguments*.

Dr. Benson. *Martin's* own account, which was addreſſed to *La Croze*, which it was highly incumbent upon him to have contradicted, if he could, but which ſtands to the preſent hour, even uncontroverted,—that he had made, to Mr. *Martin*, no ſuch manifeſtation at all. Nor was it, indeed, poſſible that *La Croze* could " make manifeſt" his aſſertion, notwithſtanding the over-forward zeal which haſtily precipitated him into it, either " to " Mr. *Martin*," or to " many learned men," or to any perſon whatever. For,

2. This MS is NOT *a tranſcript from the* Complutenſian *Bible* :—as will evidently appear by the following obſervations.

In the Goſpel of St. *Matthew*, Chap. ii. Verſe 13, the MS of *Berlin* (in queſtion) reads αποκτειναι ; but the reading of the Bible of *Complutum* is απολεσαι, in the correſponding part of that Verſe.

In ii. 17, of the ſame Goſpel, the *Berlin* MS has υπο κυριε δια Ιερεμιε ; but the *Complutenſian* Edition has, in the ſame paſſage, υπο Ιερεμιε τε προφητε.

In v. 32, the *Berlin* MS reads οτι πας ο Dr. BENSON. απολυων, but the reading of the *Complutenſian* Edition is οτι ος αν απολυση.

In vi. 13, the *Complutenſian* Edition has the Doxology compleat—" *For thine is the* " *kingdom, the power, and the glory, for ever* " *and ever:*" of which the *Berlin* MS has not a ſingle word. (e)

In vii. 18, the *Berlin* MS has εδε παλιν δενδρον; but the *Complutenſian* Edition has only εδε δενδρον.

In vii. 24, the *Berlin* MS reads ομο.ωθησεται: but the *Complutenſian* Edition only ομοισω.

In ix. 30, the MS of *Berlin* reads ανεωχθησαν αυΐων παραχρημα, but the *Complutenſian* does not exhibit the word παραχρημα, in that paſſage.

In xv. 22, the MS of *Berlin* reads ετραξεν επισω αυτε; but the *Complutenſian* Edition has, in the ſame paſſage, ετραυΐασεν αυτω.

M 4   In

(e) This Doxology ſtands in the margin of the *Complutenſian* Teſtament.

Dr. BENSON,   In xvii. 2, the *Berlin* MS has ως Χιων; but the *Complutenfian* reads, inftead thereof, ως το φως, in the parallel paffage.

In xxvii. 29, the MS of *Berlin* reads εν τη δεξια, but the Edition of *Complutum* hath, in the parallel paffage, επι την δεξιαν.

In *eight* of thefe examples, this MS agrees with one, or more, of the MSS of *Robert Stephens*; in one example, with a MS of *Cafaubon*; in *two*, with the *Codex Montfortius*; in *one*, with the MSS of *Sauberius*; in *three*, with the celebrated MS of *Cambridge*; and in the laft example, with the ftill more celebrated MS of *Alexandria*.

If thefe variations of the *Berlin* MS from the *Complutenfian* Edition, felected, by the help of *Saubertus*, from the Gofpel of St. *Matthew*, alone, be fo numerous, (and yet the Lift here given, does not comprife them all) how greatly might that number be increafed, by an examination, of this kind, purfued through the whole of the New Teftament! But, as the tafk would be irkfome, fo the
attempt

attempt is, happily, unneceſſary. The variations, which have been already adduced,
concord too nearly with the readings of other
MSS, to be mere errors of the tranſcriber.
They are too correct, in their language, and
too pointed in their meaning, to be the errors of an " ignorant tranſcriber." And they
differ too widely, are in every reſpect too
diſcordant, from the text of the *Complutenſian*, to warrant even a poſſibility, that the
MS of *Berlin* can be, at all, " a tranſcript
from that Edition."

With reſpect to the information, which
M. *La Croze* has further condeſcended to give
us,—namely, that the " αποςολος is, *in his o-
" pinion*, of no great authority," becauſe it
is a *Lectionary*, and becauſe Lectionaries
" are more ſubject to alterations than
" other eccleſiaſtical Books,"—it might be
aſked, whether in any Lectionary, of any
Church, any text would, at any time, be inſerted, which that Church did not accept as
genuine? But queſtions of this kind need
not be propoſed, or multiplied, in the preſent
caſe. For the αποςολος is NOT a *Lectionary*,
                                        in

Dr. Benson. in any other fenfe than as the Bible itfelf may be called a *Lectionary*, namely, from being *read in the Church*. The απορολος is a " Collection (*f*) of the Epiftles of the " New Teftament, written feparately ;" that is, feparately from the Gofpels. The απορολος, then, is the very volume of the E- piftles themfelves, comprifing, among the reft, this Epiftle of St. *John*. And the *opinion* of *La Croze*, founded on fuppofed alterations in Lectionaries, can have no place in the prefent queftion.

As to Dr. *Benfon's* fuggeftion, that this MS is ALSO, a " tranfcript from a printed " *Greek* Teftament ;" it feems hardly reconcileable with his other affumption, of its being, withal, " a tranfcript from the *Complutenfian* Edition." Taken *as a whole*, the accufation feems, in no fmall degree, inconfiftent with itfelf. Confidered *in parts*, the latter claufe of it has already been proved to be utterly untrue ; and the former, being made without fpecification, is empty, and

(*f*) Dr *Thomas Smith's* Mifcellanea, *Lond.* Edit. A. D. 1686, p. 155. See alfo MARTIN's *La Verite*, p. II, C. 5.

and unfounded. As an idle charge, and Dr. Benson. brought at random, it is not worth the pains to dwell upon it. It is too vaguely stated to receive an answer, and too absurdly expressed to deserve one.

XL. " *And, finally, as to the* Com-
" plutensian, *which was the* first *edition*
" *of the* Greek *Testament; which,*
" *(though printed)* Stephens *has num-*
" *bered as the first of his MSS.*"---

The *Complutensian* was *not*, properly, the first Edition of the *Greek* Testament. The *Basil* Edition of *Erasmus* was published in A. D. 1516, antecedently to the Bible of *Complutum;* which, although *printed* in A. D. 1514, was not given to the world until several years afterwards. Nor has *Robert Ste-phens* " numbered the *Complutensian* as the " *first* of his MSS," or as *any* of his MSS. Take his own (*g*) words: " Ut primò, " *Complutensem* EDITIONEM intelligas, quæ " olim ad antiquissima exemplaria fuit EX- " CUSA."

XLI.

(*g*) Preface to *R. Stephens*'s Edition, in question. (Appendix, No XII.)

XLI. " *From whence*" [viz. from the Complutensian Edition] " *most* " *probably, he*" [Robert Stephens] " *took* " *this disputed passage, and inserted it into* " *the sacred text.*"

If Dr. *Benson* had stopped to compare the text of this disputed passage, as it stands in the *Complutensian*, with that of the Edition of *Robert Stephens*, he, *perhaps*, would not have hazarded this observation.

The *Greek* Text of *R. Stephens*'s Edition of 1. *John*, v. 7, 8.	The *Greek* Text of the *Complutensian* Edition of the same Verses.
7. Ὅτι τρεις εισιν οι μαρ[υρ]- δ. ε. ζ. θ.]ουν]ες ἐν τῳ ὀρα- ι. ια. ιγ.]νγ', ὁ ϖα]ηρ, ὁ λογϴ', και το αγιον ϖνευμα, και ετοι οι τρεις * εἰς τὸ α. * εν εισι.	7 Οτι τρεις εισιν οι μαρ]υροντες εν τω κρανω, ο ϖα]ηρ και ο λογος και το αγιον ϖνευμα, και οι τρεις εις το εν εισι.
8. Και τρεις εισιν οι μαρ]υρ-ουν]ες εν τη γη, το ϖνευμα, και το υδωρ, και το αιμα, και οι τρεις εις το εν εισι.	8. Και τρεις εισιν οι μαρ]υρουν]ες επι της γης το πνευμα και το υδωρ και αιμα.

In the *seventh* Verfe of this Epiftle; then, the Edition of *Robert Stephens* reads ναι ειοι οι τρεις ,—That of *Complutum*, και οι τρεις, only. The Edition of *Robert Stephens* alfo reads εν ειοι , whilft that of *Complutum* conveys not only different words, but, in fome refpects, a different meaning, from that of *Robert Stephens,* by reading εις το εν ειοι.

Dr. Benson.

In the *eighth* Verfe, the Edition of *Robert Stephens* reads εν τη γη , but that of *Complutum* επι της γης,—a different prepofition, governing, in the following fubftantive, a different cafe. In the Edition of *Robert Stephens,* the laft claufe of this Verfe, και οι τρεις εις το εν ειοι, is read entire; but there is not one word of it found in the *eighth* Verfe of the Edition of *Complutum.*

Befide thefe palpable difcordances, which render the pretence of one of thefe Editions having been a Tranfcript of the other, improbable, beyond all feeming; a little attention to the method, in which *Robert Stephens* proceeded, throughout his Edition of A. D. 1550, will prove the abfolute impracticability of this fuppofition.

When

When any particular word, or words, were found in a few of his Copies, which did not exist in the generality, or in the greater part, of them, *Robert Stephens*, on inserting such word, or words, in the text of his work, constantly pointed to the margin, by the help of his index, the *obelus*; where his reader might find the MS, or MSS, particularly specified, on the authority of which he had made the insertion. And when, upon placing his *obelus* in the text, the passage, or word, to which it was prefixed, was found in but a very few (as in one, or two) of his Copies, it was his invariable custom to signify this deficiency, in the margin, by the following description——εν πασι (οι παντα) πλην τε β (for instance) *viz. This word, or passage, is wanting in all my authorities, except the Copy marked* β or, for the sake of brevity, by the single initial π. (instead of εν πασι or παντα) followed by the rest of the reference. Thus in St. *Matthew*, xii. 35, the *obelus* is placed over the words της καρδιας; and in the margin is written εν πασι, πλην εν τω η, or *These words are wanting in all my authorities, except the MS,* η. In St. *Mark*, viii. 2, the mark of

reference

reference is placed over the word ημερας, and Dr. BENSON.
the correſponding marginal Note is, παντα
πλην τε γ, or, *Wanting in all, except the MS
marked γ.* And laſtly in St. *John,* iii. 25,
the reference is affixed to the word Ιεδαιων;
and in the margin is found ω. πλην τε α, or,
wanting in all, except the Copy α, which is the
Complutenſian Edition. (b)

Now, what is the Note, or Reference, of
Robert Stephens, in the margin of this diſputed Verſe, couſidered in relation to the
Complutenſian Edition? Not, εν πασι, or πανία,
πλην τε α, (or, abbreviated, ω. πλην τε α) which
is the conſtant cuſtom of *Robert Stephens,*
where *one,* only, of his authorities ſuppoits
a particular reading: Not, " *Wanting in all*
" *my copies, except the* Complutenſian,"—
which, certainly, would have been the caſe,
if the ſuppoſition, advanced by Dr. *Benſon,*
and now under conſideration, weie juſt.
But his Note, or Reference, is to this effect,
and may be thus fairly paraphraſed. *The
words,* εν τε ερανω, *in this Verſe, are wanting
in*

Dr. BENSON. *in* feven *of my MSS. The* Complutenfian *Copy, and others of my authorities, have the whole Verfe in full length, fave that the* Complutenfian *has, at the clofe of the Verfe, a reading peculiar to itfelf, viz.* ας το ει, *which does not belong to any of the reft.* If *Robert Stephens*, whilft living, had even entertained fome latent fears, left a fuppofition of the kind, now under confideration, however prepofterous, might, at fome future time, attempt to impofe itfelf upon the world; it feems that he could not have employed thofe marginal Notes, and References, which he had adopted, more appofitely, than he thus has done, to meet it with a flat negation. It was not well within his power to have done more for our fatisfaction herein, unlefs he had been uneafy enough to have detailed thofe fears, at large, to the world, by anticipation; and had bufied himfelf, in much circumlocution, to caution his readers, beforehand, not to pay any heed to fuch an impofition, if it fhould be attempted to be paffed upon them.

Thefe impediments, Sir, being thus removed,

moved, I am enabled to fum up this argu- Dr. Benson.
ment, in *both* its parts, in a few words. Had
Robert Stephens " taken this difputed paffage
" from the *Complutenfian* Edition," he would
not have remarked, as a circumftance peculiar to *that* Edition, that it read εις το εν, in
a *part* of the Verfe in queftion; if the *whole*
Verfe had been peculiar to it, and had not
been found in any of his other authorities.
But he has *not* inferted the difputed paffage,
as it ftood in the text of the *Complutenfian.*
And he *has* remarked the εις το εν, as a circumftance *peculiar* to a *part* of the Verfe, in
the *Complutenfian* Copy. The confequence
is peremptory; it will not be evaded, and it
cannot be repelled: namely, that *Robert Ste-*
phens did NOT take this difputed paffage from
the *Complutenfian* Edition.

XLII. " *The Editors*" [of the *Com-*
" *plutenfian* Edition] " *fay, in general,*
" *that they followed the beft and moft an-*
" *cient MSS of the* Vatican.—*But Mr.*
" Wetftein *(i) renders it dubious whe-*
N " *ther*

(i) *Prolegomena* to folio Edition, A. D. 1751, page
116.

Dr. Benson.

" *ther they had any* Vatican *MSS,—not*
" *only, from their varying, in so many*
" *places, from the best* Vatican *copy, but*
" *because* Leo X *did not come to the Pope-*
" *dom, time enough to have furnished*
" *them, in* Spain, *with such MSS before*
" *they undertook that work.   For he (be-*
" *ing then sick) was chosen Pope not a*
" *year before that Edition was published.*
" *And they are supposed to have been about*
" *fifteen years in preparing and publishing*
" *it."*—(p. 641.)

The Editors of *Complutum* positively, and
in the strongest terms, declare, that they had
the use of several *Vatican* MSS, which were
sent, from *Rome*, to Cardinal *Ximenes*, for
that purpose.

" Let it be known" (say they (*k*) in their
preface) " to the reader, that we have had,
" for the benefit of this work, the use of
" several MSS, of such very great antiquity,
" and correctness, that it seems a kind of
" impiety

(*k*) Appendix, No. XIV.

" impiety to doubt their truth : which the
" moſt holy Father, &c. *Leo* X. deſirous to
" favor our undertaking, ſent from the Apoſ-
" tolic Library, to the moſt reverend the
" Cardinal of *Spain* ; under whoſe authority,
" and by whoſe commands, we have com-
" mitted this work to the preſs."

The world, ſurely, owes to theſe illuſtrious Editors ſo much reſpect, at leaſt, as to
credit a declaration, made with ſuch ſolem-
nity, unleſs there ſhall appear, from circumſtances, a moral impoſſibility of its truth.
But the objections, here culled out of *Wetſtein*,
are far from importing any ſuch impoſſibility.
It by no means follows, that theſe Editors
had no *Vatican* MSS, becauſe they varied, in
many places, from the beſt *Vatican* Copy.
It would be juſt as ſound a concluſion, to
affirm, that *Robert Stephens* had not the *Complutenſian* Bible, becauſe he has varied, in
many places, from that Edition.   And, as to
there not being a *Leo* X. at *Rome*, " time
" enough to have furniſhed them, in *Spain*,
" with ſuch MSS, before they undertook
" that work ;" it may be anſwered, that

there

Dr. BENSON. there was a Cardinal (*l*) *de Medici* there, time

(*l*) He was created Cardinal, by *Innocent* VIII, at 41 years of age (*Bayle*, Dict. Historique, Tom. II. p. 299. Edit. *Rotterdam* A D. 1697.)

The learned friend, to whom I am indebted for the account of the *Dublin* MS, set forth in p 150—153 of this work, has favored me with the following reflections, on the subject of these *Vatican* MSS.

"I think it probable, that the *Vatican* MSS were lent
" to *Ximenes*, during the Popedom of his countryman
" *Alexander* VI, who died in August, A. D. 1503,—
" that, during the ensuing scenes of turbulence, they
" were not re-demanded, until at last they were abso-
" lutely forgotten, and that they lie dormant in some
" Library, or Monastery, in *Spain*, where, on examina-
" tion, they may yet be discovered. I know when
" *Francis* I died, and when *Leo*'s Popedom commenced,
" But the reigning Prince, or Pope, is always thanked
" for the favours conferred by their predecessors, while
" it is to their indulgence we owe their continuance, or
" from their grace we must expect their repetition. R.
" *Stephens* acknowledges that his MSS came from the
" Library *then belonging* to *Henry* They were lent by
" *Francis* So might the *Complutensian* Editors thank
" *Leo* for the MSS, which they had from his *Vatican*,
" although they received them from *Alexander*. *Ximenes*
" was long projecting his work, and long preparing his
" materials Is it not probable, that he would take the
" opportunity of soliciting the loan of the *Vatican* MSS
" (if they were LENT to him) when his countryman
" filled St. *Peter*'s chair? But, as Books, and MSS,
" were not *Alexander*'s passion, I suspect that he SOLD
" them to *Ximenes*, and that the *loan* was a fable, con-
" trived to conceal the infamy of the transaction."—

This is a most judicious conjecture. And it seems that no objection can be brought against it, save the ex-pressions of the *Complutensian* Editors; who positively say, in their preface, that *Ximenes* received them from *Leo*.
" *Quæ* Leo *decimus educta*, &c. MISIT *ad Cardinalem*
" *Hispaniæ*."—

time enough to furnifh thofe MSS to his Brother Cardinal, *Ximenes*, for his affiftance in this undertaking. And becaufe, in that long feries of *fifteen* years, which faw thefe learned Editors fecluded from the world, and anxioufly intent on their great work, their original benefactor had been exalted to the Papal throne, and affumed the *new* name of *Leo* X; they would not, in their Preface, mention him by his former, lefs honorable, appellation, but by the auguft, and pre-eminent, title, which diftinguifhed him in A. D. 1514, when their *Polyglott* came forth from the Prefs. As *men*, this leffer kind of *Metonymy* would be natural.—As *Papifts*, it would be inevitable.

XLIII. " *Since that*, Pope Urban,
" *having recommended thofe MSS in the*
" Vatican, *to be examined, it was found*
" *that all of them, which have the Epif-*
" *tle of* St. John, *want this feventh*
" *Verfe of the fifth Chapter.*"

Dr. *Benfon* has not been fo juft to his
readers,

Dr. BENSON. readers, (*m*) as to inform them on what authority this affertion is founded.

But, admitting, for the prefent, and for
the fake of argument alone, that the MSS,
NOW in the *Vatican*, have not the text in
queftion,—does it follow from thence, that
there were no MSS in that Library, BEFORE
the time of Cardinal *Ximenes*, which had the
Verfe? Dr. *Benfon*, indeed, is forward enough
to tell us, that " thofe MSS," thofe identical exemplars which were ufed by the Editors of *Complutum*, were " examined," and
that " all of them, which have the Epiftle,
" want the Verfe." Will he prove it to us ?
He does not attempt it. He trufts to find
readers as full of zeal as himfelf; and then
—no proof will be required.

The truth is, the MSS which were *fent*
(not lent—for there is a great difference in
the two words, and the expreffion in the
original, is *mifit*) to *Ximenes*, for the ufe of
the

(*m*) The fearch, alledged to have been made by *Caryo-
philus*, is fuppofed to be here alluded to. But even *Wetftein*, himfelf, pays little, or no, credit to it. (*Prol.*
p. 61.)

the *Complutenſian* Editors, were not ordered, Dr. BENSON. as far as we know, to be returned, nor are we certified that they ever were returned, to the Library of the *Vatican*. We know, that the MSS, which were *borrowed*, by *Robert Stephens*, from the Royal Library, at *Paris*, have never found their way back thither, or, at leaſt, that they are not now in that Library: for the MSS, which Father *Le Long* ſpoke of, have already been proved (*n*) NOT to be thoſe which had been uſed by *Robert Stephens*. And the ſame concluſion may, with far more probability, for many obvious reaſons, be formed, as to the *Vatican* MSS, uſed by the Editors of *Complutum*.

XLIV. " *And Father Simon has ob-*
" *ſerved very juſtly, That, when the pub-*
" *liſhers of the Complutenſian edition pub-*
" *liſhed this diſputed text, they followed*
" *the reading of the latin copies here.*"

This objection ſuppoſes that *Ximenes*, and his congregated (*o*) Divines, not finding the

N 4 text

(*n*) Pages 127 to 138.
(*o*) They were no leſs than 42 in number, as hath been before obſerved, and the expences of *Ximenes*, in

Dr. Benson. text of the *heavenly Witneſſes* in any *Greek* MSS, confederated to forge this new text, in order to make their *Greek,* correſpond with the *Latin,* Copies : nay, it poſitively affirms that they did ſo.

Thus ſtands the *liberality* of this objection. Let us now enquire into its truth.

The text of the *Latin* Copies is " Et hi " tres unum ſunt,"—*And theſe three are one.* But what is the text of the *Complutenſian* Edition, in the parallel paſſage? Not ꞷτοι οι τρεις ꞓν ꞓιꞂι, which would have been exactly conſonant to the *Latin* text, (hi tres unum ſunt) *theſe three* ARE *one* ; but οι τρεις ꞓις το ꞓν ꞓιꞂι, *theſe three* AGREE IN *one.* Can any perſon be ſo much much a *Bæotian,* as to imagine, that, if theſe Editors had meant to forge a
Greek

---

the whole of this publication, are affirmed to be *Ducatorum ſexcenties Millena millia.* The Writer of the Appendix to the *Hiſt. Lit.* of *Cave,* ſays, *Quinquaginta millia aureorum.* Edit. *Lond.* A. D. 1688, p. 201.

The delighted mind of *Ximenes* is ſaid, by *Gomez,* in his life of this Cardinal, to have expreſſed the happineſs, which it poſſeſſed, on ſeeing this great work compleated, in theſe animated words—" *Grates tibi ago, ſumme Chriſte, quod rem, magnopere à me curatam, ad optatam finem perduxeris.*" *Hody,* De Bibl. Text. Orig. p. 462.

Greek text, " to follow the reading of **Dr. Benson.**
" the *Latin* Copies," they would have not
have forged one which would have followed
thofe Copies exactly? Is it poffible to believe,
that, if thefe Editors had intended to frame,
in the *Greek* language, a tranflation of the
Latin Text, they would have produced fome-
thing fo utterly diffonant from it?—that fo
many men of learning, who had fpent *fifteen*
years in collating *Greek* MSS, in order to
compile a *Greek* Teftament, were yet fo utterly ignorant of the *Greek* language, as to
bring forth a grofs mif-tranflation, and, withal, one fo foreign to their purpofe?—The
truth is, that M. *Simon*, and Dr. *Benfon*,
would not have argued thus abfurdly in any
other cafe. There is, upon a fair ftatement
of the proofs, every reafon to believe (as
hath been remarked in a former letter) that
the verfe ftood, in thofe MSS which the
Complutenfian Editors confulted, (*p*) exactly
as they have delivered it to us; and that
they did not think themfelves at liberty to
vary from their MSS, either to " follow the
" reading

(*p*) The *feven* MSS of L. *Valla* read εις το εν εισι, in
the laft claufe of this verfe, as well as the MSS ufed by
the *Complutenfian* Editors.

Dr. BENSON. reading of the *Latin* Copies," or of any other copies whatſoever.

Between this objection, herein laſt ſtated, and that to which I now proceed, ſeveral miſcellaneous obſervations intervene, which Dr. *Benſon* ſtiles " incidental and internal marks " which may render it" [the authenticity of the Verſe] " ſuſpected." Some of theſe obſervations are too frivolous to require any animadverſion. Thoſe, which ſeem to deſerve it, will receive their anſwer hereafter.

XLV. " *This diſputed text was not in* " *the Italic, or old Latin Verſion, before* " *the time of Jerome.*" (p. 643.)

The whole tenor of the authorities, from the *Latin* Fathers, who were prior to, and coeval with, and from ſome, who were ſubſequent to, the age of *Jerome*, which have been already *(q)* ſet forth, proves the abſolute falſehood of this aſſertion. It may not, however, be improper to ſtate this matter, here, at large.

The

(q) Pages 26 to 40.

The *old Italic* Verſion, then, or the *Itala* Dr. BENSON.
Vetus, was ſucceeded, in the *Latin* Church,
by the Tranſlation of *Jerome*. But it was
not ſuperſeded by that Tranſlation, as to
general uſe, until about the end of the *ſeventh*
Century, *(r)* or until nearly 300 years after
Jerome's death. The references, therefore,
to, and the quotations of, this Verſe, which
were made by *Tertullian*, by *Cyprian*, by
Phæbadius, and *Marcus Celedenſis*,—by *Eucherius*, *Vigilius*, *Fulgentius*, and *Caſſiodorius*,—
and which have been already produced, *(s)*
were not, in any inſtance, taken from *Jerome*'s Verſion. For the three, firſt named,
of theſe Writers lived before *Jerome*'s Verſion was made. The two next in order,
were ſo nearly the contemporaries of *Jerome*,
that they can hardly be ſuppoſed even to
have ſeen his Verſion. It ſeems, moreover,
certain, from an examination of their works,
as well as from the poſitive affirmation of
Wetſtein, *(t)* that *Vigilius*, and *Fulgentius* did
not quote from the Verſion of *Jerome*. And
the

(r) See the anſwer to objection LVI of Dr. *Benſon*,
hereafter ſtated.
(s) Pages 26 to 40.
(t) *Proleg.* p. 81. He admits that ALL theſe authors,
here mentioned, uſed the *old* ITALIC Verſion in their
quotations.

Dr. Benson. the very learned *Maffeius* (*u*) affirms the same thing of *Caffiodorius*, in the moſt poſitive terms. Theſe references, and quotations, then, being, all, made whilſt the *old Italic* Tranſlation was in general uſe in the *Latin* Church, and NOT being taken from that of *Jerome*, ſeem to beſpeak their own derivation in the cleareſt manner; and to prove the very oppoſite concluſion to that which is advanced in the objection: namely, that *this diſputed text* WAS *in the Italic, or old Latin Verſion*, not only BEFORE *the time of Jerome*, but from the firſt hour of that Verſion being delivered to the Chriſtian world.

XLVI. " *It*" [the Verſe in queſtion] " *is not in any of the oriental Verſions, as* " *the ſyriac.*"—

There were TWO, *ancient*, *Syriac* Verſions. The latter of them was made in the time of *Xenayas*, (who was Biſhop of *Hierapolis*, and

(*u*) " *Evidenter enim patet, ex quamplurimis harum* " *Complexionum locis, Caffiodorium* ALIA *verſione a* Hieronymiana *uſum eſſe*"—are the words of *Maffeius*. (Appendix, No. X.)

and died in A. D. 520) and consequently in Dr. BENSON. the end of the fifth, or in the beginning of the sixth, century. Concerning the age of the former of these Versions, there hath been a great diversity of opinion. To pass over the sentiments of more ancient critics, the learned *Michaelis* (*x*) wishes to carry its date up to the *third* century, at least; while *Wetstein* (*z*) degrades it to the *seventh* century. Truth is, generally, *a medium between two extremes*; and it seems to be peculiarly so in the present case. For, from the testimony of *Bar Hebræus*, in his *Horreum mysteriorum*, that a *more accurate* Translation of the New Testament into the *Syriac* language, was made in, or about, the beginning of the sixth century, in the time of *Xenayas*; it seems evident, that one more ancient, although less accurate, subsisted before that time.

(*x*) *Introd. Lectures*, Sect. 49, Ed. *Lond.* 1761. The other arguments of this very learned professor, on this head, have no real weight. *Ephrem* quoted from the *Greek* MSS themselves, which were then frequent in *Syria*, translating, as he quoted, for the benefit of his unlearned country-men. And the story of the *Edessa* Copy is a mere dream.

(*z*) *Proleg.* Tom. 1 p 109 —In page 113, he forgets himself so far as to say, that the *latter* (or second) *Syriac* Version was made in A. D. 506,—thus making, by his own account, the *offspring* older than the *parent*.

Dr. Benson. time. Whilst, on the other hand, it seems equally certain, that this, more ancient, *Syriac* Version was made subsequent to the age of *Chrysostom*, who died in A. D. 407; not only because it is divided according to the Canons of *Eusebius*, and contains his letter to *Carpianus* : but because it sets forth the *Doxology* in *Matt.* vi, 13, which was not found (*a*) in that Gospel until the time of *Chrysostom*.

The (more ancient) *Syriac* Version, then, is posterior, in point of time, to the *Italic* Translation, and to the Version of *Jerome*; both of which, it has been already shewn, have constantly exhibited the Verse in question. The *Syriac* is, moreover, faulty, and incorrect, almost beyond belief. Not words, or sentences, only, but even whole verses, are left out, or passed over, by the Translator, in various parts of his Version (beside the passage now in dispute) which are admitted by all to be genuine. It may not be improper, perhaps, to specify a few instances of these omissions.

In

(*a*) See (int al) *Erasm.* Annot. in Nov. Test. A. D. 1522, p. 31 and 32.

In St. *John*'s Gofpel, the following Verfes Dr. Benson. are wholly left out of this Verfion :—

" And if I go, and prepare a place for
" you, I will come again, and receive you
" unto myfelf; that where I am, ye may
" be alfo."   (C. xiv. 3.)

" He fhall glorify me : for he fhall receive
" of mine, and fhall fhew it unto you."
(C. xvi. 14.)

In the *Acts* of the Apoftles :—

" And *Philip* faid, If thou believeft with
" all thine heart, thou mayeft.   And he
" anfwered and faid, I believe that *Jefus*
" *Chrift* is the Son of God."   (C. viii. 37.)

" Notwithftanding, it pleafed *Silas* to
" abide there ftill."   (C. xv. 34.)

" And when he had faid thefe words, the
" *Jews* departed, and had great reafoning
" among themfelves."   (C. xxviii. 29.)

In

Dr. BENSON.　In the 1. Epiſtle of St. *Peter*.

　　" If ye be reproachèd for the name of
" *Chriſt*, happy are ye: for the ſpirit of
" glory, and of God, reſteth upon you.
" On their paɪt he is evil ſpoken of, but
" on your part he is glorified." (C. iv. 14.)

　　Theſe are examples, which have eſcaped
even the critical eye of *Theodore Beza*.　His
(b) annotations point out others, almoſt in-
numerable.

　　Inſtances of omiſſions, in Copies, in general, when brought to prove that the words,
ſo omitted, did not exiſt in the original, aɪe
but ſuſpicious evidence.　Inſtances of omiſſions, in a Copy ſo full of omiſſions as this,
will ſcarcely amount to evidence at all.

　　XLVII. " ·Nor is it in the Arabic,
" Æthiopic, or Perſic."——

　　　　　　　　　　　　　　　　Theſe

(b) Beza's Annotations, *paſſim*. *Martin's* Diſſerta-
tɪon, Paɪt. 2. C. I.

Thefe Verfions were copied from (c) the Dr. Benson.
Syriac, and, therefore, muft have adopted
its faults; increafed, moft probably, by others
of their own.

XLVIII. " *Nor in the Coptic.*"

The Verfion abounds more, if poffible,
with faults, and omiffions, than the *Syriac*.
The fame remark applies to both.

The following omiffions of compleat
Verfes, in this Tranflation, feem to merit a
particular reference : viz.

In the Gofpel of St. *Matthew*.

" But I fay unto you, Love your enemies,
" blefs them that curfe you, do good to
" them that hate you, and pray for them

O   " which

(c) M. *Simon*, Hift. des Verfions, C. 17 and 18, and
in Book 11, C. 15, of his Hift. of the Verf. of the Old
Teftament · and *Du Pin*, Differt. Prelim. p. 82. *Wetftein*,
however, *Proleg.* 110, affirms, " tefte *Renodotio*," that
the Æthiopic Verfion proceeded from the *Coptic*. And
Michaelis affirms (Sect. 54) that fome of the *Arabic* Verfions, alfo, were rendered from the *Coptic*. It is of fmall
importance to the *prefent* difquifition, whether *Wetftein*,
and *Michaelis*, are right, or not, in thefe conclufions.

Dr. Benson. " which defpitefully ufe you, and perfecute
" you." (C. v : 44)

" At the fame time came the Difciples
" unto *Jefus*, faying, who is the greateft in
" the kingdom of Heaven? (C. xviii : 1.)

" But *Jefus* anfwered, and faid, Ye know
" not what ye afk. Are ye able to drink
" of the cup, that I fhall drink of, and to
" be baptifed with the baptifm that I am
" baptifed with ? They fay unto him, We
" are able.

" And he faith unto them, Ye fhall drink,
" indeed, of my cup, and be baptifed with
" the baptifm that I am baptifed with :
" but to fit on my right hand, and on my
" left, is not mine to give ; but it fhall be
" given to them, for whom it is prepared of
" my Father." (C. xx · 22, and 23.)

" And they crucified him, and parted his
" garments, cafting lots : that it might be
" fulfilled which was fpoken by the Pro-
" phet, They parted my garments among
" them,

" them, and upon my vefture did they caft Dr. BENSON.
" lots." (C. xxvii : 35.)

In the Gofpel of St. *Mark.*

" If any man have ears to hear, let him
·" hear." (C. vii : 16.)

" But if ye do not forgive, neither will
" your Father, which is in Heaven, forgive
" your trefpaffes." (C. xi : 26.)

In the *Acts* of the Apoftles.

" And *Philip* faid, If thou believeft with
" all thine heart, thou mayeft. And he
" anfwered, and faid, I believe that *Jefus*
" *Chrift* is the Son of God." (C. viii : 37.)

" But the Chief Captain, *Lyfias*, came
" upon us, and, with great violence, took
" him away out of our hands." (C. xxiv :
" 7.)

More inftances need not be adduced, to
fhew, that no argument is to be drawn from

O 2   any

DR. BENSON. any omiſſion oᶠ any Verſe, by any Tranſcriber, like this *(d)*.

XLIX. *" No, nor in the ancient copies*
" of the Armenian Verſion."—

The *Armenians* were converted to the
Chriſtian faith, in the third century; at which
time Chriſtianity became the eſtabliſhed religion of all *Armenia*, under *Tiridates*, who
was then the King of that country. Until
this æra, the *Armenians* had poſſeſſed no
alphabet of their own; but had made uſe
of *Perſian*, or *Greek*, characters in writing.
Not long after the introduction of Chriſtianity into that country, the famous *Mieſrob*,
who flouriſhed in the end of the fourth, and
in the beginning of the fifth century, invented the characters, which have ever ſince
been uſed by the *Armenians*. To this won-
derful man *Armenia* owes the Verſion of the
Scriptures, alſo, which it now poſſeſſes, as
well as its alphabet; which Verſion was
finiſhed

(*l*) *Wetſtein* aſcribes this Verſion to the fifth, or ſixth
century. (*Proleg.* 110.)

finifhed (e) very early in the fifth century.   Dr. BENSON.

This, however, was not the firft, but the *third*, Tranflation of the Scriptures, which had then been made by this extraordinary man, affifted by *Ifaac*, the great Patriarch of *Armenia*. The two former Verfions had been rendered from the *Syriac*; becaufe *Meruzan*, who was, at that time, the *Perfian* Governor of *Armenia*, and an enemy to Chriftianity, had deftroyed all the *Greek* MSS in the land : and had even prohibited the *Greeks*, who lived in part of *Armenia*, from ufing (f) any other than the *Syriac* language. But, in a few years afterwards, the *Armenians*, being delivered from all fear of *Meruzan*, and being anxious to know whether their Ver-

O 3   fion

(e) *Michaelis*, Sect. 57, fays, that this Verfion was finifhed in A. D. 410.—

Sir *Ifaac Newton* (Objection XXVIII, hereafter ftated) affirms that it hath been ufed by the *Armenians* ever fince the age of *Chryfoftom*, who died in A. D 407 Thefe accounts differ but very little in their æras, and may be reconciled by a very eafy fuppofition which is, that the different books of Scripture were delivered out to the clergy, and people, of *Armenia*, AS THEY WERE SEVERALLY TRANSLATED, [viz. in A D 405, &c] although the WHOLE VERSION was not FINISHED until A. D. 410.

(f) *Hift.* Mosis CHORENENSIS, Edit. *Whifton*. Lib. iii, C. liv, p 300.

Dr. Benson. fion, having been then rendered from the *Syriac* alone, contained the *true words of life,* fent deputies to the *Greek* Council, which was held at *Ephefus*, in A.D. 431. Thefe deputies, being returned from *Ephefus* (fays *Mofes Chorenenfis*) " *delivered to* Isaac (the " Patriarch) *and to* Miesrob, *the letters,* " *and decrees, of that Affembly, together with* " *a copy of the Scriptures* CAREFULLY WRIT- " TEN. *When* Isaac, *and* Miesrob, *had* " *received this copy, they chearfully took upon* " *them the labor of tranflating again that fa-* " *cred volume, which they had tranflated twice* " *before. But finding themfelves fomewhat* " *deficient in knowledge*" [of the *Greek* tongue] " *they fent us to the famous School at* Alex- " andria; *there to learn compleatly that ex-* " *cellent language.*" Such was the great induftry, which the *Armenians* of the fourth, and fifth, centuries, ufed in order to obtain an accurate Verfion of the Scriptures; rendering them twice from the *Syriac* Verfion, and the third time from the *Greek* MSS.

This Verfion was not known, in any *printed* Copy, until the laft century; when it was committed to the prefs, by order of an *Ar-* *menian*

menian Council, held in A. D. 1662. *Uscan,* Dr. Benson.
an *Armenian* Bishop, was deputed by that
Council, to superintend, in *Europe,* an impreffion of their Bible, in their own language.
He executed his commiffion, in A. D. 1668,
at *Amfterdam:* and this impreffion contains,
without any mark of doubt, or fufpicion,
annexed to it, the Verfe, 1. *John,* v. 7.

Thus far, Sir, I have the good fortune to
concur with *Michaelis;* who feems to have
given by much the beft hiftory of this Verfion, that has ever yet appeared. I am truly
concerned to feel myfelf compelled to dif-
fent from him, totally, in EVERY other part,
(which fhall hereafter be ftated) of his reafonings in refpect to this excellent Verfion.
For,

1. *Michaelis* affirms, on the authority of
Sandius, that " he" [*Ufcan*] " did not find the
" paffage, 1. *John,* v. 7, in his MS, although
" it ftands in *Ufcan's* edition."

But the account, fo given by *Sandius,* was
evidently (to fay the leaft of it) a miftake. For
M. *Simon* was acquainted, at *Paris,* with *Ufcan,*

O 4   whilft

Dr. Benson. whilft he was employed in executing his important commiffion.   And M. *Simon* (who
was not only a very learned, but, on the
whole, a candid, opponent of this verfe) exprefsly admits, that *Ufcan*'s impreffion could
not but be very accurate. " *The Bifhop*,"
(fays he) " *who was a judicious, and difcreet,*
" *perfon, brought with him* THE MOST COR-
" RECT *MSS, which he carefully followed.*
" *And thefe particulars I learned* FROM THE
" BISHOP HIMSELF." (g)

There is no difficulty in determining,
whether the preference, in point of credit,
is to be given to *Sandius*, or to M. *Simon*, in
the prefent cafe.   If all other circumftances
were equal between thefe two witneffes
(which M. *Simon*'s great fund of learning
forbids us to fuppofe) the fact of M. *Simon*'s
being a ftrenuous opponent of the authenticity of this verfe, decides the queftion entirely in favor of his teftimony.   The account of *Sandius* is the attack of a zealot,
fupporting his own partialities.   The teftimony

(g) *Hift. des Verfions*, C. 16, and 17.—Alfo *Millii*
Proleg. Edit. *Oxon.* A. D. 1707, p 742.

mony of M. *Simon* is the CONFESSION of an
adverfary, overthrowing his own prepof-
feffions. The ballance of evidence cannot,
for a moment, hefitate in inclining to the
latter.

2. *Michaelis* argues, that " as this verfe
" was not in the oldeft *Armenian* MSS,
" *Haitho* (King of *Armenia*, from A. D.
" 1224 to 1270) who underftood *Latin*,
" feems to have added it from the Vulgate."

This is begging the queftion. It does not
appear, by any kind of proof, that this verfe
was *not* in the oldeft *Armenian* MSS. So
far, indeed, is this affumption from being
true, that the very contrary appears from
the teftimony of M. *Simon*, himfelf, which
hath been juft related.

3. But *Michaelis* further infifts, that *Haitho*
was " a fuperftitious Prince, that he tranf-
" lated all *Jerome's* prefaces, and turned
" Friar before his death."

And fo he might. His being fuperftitious

(if

Dr. Benson. (if there be any meaning in that epithet, in the present instance) translating *Jerome*, and turning Friar, does not prove that this verse was not in the MSS of his nation long before he was born.

Indeed, the existence of this passage, in the ancient MSS of *Armenia*, seems clearly to appear from an acknowledgment of *Michaelis*, which follows the charges, which have just been considered. He there confesses, that, " *thirty-seven* years after *Haitho's* " death, this verse is quoted in a Council " held in *Armenia*, and in other (*h*) *Arme-* " *nian* records. Now, this quotation, by the Council, so early after the death of *Haitho*, and without any remark, or comment, upon it, is a very strong argument in favor of this verse. Had it not existed in the *Armenian* Bibles, *before* the time of *Haitho*, the members of that Council would certainly have annexed, to their quotation of it, some note, to the reader, to inform him that it had been once lost out of their
MSS;

(*h*) *Galani* Concilia, Lib. 1. p. 436—478. And Thes. Epist. *La Croze*, p. 4, and 69.

MSS; or some mark of acknowledgement Dr. Benson.
to the memory of *Haitho*, for having (as
they would, in that cafe, have expressed
themselves) *restored* this verse.

4. *Michaelis*, lastly, urges (Sect. 58)
that " *Uscan* acknowledges, in his Preface,
" that he had altered some things from the
" Vulgate."

But this observation proves nothing, as to
the present question. For *Uscan* makes no
acknowledgement, of that kind, respecting
this passage of St. *John*.

And this fact, that *Uscan* had made no
alteration as to this verse, is further established by M. *Simon* :—who relates, that *(1)*
an *Armenian*, named *Nicon*, published a treatise on this subject, wherein he accused his
countrymen of having interpolated several
passages in their Bibles. And he mentioned
Luke, xxii : 43, 44, and diverse other texts,
as particular instances of such interpolation.
But he brought no charge, of this kind,
against

(1) *Lettres Choisies*, Ep. 24. (Bibl Critique, Tom. iv.)

Dr. Benson. againſt the verſe now in debate :—which is a fuꞯther proof that it anciently was, as it now is, found in that Verſion.

Thus, then, Sir, I have produced the *direct* authority of M. *Simon*, to the exiſtence of this paſſage in the ancient *Armenian* Verſion. I have further enforced that direct teſtimony, by *circumſtantial* proof. In ſo doing I have, as I truſt, not only collected a body of evidence, to this point, which will not be controverted ; or, if controverted, will not be ſet aſide :—but have, moreover, adduced a freſh inſtance of Greek authority, the authority of a Council, in favor of the originality of the text, 1. *John*, v. 7.

I ſhould now, Sir, beg leave to diſmiſs this objection, did it not ſeem requiſite, previouſly, to take a ſhort, general, review of the concluſions, at which we ſeem to have arrived, on this ſubject of the *ancient Verſions* of the New Teſtament.

The ancient Verſions, then, of the New Teſtament into various languages, are,—arranging

ranging them in order of time––the OLD

ITALIC, (or *Itala Vetus*) the VERSION OF
JEROME, the SYRIAC, the ARMENIAN, and
the COPTIC. These were all made in, or
before, the *sixth* century. Of the rest, some
are too modern, as the *French*, the *Russian*,
and the *Sclavonic*, (which, however, will be
mentioned in the next, succeeding objections)
to deserve the appellation of ancient Versions. And others, as the *Arabic*, *Persian*,
and *Ethiopic*, are merely transcripts from
some of those, which have just been mentioned, and therefore are not entitled to a
special enumeration. The *Frankish*, erroneously stiled the *Gothic (k)* by some of the
learned, is out of the present question ; for
it contains the Gospels only. The *five*, then,
herein first mentioned, are ALL the ancient
Versions of the Epistles of the New Testament, from their *original Greek*, which affect
the present debate. And here,––although
Dr. *Benson* has thought proper, in the outset
of *(l)* his observations on this part of the
subject, to affirm, that " *the ancient versions*
" *have*

(k) *Michaelis*, Sect. 70, and 71.
Continet iste codex quatuor Evangelia, sed in titla. ' WET-
STEIN, *Proleg* p. 114)
(l) Page 643.

Dr. Benson. " *have* NOT *this difputed text,*" yet—it feems, from what has been premifed, undeniably certain, that THREE, out of the whole FIVE, of thefe ancient verfions, and TWO out of the THREE *moft ancient* of them all, have uniformly exhibited the verfe, now in queftion !—

L. " *It is not in the Ruffian.*"—

The modern *Ruffian*, is a younger branch of the ancient *Greek* Church. The *Ruffians* were converted to Chriftianity, by the *Greeks*, about the clofe of the tenth Century. From the *Greeks* they received, not only the Scriptures, but their ecclefiaftical difcipline; and they acknowledged the *Greek* Patriarch, at *Conftantinople*, as the head of their Church, until the feventcenth Century, when they elected a Patriarch of their own country, but ftill without caufing, or wifhing to caufe, thereby, any abfolute feparation from their Mother-Church.

It has been already (*m*) proved, that the
ANCIENT

(*m*) Pages 48—50.

ANCIENT *Greek* Church (as it may be ftiled Dr. Benson.
for the fake of diftinction) has given the moft
decided judgment in favor of the authenticity of this Verfe, by inferting it in its public Confeffion of Faith, and by reading it,
conftantly, in its public fervice. The ufe,
in that Church, of the απoσoλoς, (n) of which
this Verfe formed a part, has been traced up
to the *fourth*, or *fifth*, Century after Chrift,
without finding, even there, the time when
it began to be fo ufed: from whence, as
hath been before remarked, the thinking
mind feels itfelf compelled to carry up the
commencement of that ufe almoft to, if not
entirely as far as, the age of the Apoftles.]

Thus, then, the cafe ftands with the ancient *Greek* Church. It might have been
prefumed, without feeking for further proofs,
that the *Ruffian*, or modern *Greek*, Church,
thus deriving its rudiments of Chriftianity
from the ancient one, would, with its Mother
Church, acknowledge this Verfe to be genuine. But, happily, we need not leave any
thing, even here, to prefumption. The
                                        Verfe,

(n) See pa. 49—50, and 169.

Dr. Benson. Verse, in question, possesses its place in all the *Russian* (o) New Testaments; and is, moreover, cited in the public *Confession of Faith*, or Catechism, of the *Russian* Church, in the following express manner :—

     " What the Father is according to his
" nature, the same is the Son, and the Holy
" Ghost. Now, as the Father is, in his
" nature, true, and eternal, God, and Creator
" of all things, visible, and invisible, such is
" the Son, and such the Holy Ghost, being
" consubstantial one with another ; accord-
" ing to what the Evangelist, St. *John*,
" teaches, when he says, *There are three*
" *which bear record in Heaven, the Father,*
" *the Word, and the Holy Ghost, and these*
" *three are one.*"

This Confession, (p) or Catechism, was drawn up by the *Russians*, and approved of by *Parthenius*, Patriarch of *Constantinople*, in A. D. 1643 ; was printed in *Greek*, and *La-*
tin,

(o) The *Sclavonian* Bible, of A. D 1663, has this text printed in its margin, only All the *Russian* Bibles have it in the body of the page.
(p) *Martin's La Verite*, Part 2. C. 10.

zin, at *Leipfic,* in A. D. 1695, and at *Mofcow,* Dr. BENSON. in A. D. 1709.

LI. " *Nor in the old French Verfion.*"

There was no ancient *French* Verfion of any part of the New Teftament, except the *Frankifh,* which was formerly called the *Gothic,* through miftake. And that Verfion, (although not ancient) does not, as was obferved *(q)* before, affect the prefent queftion. That which was made by the *Waldenfes,* on their feparation from the Church of *Rome,* about A. D. 1160, feems to have been *(r)* the next, in point of time, to the *Frankifh,* herein before mentioned. But this Verfion of the *Waldenfes,* together with the Tranflation of *Guiart des Moulins,* in A. D. 1294, and of others, in ftill later times, have no claim to the appellation of *old,* or ancient, Verfions.

LII. " *And there is even a great num-*
P " *ber*

(q) Page 205.
(r) K. Vide KORTHOLTI *de variis Scriptur. Edit.* page 311.—

" *ber of MS copies of the vulgar latin,*
" *in various parts of Europe, in which*
" *this text is not found.*"

And there is a ftill *greater* number, beyond all comparifon, in which this text is found. Dr. *Benfon*, if living, would not content to have the caufe decided by the greater number of thefe *Latin* MSS. The argument, therefore, was merely *ad captandum*; and proves nothing either to the advantage, or to the credit, of the propofer.

LIII. " *It*" [the Verfe in queftion]
" *is not once quoted in the genuine works*
" *of any one of the greek fathers. For*
" *inftance ; It is not found, in Clemens*
" *Romanus, Barnabas, Hermas, Ignatius,*
" *Juftin Martyr, Irenæus, Clemens A-*
" *lexandrinus, Eufebius, Athanafius, E-*
" *piphanius, Didymus of Alexandria, Bafil*
" *the Great, Gregory Nazianzene, Gre-*
" *gory Nyffene, Chryfoftome, Cyril of*
" *Alexandria, &c.*"

Before we enter on this wide field of va-
cuity,

cuity—this region of night, and nothing,— Dr. Benson. let the two following, general rules be laid down, as guides to lead us through it with fafety, and difpatch.

1. That where a part only (perhaps but a fmall part) of the works of any ancient Father has defcended to us, we are not at liberty to conclude, that a particular paffage of Scripture has *not been quoted* at all by fuch ancient Father, merely becaufe it is *not* found in that *part* of his works, which hath come down to the prefent age. And

2. That where fuch ancient Fathers have *not* cited, in thofe parts of their works which remain to our times, other texts, confeffedly genuine, which would have been as applicable to the fubject then in difcuffion, as this paffage of St. *John,*—no conclufive argument is to be drawn, from fuch filence, againft the originality of the text in queftion.

Thefe two general rules being premifed, let us now proceed to particulars. And firft—

“ It

Dr. BENSON.   " It is not found in *Clemens Alexandrinus.*"

A part only of his works hath come down to the prefent age. In that part he occafionally treats of the *Trinity*; but he has not, on that fubject, cited the text of the Baptifmal Inftitution, (*s*) which would have been as applicable to his defign as this paffage of St. *John*. By both the preceding rules, therefore, no conclufive argument is to be drawn from his filence, againft the originality of the Verfe in queftion.

" Nor in *Alexander*, Bifhop of *Alexandria*,
" *Eufebius, Epiphanius*, or *Gregory Nazian-*
" *zene.*"

Nor has the firft of thefe, in his Epiftle againft *Arius*; the fecond in his Tract againft the *Sabellians*; the third, in his defence of the Trinity, againft *Noetus*; or the laft in his Treatife on the Divinity of *Jefus Chrift*; cited the words of the Baptifmal Inftitution.
(*t*) The

(*s*) " Go ye, therefore, and teach" (or, *make difciples of*) " all nations, baptizing them in the name of the Fa-" ther, and of the Son, and of the Holy Ghoft." *Matthew,* xxviii. 19.

(*t*) The second of the preceding general Dr. Benson. rules applies itself to all these Fathers.

" Nor in *Athanasius*."—

Whether the Dialogue between *Athanasius*, and *Arius*, belongs to this Author, or not, the *Synopsis*, (*u*) herein before mentioned, may, with great probability, be attributed to him : the writer of which has plainly referred to the text in question.

As to the rest of the *Greek* Fathers, recited in the objection, they fall under the former of the foregoing rules. Their works have not descended to us compleat. And it seems that we are not at liberty (as is there observed) absolutely, and entirely, to conclude, that this verse has NEVER been quoted by them, merely because it is not found in that part of their works, which hath survived to the present times.

LIV. " *They quoted this first epistle of*

P 3 *St.*

(*t*) *Martin's* Differtation, Part 2. C. 3.
(*u*) Page 102.

Dr. Benson.   " *St. John, the fifth chapter, and even*
" *the fixth and eighth verfes.*" (p. 644.)

By the univerfality of thefe expreffions, it fhould feem that Dr. *Benfon* believed, or wifhed his readers to believe, that *all* the *Greek* Fathers herein befoie named, had quoted the fixth, and eighth, verfes of this Chapter. But that is a miftake, or a mifieprefentation; for only three of thefe Fathers feem to ftand in this predicament, namely *Clemens Alexandrinus, Gregory Nazianzene,* and *Cyril* of *Alexandria.*

As to the firft of thefe, no part of his Commentary (if indeed (*x*) it be his) on this Epiftle, hath defcended to the prefent age, except a few fcattered fragments. Thefe fragments make no mention of the five firft verfes of this Chapter; they juft touch upon the fixth, giving only the firft words of it. They then pafs from the eighth, to the end of

---

(*x*) Dr. *Cave* does not believe thefe fragments to have been the work of *Clemens Alexandrinus.* (Hift. Lit. *Lond.* Edit. A. D. 1688, p. 56.)

    Thefe fragments may be found (fuch as they are) in *Max. Bibl. Patrum*, Vol. 3. pa. 232.

of the eleventh, verse; then omitting the Dr. Benson. two next following verses, and part of the fourteenth, they end with the last clause of the nineteenth, verse. From such disjointed members of a Commentary, even if allowed to be the work of *Clemens Alexandrinus*, no-thing conclusive can be inferred.

With respect to the other two *Greek* Fa-thers, they seem to fall under the objection of *omissions in general*, which will be con-sidered hereafter.

LV. " *As to the latin fathers, The* " *author of the treatise about the baptism* " *of heretics, supposed to be co-temporary* " *with St.* Cyprian, *hath quoted the* " *sixth and eighth verses; but taken no* " *notice of the seventh. Which, as it* " *shews he knew nothing of the seventh* " *verse, affords a very strong and cogent* " *argument for the supposition, that nei-* " *ther had* Cyprian *this text in his* " *copies.*"

Du Pin says of the Author of this Trea-

tise,

Dr. Benson. tife, (*y*)—" He was, PERHAPS, a Contem-
" porary with St. *Cyprian*."—Dr. *Pearson*
(*z*) calls it, *the work of an unknown Author*.
Such teftimonies as thefe are no pioofs, even
of the *antiquity* of this Treatife. But whether
ancient, or modern, the conclufion, here
drawn by Dr. *Benfon*, is unwarranted, and
groundlefs. The Writer of the Treatife, in
the paffage iefeired to, fpeaks, as was ufual
with the Divines of that age, of three forts
of Baptifm ; namely, by the *Water*, by the
Spirit, and by the *Blood*. On this topic he,
properly, quotes the *fixth*, and *eighth*, Verfes
of this Chapter of St. *John*. The words of
the *feventh* Verfe did not ielate to his fubject. (*a*)

LVI. " Didymus *of* Alexandria, *in*
" *the fourth* ; Bede *in the eighth* ; *and*
" Oecumenius, *in the eleventh, century,*
" *wrote, each of them, a commentary up-*
" *on this firft epiftle of St. John. But fo*
" *far*

(*y*) *Du Pin*, Vol. 1. *Lond.* Edit. A D. 1692, p. 155.
(*z*) *Cyprian's* works. Ed. *Pearfon* (int. op. falf) p. 71.
(*a*) Appendix, No. XVII, where this part of the
Treatife is fet forth from the original.

" *far were they from explaining this dif-* Dr. Benson.
" *puted text, that they have not so much*
" *as mentioned it. Which shews, that*
" *they either knew nothing of it, or did*
" *not believe it to be genuine.*"

Didymus did not write a regular Commentary, but some loose, and desultory, Notes on this Epistle of St. *John*. In these Notes, all the Verses, from the *fifth* to the *fourteenth*, of this Chapter, are wanting. The inference, then, that *Didymus* " knew no-" thing of this text, or did not believe it to " be genuine," because he has not made special mention of it in his Commentary, will apply just as forcibly to *all* the other Verses thus omitted, as to the *seventh*. If the argument proves any thing, it concludes equally against all these Verses. But it proves too much; and, of course, proves nothing. (*b*)

As to *Bede*, who comments upon the *sixth*, and *eighth*, but passes over the *seventh*, Verse, his silence affords grounds for a slight suspicion,

(*b*) *Wolfius*, Cur. Philol. vol. v. p. 301.

Dr. Benson. picion, that he did not know this text, or that he did not believe it to be genuine. But the suspicion seems to vanish, on a due consideration of the following observations.

1. *Bede* was not ignorant of the existence of this text. He had read the works of *Cyprian*, and *Fulgentius*; and he, virtually, admits the testimony of the four hundred *African* Bishops, recorded by *Victor Vitensis*: for he has cited all these Authors in his works. But what seems decisive as to *Bede*'s knowledge of the Verse, is, that the Version of *Jerome*, in which this text has always possessed its place, had not only been adopted by the learned, but publicly read in the Churches, for more than a century before *Bede* began his Commentary. "*Remigius*," (says (c) M. *Simon*) "*Rabanus, Haimo, An-* "*felmus*, &c. and, finally, *all* other Eccle- "siastical Writers for more than *nine hundred* "years past, have adhered so closely to the "New" (*Jerome*'s) "Edition, that all other "Versions

(c) Hist. Crit. des Versions, C. vii, viii, and ix; and *Le Long*, Bibl. Sacr. C. iv. Sect. i. Edit, *Paris*. A. D. 1723, p. 229.

" Verfions have been utterly loft, at leaft Dr. Benson.
" as to their ufe."

Nor does this obfervation depend upon
the teftimony of M. *Simon* alone. It ftands
upon the moft folid foundation, the authority of *Bede* himfelf; who very frequently
refers to *Jerome*'s Verfion, entitling it nostram *editionem*," and nostros *codices*;"
and defcribing *Jerome* by the affectionate
appellation of " *Interpres nofter*." (*d*) The
fuppofition, then, that *Bede* " knew nothing
of this text," cannot be maintained, even
for a fingle moment.

2. Nor does the other fuppofition, founded alfo on the filence of *Bede*, namely, that
he did " not believe this text to be genuine,"
feem more defenfible than that which preceded it. For *Bede* poffeffed no fmall fhare
of the learning of thofe days, particularly as
to the *Greek* language; and his practice, in
other parts of his Commentary, was, conftantly

(*d*) See his works, *paffim*.
Bede was, alfo, the preceptor of *Alcuinus*, of whofe
Correctorium (which contained this Verfe) mention is
made in p. 43 of thefe Letters.

Dr. Benson. ſtantly to advertiſe his readers, whenever any paſſage occurred in the vulgar copies, which was not found in the *Greek* MSS. But he has fixed no imputation of this kind on the Verſe in queſtion. He has paſſed it over in ſilence. And how is that ſilence to be accounted for? He either found this Verſe in his *Greek* Copies, or he did not. If he *did not find it there*, it muſt be preſumed that he would have appriſed his readers of the deficiency in this, as he did in other inſtances. His ſilence, alone, in ſuch a caſe, would not have been ſufficient. Where it is a duty to ſpeak, to be ſilent is to be criminal. We cannot preſume thus of the " Venerable *Bede*," without having more ſubſtantial grounds, for the preſumption, than mere conjecture.

The concluſion, then, ſeems to be, that *Bede* DID FIND *this Verſe in his* Greek *Copies*. His practice, in other caſes, warrants, the ſanctity of his character even hallows, this concluſion. Standing ſingly, theſe circumſtances form, each, a probable proof,—united, they preſs conviction home upon the mind,—

that

that BEDE *believed this Verse to be genuine* ; Dr. BENSON. and that, from whatever other motive his silence, in regard to it, may be conjectured to have proceeded, he had no scruples to communicate respecting its authenticity, and truth.

As to *Oecumenius*, who lived so late as the *eleventh* Century, no inference can be drawn from any *omission*, on his part, which can impeach the originality of this Verse. It has been already shewn, by *a cloud of witnesses*, by proofs too numerous to be here repeated, that this text DID exist, in his times, in the Epistle of St. *John*.

Thus far, Sir, for those objections of Dr. *Benson*, which appropriate themselves to particular objects, and may be met by particular answers. And thus I beg leave to dismiss, for the present, at least, his Dissertation: which for intrepidity of assertion, disingenuousness of quotation, and defectiveness of conclusion, has no equal,—stands aloof beyond all parallel,—as far as my reading extends, either in ancient, or in modern, times!

I am, Sir, &c.

LETTER IV.

SIR,

I NOW proceed to a confideration of the NEWTON. objections, which have been urged againſt the authenticity of the Verſe, 1. *John*, v. 7, by the late Sir ISAAC NEWTON.

The learned Dr. *Horſley* has juſt given theſe objections to the public, in the *fifth* Volume of his Edition of the works of this illuſtrious man; to which he has prefixed the following advertiſement.

" *A VERY imperfeĉt copy of this traĉt,*
" *wanting both the beginning and the end, and*
" *erroneous in many places, was publiſhed at*
" *London in the year* 1754, *under the title of*
" *Two Letters from Sir Iſaac Newton to Mr.*
" *Le Clerc. But in the Author's MS. the*
" *whole*

Newton. *" whole is one continued difcourfe; which, al-*
" though it is conceived in the epiftolary form,
" is not addreffed to Any *particular perfon.*

" It is now firft publifhed entire from a MS.
" in the Author's *hand-writing, in the pof-*
" feffion of the Rev. Dr. Ekens, Dean *of*
" Carlisle." *(a)*

The objections, urged by this moft refpectable antagonift of the verfe, in queftion,
are, principally, as follows.—

I. *" The arguments alledged for the*
" teftimony of the Three in Heaven, *are*
" the authorities of Cyprian, Athanafius,
" and Jerome, *and of many Greek MSS,*
" and almoft all the Latin ones."—(p.
495.)

This enumeration is candid, and has no
fault but that of being incompleat. Befide
thefe authorities, and within the limit, as to
time, of the century, in which *Jerome* lived,
the

(a) Dr. *Horfley* has obligingly informed me, that he
finds nothing in the MS to afcertain the time when this
tract was compofed.

the reading of this Verſe in the απορολος, the NEWTON.
direct refeiences to, or expreſs citations of,
it, by *Tertullian, Phæbadius, Marcus Celeden-*
ſis, Auguſtine, Eucherius, and *Vigilius,* and its
exiſtence in the *Armenian,* and *Old Italic,*
Verſions, *(b)*—are concurrent teſtimonies of
its authenticity : all of which, nevertheleſs,
are here totally paſſed by, and omitted.

  II. " *Cyprian's words run thus :* The
" Lord faith, I and my Father am One.
" And again of the Father, Son, and
" Holy Ghoſt it is written ; And theſe
" Three are One. *The Socinians here*
" *deal too injuriouſly with Cyprian, while*
" *they would have this place corrupted :*
" *for Cyprian in another place*" [Epiſ.
ad *Jubaianum*] " *repeats the ſame thing.*
" *Theſe places of Cyprian, being in my*
" *opinion genuine, ſeem ſo appoſite to prove*
" *the teſtimony of the Three in Heaven,*
" *that*"—(p. 497.)

This extract contains another, pleaſing, inſtance of candor in this illuſtrious objector.
Theſe paſſages in *Cyprian* are, undoubtedly,

     Q

Newton as, " genuine," as they are clearly " appo-
" fite to prove the teftimony of the *Three in*
" *Heaven.*"—

> III. " *I fhould never have fufpected a*
> " *miftake in it,*" [viz. the teftimony of
> the *Three in Heaven,* as fet forth by
> *Cyprian*] " *could I but have reconciled*
> " *it with the ignorance I meet with of*
> " *this reading in the next age, amongft*
> " *the Latins of both Africa, and Europe,*
> " *as well as among the Greeks.*"—

Cyprian fuffeied martyrdom in the latter
pait of the third century. The " *next age,*"
theiefoie, to that of *Cyprian,* is the fouith
century. And in that centuiy, *Phæbadius*
among the *Latins* of Europe, *Jerome* among
thofe of *Afia,* and *Marcus Celedenfis,* and *Auguftine,* among thofe of *Africa,* have directly
quoted, or refeired to, this teftimony of the
Three in Heaven. The fame centuiy, alfo,
holds forth to us the difputation (whether
real, or feigned) between *Arius,* and *Athanafius,* the *Synopfis* of St. *John*'s Epiftle, and the
ufe of the απορολος, among the *Greeks* : (c)
which,

(c) Pages 30—56, and 101—103.

which, all, exhibit the fame teftimony. NEWTON.

Sir *Ifaac Newton*'s argument, then, is this. " *There is an* IGNORANCE *of this verfe, in the next age to* Cyprian, *amongft both* Latins, *and* Greeks. *Had it not been fo, I fhould not even have* SUSPECTED *a miftake in* Cyprian's *quotation.*"---The anfwer to which is---The *next age to* Cyprian *was* NOT IGNORANT *of this verfe, as* Sir Ifaac Newton *improperly imagined. The quotation of it therefore by* Cyprian, *was* NOT *a* MISTAKE, *as he erroneoufly fufpected.*"---The fuppofed *ignorance*, then, upon which Sir *Ifaac Newton* here builds his fufpicion of a *miftake* in *Cyprian*'s quotations, does not exift. The *fufpicion* itfelf, confequently, falls to the ground. And thus, by Sir *Ifaac*'s own argument, the queftion is already decided in favor of the authenticity of the verfe, in queftion.

It appears evident, from thefe confiderations, that had Sir *Ifaac Newton* been acquainted with the *whole* of the evidence, which tends to fupport the authenticity of this Verfe; (a confiderable part of which feems to have been entirely unknown to

Q 2   him)

Newton. him) he would not have written this treatife, now under confideration, which ftrives
to overthrow it. The plain import of his
own argument warrants the former conclufion. His known candor infers the latter.

> IV. " *For had it been in Cyprian's*
> " *Bible, the Latins of the next age, when*
> " *all the world was engaged in difputing*
> " *about the Trinity, and all arguments*
> " *that could be thought of, were diligent-*
> " *ly fought out, and daily brought upon*
> " *the ftage, could never have been igno-*
> " *rant of a text, which, in our age, now*
> " *the difpute is over, is chiefly infifted up-*
> " *on.*"

Sir *Ifaac Newton*, in this objection, ftill
preffes the former argument of a fuppofed
ignorance of this Verfe, in the fourth century,
and during the *Arian* controverfy. The
fuppofition of fuch an *ignorance* hath been
already refuted. The argument, as to the
Arian controverfy, will be more properly
confidered hereafter. (d)

V. " *In*

(d) See objection XXXII, of Sir *Ifaac Newton*;—where
this queftion is ftated, and confidered.

V. " *In reconciling this difficulty, I* Newton.
" *consider, therefore, that the only words*
" *of the text quoted by Cyprian in both*
" *places, are,* And thefe three are one :
" *which words may belong to the eighth*
" *verfe as well as the feventh. For Eu-*
" *cherius, Bifhop of Lion in France, and*
" *contemporary to St. Auftin, reading the*
" *text without the feventh verfe, tells us,*
" *that many then underftood the Spirit,*
" *the Water, and the Blood, to fignify*
" *the Trinity."*—

Cyprian's words are (as hath been before
ftated) " *Of the Father, Son, and Holy Ghoft,*
" IT IS WRITTEN, (e) *And thefe three are*
" *one.*" Thefe words *cannot* be underftood
to have been taken, by *Cyprian,* from the
eighth verfe ; becaufe *it is* NOT *fo written,*
in the eighth verfe.

And, as to *Eucherius,* the argument here
infifted upon, overthrows itfelf. For *Eucherius* has, in another part of his works, (f)
directly cited the *feventh* verfe.

Q 3   VI. " *And*

(e) Pages 73—93.
(f) Pages 32, and 79—82.

VI. " *And St. Auſtin is one of thoſe*
" *many, as you may ſee in his third book*
" *againſt Maximus, where he tells us,*
" *that the Spirit is the Father, for God is*
" *a Spirit; the Water the Holy Ghoſt,*
" *for he is the Water, which Chriſt gives*
" *to them that thirſt; and the Blood, the*
" *Son; for the word was made fleſh.*"——
(p. 498.)

Auguſtine may be one of thoſe, who have wiſhed to undeiſtand the *eighth* Verſe, as being typical of the Trinity. And this paſſage from the *third* book of his treatiſe againſt *Maximinus* (not *Maximus*) the *Arian,* may be a proof of it. But it is no proof that he did not read the *ſeventh* verſe in his bible. In fact, he not only read it there, but has ſhewed us, in his *ſecond* book againſt the ſame *Maximinus,* that, like *Eucherius,* he knew how to interpret it, when he thought proper to bring it forward. (*g*) For his words there are (as hath been before ſtated,——
" *There are three perſons*" [in the Godhead]
" *the Father, Son, and Holy Ghoſt;* AND
" THESE

(*g*) See page 35,

" THESE THREE (*because they are of the* NEWTON.
" *fame effence*) ARE ONE. *And* THEY ARE
" *completely* ONE, *there being in them no differ-*
" *ence in nature, or in will.* THESE THREE,
" *therefore, who* ARE ONE ; *through that in-*
" *deſcribable union, in which they are joined*
" *together in the Godhead, are* ONE GOD."

Whatever might be the caſe, with the
expreſſions which are quoted in the objection,
it ſeems impoſſible that *Auguſtine* COULD
have the *eighth* verſe in view, in the laſt pre-
ceeding extract. For he therein ſpeaks of
the Father, Son, and Holy Ghoſt, who are
of the *ſame eſſence, or ſubſtance*, and in whom
there is *no difference in nature, or in will.*
Whereas the *things*, NOT *perſons*, ſpoken of
in the *eighth* verſe, are not either of the ſame
nature, or of the ſame *ſubſtance* ; nor can
they be ſaid to have any *will* at all.

VII. " *Now if it was the opinion of*
" *many, in the Weſtern Churches of thoſe*
" *times, that the Spirit, the water, and*
" *the blood, ſignified the Father, the Son,*
" *and the Holy Ghoſt, it is plain, that the*

Q 4   " *teſtimony*

" *teſtimony of the* Three in Heaven *was*
" *not crept into their books.*"

It might be the opinion of both *Eucherius,* and *Auguſtine,* as hath been already
obſerved, that the Spirit, Water, and Blood,
in the *eighth* verſe, *did* ſignify (typically)
the Father, the Son, and the Holy Ghoſt.
And yet is plain, that the teſtimony of the
Three in Heaven, in the *ſeventh* verſe, had,
neverthelefs, then *crept into their books.* For
they not only tell us, very plainly, that they
found that teſtimony *in their books*; but they
give us this information without any marks
either of ſurpriſe, or of indignation:—which
ſhews that they had no doubts either of its
antiquity, of its authenticity.

VIII. " *Even without this teſtimony,*
" *it was obvious for Cyprian, or any*
" *man elſe of that opinion, to ſay of the*
" *Father, Son, and Holy Ghoſt,* It is
" written, And theſe three are one."

It is obvious that *Cyprian,* or any other
Writer, might, and perhaps would, expound
the

the *eighth* verfe, as being typically expreffive NEWTON. of the Trinity, if he really thought fo. But he would not fay, at the fame time, " IT IS WRITTEN, *in the eighth Verfe, of the Father, Son, and Holy Ghoft,* AND THESE THREE ARE ONE,"—if he paid any regard to truth: becaufe it never was fo *written,* in any part of the eighth verfe.

The objections, which follow, as to *Facundus,* and *Tertullian,* have already been obviated; *(h)* and therefore require no further confideration.

    IX. " *So then this interpretation feems* " *to have been invented by the Montanifts* " *for giving countenance to their Trinity.* " *For Tertullian was a Montanift, when* " *he wrote this.*" (p. 500.)

This objection feems to abound in miftakes.

It is, in the firft place, far from being clear that *Tertullian* was a *Montanift,* when

                                   he

(h) Pages 64—73, and 82—84.

Newton. he wrote his Treatife againft *Praxeas*. In the life of *Tertullian*, prefixed to the Edition of his works by *Rigaltius*, (*i*) this treatife is affirmed to have been written, before the opinions of *Montanus* were adopted by *Tertullian*.

But admitting, for the fake of argument alone, that *Tertullian* was a follower of *Montanus*, when he wrote his treatife againft *Praxeas*,—what was the Trinity of the *Montanifts* ? *Epiphanius* affirms, that the *Montanifts* (*k*) held the fame opinion, as to the Trinity, which was entertained by the catholic Church, in general. While *Jerome* pofitively afferts, that the *Montanifts* (*l*) thought like *Sabellius* in that refpect,—*Trinitatem in unius perfonæ anguftias cogentes.*

And

(*i*) Edit. *Paris.* A. D. 1675.

(*k*) Περι δε πατρος, &c. De Patre, enim, et Filio, et Spiritu fancto, fimiliter cum ecclefia catholica fentiunt. Epiph. *adv. Hær.* Lib. 11. Tom. 1. Edit. *Paris.* A. D. 1622, p. 402.

(*l*) Nos Patrem, et Filium, et Spiritum fanctum, in fua unumquemque perfona ponimus. Illi, (viz *Montaniftæ*) dogma *Sabellii* fectantes, Trinitatem in unius perfonæ anguftias cogunt. Hieron. adverfus *Montanum*, vol. 11. p. 44, A. (Ed. *Erafm.* A. D. 1546.)

And now, Sir, whether of thefe interpre- NEWTON. tations of the " Trinity of the *Montanifts*," fhall we adopt, in order to *give countenance* to the preceding objection? If that of *Epiphanius*,—the *Montanifts* wanted no countenance to be given to *their* Trinity, in particular, becaufe it was the fame with that of the Chriftian Church, in general. And if that of *Jerome*,—the *Montanifts* had NO TRINITY, to which they could give countenance; becaufe, being *Sabellians*, they did not hold the doctrine of a Trinity at all.

The facts, however, upon the whole, feem to be, that *Jerome*'s account of the *Montanifts* is the true one. For *Jerome* lived in the vicinity of the ancient *Phrygia*, where the errors of *Montanus* were almoft univerfally followed: from which circumftance the appellation of *Cataphryges* is frequently applied to the *Montanifts* by ancient writers. And that *Tertullian* was *not* a *Montanift* (as hath been already obferved) when he wrote the treatife againft *Praxeas*; but a believer, with *Jerome*, in the catholic doctrine of a Trinity, of *three perfons*, and *one God* (*qui*

TRES

NEWTON. TRES UNUM SUNT, are *Tertullian's* own words) as then, and now, taught by the catholic [or univerſal] Church of Chriſt.

X. " *What is ſaid of the teſtimony of* " *Tertullian, and Cyprian,"* [viz. that their words were only a forced interpretation of the eighth verſe] " *may be much* " *more ſaid of that in the feigned diſpu-* " *tation of Athanaſius with Arius at Nice.* " *For there the words cited are only* Theſe " three are one, *without naming the* " *perſons of the Trinity before them."* (p. 500.)

The expreſſions of this Dialogue, or Diſputation, (as hath been before ſtated) are, (m) " *Is not that lively, and ſaving, baptiſm, where-* *by we receive remiſſion of ſins, adminiſtered in the* *name of the Father, the Son, and the HolyGhoſt?* *And moreover St.* JOHN *ſays,* AND THESE THREE ARE ONE."

The words thus cited, then, are NOT *Theſe* *three are one,* WITHOUT *naming* (for they DO expreſsly

(m) Page 101.

exprefsly name) *the perfons of the Trinity be-* NEWTON. *fore* (and immediately before) *them.*

XI. " *They*" [alfo] " *are*—και οι Ͳρεις " το εν εισιν—*and they are taken out of the* " *eighth Verfe.*"

This conclufion is by no means to be admitted. The premifes warrant the very contrary deduction, viz. that the words, cited in this Dialogue, are *not* taken from the eighth verfe. For the claufe, here referred to, wherever it ftands in the eighth Verfe, is (not το εν only, but) εις το εν, univerfally.

XII. " *The Greeks interpreted the Spi-* " *rit, Water, and Blood, of the Trinity,* " *as well as the Latins; as is manifeft* " *from the annotations they made on this* " *text in the margin af fome of their* " *MSS. For in the margin of one MS.* " *in the Library of the King of France* " *(about* 500 *years old) over againft the* " *former claufe of the eighth Verfe are* " *written*—The Holy Ghoft, and the " Father, and He of himfelf—*and over* " *againft*

NEWTON.

" *againft the latter claufe,* One Deity,
" one God. *And the margin of the fame*
" *Verfe, in another in M. Colbert's Libra-*
" *ry, thefe words,* One God, one God-
" head—The teftimony of God the
" Father, and of the Holy Ghoft."
(p. 501.)

Some of the *Latins* did, we know, interpret the expreffions of the eighth Verfe in
this manner. And fome of the *Greeks* might
do the fame. But it will not follow, from
thence, that they had not the *feventh* Verfe
in their MSS. *Eucherius,* for inftance, *Auguftine,* and *Facundus* have adopted this myftical interpretation of the *eighth* Verfe.
And yet it is moft certain, that *Eucherius*
DID read the *feventh* Verfe in his Bible.
The quotations, which have been before referred to, from *Auguftine,* will hardly permit
a ferious doubt as to its being found in his
Bible, likewife. And the fame conclufion
has been already drawn, (*n*) in refpect to the
Bible of *Facundus*; and ftands as it feems,
upon the moft folid foundations.

XII. " *Thefe*

(*n*) Pages 32, 35, and 79—84.

XII. " *Thefe marginal notes fufficient-* Newton.
" *ly fhew how the Greeks ufed to apply*
" *this text*" [the eighth Verfe] " *to*
" *the Trinity, and, by confequence, how*
" *the author of that difputation is to be*
" *underftood.*"

This conclufion is defective in all its parts. If the two marginal notes, in queftion, fhall be admitted to fhew that the *two* refpective poffeffors, or copyifts, of thofe *two* particular MSS. applied the *eighth* Verfe to the Trinity; they will be ftill very far from proving the fame thing of the *Greeks*, in general. But even if both thefe propofitions fhould be granted, the confequence, juft alledged, will be as remote as ever from the premifes. For " the Author of this *Difpu-* " *tation*, is *not* to be underftood," as applying the eighth Verfe to the Trinity, in this paffage; becaufe, as hath been before obferved, he has *not* cited, in this paffage, the words of the eighth Verfe.

XIV. " *But I fhould tell you alfo, that* " *that Difputation was not writ by Atha-* " *nafius,*

" *nafius, but by a later author; and there-*
" *fore, as a fpurious piece, ufes not to be*
" *much infifted on.*"

The queftion, whether this Difputation
is fpurious, or, in other words, whether it
was written by *Athanafius*, or not,—has been
much debated, but does not feem to be as
yet determined. The *time, when* it was written, is of much more importance in the prefent enquiry. And that feems to have been
already fixed, by the aid of the Treatife itfelf, (*o*) to the joint reign of *Conftantine* and
Conftantius, which ended in A. D. 337. The
circumftances of its being written in the
Greek language, of its very high antiquity,
and of its referring to St. *John* by name,
will always give a moft powerful influence
to the teftimony of this Dialogue, or Difputation, in favor of the authenticity of the
Verfe, 1. *John*, v. 7.

XV. " *The firft upon record, that in-*
" *ferted it, is Jerome, if the Preface to*
" *the canonical epiftles be his.*"

The

(*o*) Page 101—102.

The preface to the canonical Epiſtles, it NEWTON. is truſted, hath been already proved (*p*) to be *Jerome*'s. And yet he is NOT *the firſt upon record, that inſerted* the Verſe. It was received by the *Latin* Church long before *Jerome*'s Tranſlation was made, and indeed long before *Jerome* himſelf was born; becauſe it hath always ſtood in the old *Italic* Verſion, which was made in the (*ſecond,* if not in the) *firſt* century after Chriſt. This matter hath been already ſtated at large. (*q*)

XVI. " *For which he*" [Jerome] " *compoſed not a new tranſlation of the* " *New Teſtament, but only corrected the* " *ancient vulgar Latin.*"—(p. 502.)

He compoſed a new Tranſlation of the New Teſtament, from the *Greek. Auguſtine* calls it ſo, who was *Jerome*'s contemporary, and correſpondent. " *We heartily thank God* " *for your* TRANSLATION." (*r*) Nay *Jerome* himſelf calls it ſo, in effect. His expreſſion

R

(*p*) Pages 92—110.
(*q*) Pages 186—188.
(*r*) Page 106.

NEWTON. preſſion, upon this ſubjeĉt, is not *correxi*, or *caſtigavi*, but REDDIDI, (s) repeatedly.

XVII. " *He*" [Jerome] " *complains,*
" *in the ſame Preface, how he was there-*
" *upon accuſed, by ſome of the Latins,*
" *for falſifying Scripture.*"——

Permit me, Sir, to take this objeĉtion in detail. It may aſſiſt us, perhaps, in coming to an early, as well as a ſatisfaĉtory, concluſion.

Jerome, then, in his Preface to the Canonical Epiſtles, complains of the malicious accuſations of his enemies. *They pronounce me* (ſays he) *a falſifier of Scripture*—" *me* " *falſarium pronunciant.*" But have they ſpecified their accuſations, and mentioned the particular parts of Scripture, which they

affirm

(s) Pages 33, and 99.

Jerome, it is true, upon one occaſion uſes the word, *emendatione*, when ſpeaking of his own New Teſtament. And the learned *Hody* (p. 351) has argued, from that expreſſion, that *Jerome* did not make a *new* Tranſlation, but only corrected the old one. And, indeed, had *Jerome* never uſed *any other* expreſſion, reſpecting his work, than that,—*Hody*'s argument would have been as ſtrong, and valid, as it now ſeems weak, and unſatisfactory.

affirm to have been falsified by him ?—They NEWTON. *have specified* them. They have, in the Old Teſtament, particulariſed his inſerting *bæde-ta*, for *cucurbita*, in the Book of *Jonah*,—his accuſations of the *Septuagint*,—and his objections as to the Prophet *Daniel*. And, as to the New Teſtament, among many other charges, they have accuſed him of following the tenets of *Origen* in his Commentary on St. *Paul*'s Epiſtle to the *Epheſians*,—they have objected to his notions concerning pre-deſtination,—his interpretation of *No man ever yet hated his own fleſh*,—his expoſition of *From whom the whole body fitly framed together*,—his opinion concerning the re-miſſion of ſins by baptiſm,—his conjectures as to the condition, and office, of Angels,—and his explanation of the reſurrection of the body.—But have they ſaid any thing againſt his retention of the Verſe, 1. *John*, v. 7, in his Tranſlation ? Not a ſingle ſylla-ble.—How, then, do theſe accuſations prove, that the accuſers of *Jerome* were offended with his inſertion (or, to ſpeak more proper-ly, his *retention*) of this Verſe in his Teſta-ment ?—They do NOT prove it at all, in any manner, or in any reſpect, whatſoever !

Nor

NEWTON. Noɪ have we, furtheɪ, any reaſon even to ſuſpect, that theſe, or any other, accuſations were brought againſt *Jerome*, on account of *any part* of his Tranſlatɪon of the firſt Epiſtle of St. *John*. Thoſe accuſations are thus recorded by *Jerome* himſelf.

" But now, becauſe, according to our " Saviour's precept, I am deſɪrous to labor " for the meat whɪch periſheth not, and to " clear the primitive paths of the Scriptures " from thorns, and brambles, an accuſation " doubly injuɪɪous is brought againſt me. " Anxious to correct the falſifications of " others, I am, myſelf, called *a falſifier*" [FALSARIUS *dɪcor*] " of Scripture; and am " charged with ſowing errors, inſtead of " plucking them up." (ɪ)

" Inaſmuch as I am called a *falſary*" [FALSARIUS *vocor*] " I am contented to deny

(ɪ) " *Nunc autem, quɪa juɪta ſententiam Salɪatorɪs, volꝛ* " *operarɪ cɪbum quɪ non peɪɪt, et antiquam divɪnorum volu-* " *mɪnum vɪam ſentɪbus, vɪrgultɪſqɪe, puɪgare, error mɪhɪ* " *gemɪnus ɪnflɪgɪɪur Corɪector vɪtɪorɪm,* FALSARIUS *dɪcor,* " *et errores non aufeɪre, ſed ſerere.* ' (Præf. alt. ɪn Lɪb. *Job.*)

" deny, without retorting, the accusa- NEWTON.
" tion." (*u*)

I will beg leave, Sir, to state the rest of *Je-*
rome's complaints of this kind, in his own language.   My own may not do him justice.

" Sed et vos, famulas *Christi*, rogo, quæ
" Domini discumbentis preciosissima fidei
" myrrha ungitis caput, quæ nequaquam
" Salvatorem quæritis in sepulchro, quibus
" jam ad Patrem *Christus* ascendit : ut con-
" tra *latrantes canes*, qui *adversum me rabido*
" *ore desæviunt*,——orationum vestrarum cly-
" peos opponatis." (*x*)

" *Obtrectatoribus* meis——qui canino dente
" me rodunt." (*y*)

" Cogor PER SINGULOS SCRIPTURÆ
" DIVINÆ LIBROS adversariorum respon-
" dere maledictis." (*z*)

R 3

" Quanto

(*u*) Ad *Pammach.* vol. ii, Edit. *Eras.* A. D. 1546,
pa. 123, B.
(*x*) Præf. in Lib. Regum.
(*y*) Præf. in Lib *Paralip.*
(*z*) Præf. in Lib. *Job.*

Newton. " Quanto plus amatis" [*Chriſtum*] " O
" *Paula*, et *Euſtochium*, tanto magis ab eo
" petite, ut pro *obtrectatione præſenti*, qua
" me *indeſinenter æmuli laniant*, ipſe mihi
" mercedem reſtituat in futuro : qui ſcit me
" ob hoc, in peregrinæ linguæ eruditione
" ſudaſſe, ne *Judæi* de *falſitate* ſcripturarum
" eccleſiis ejus diutius inſultarent." (*a*)

" Quis enim doctus, pariter, vel indoctus,
" cum in manus volumen aſſumpſerit, et a
" ſaliva, quam ſemel imbibit, viderit diſcre-
" pare quod lectitat, non ſtatim erumpat in
" vocem, me *falſarium*, me clamitans eſſe
" ſacrilegum, qui audeam aliquid in veteri-
" bus libris addere, mutare, corrigere." (*b*)

Theſe accuſations, then, of *Jerome*, as a
falſary, were brought againſt him BEFORE
he publiſhed either his Tranſlation of the
Canonical Epiſtles themſelves, or his Preface to them, which is now under conſideration. And they were not increaſed, or even
repeated, (as far as is known) *after* his publication

(*a*) Præf. in *Eſaiam*.
(*b*) Præf. in quatuor Evangelia.

lication of thofe Epiftles. *Jerome*, therefore, was *not* THEREUPON (that is, upon
the publication of this Preface, or upon the
retention of the Verfe 1. *John*, v. 7, in his
New Teftament) accufed of falfifying Scripture; as is afferted in the above objection.
The tranfient mention of his accufers, in
this Preface, is merely the retrofpection of
a feeling mind, ftill fmarting under a fenfe
of former injuries; and bears no reference
whatfoever to his Tranflation of any part
of the firft Epiftle of St. *John*.

XVII. " *In this defence he*" [Jerome]
" *feems to fay, that he corrected the Vul-*
" *gar Latin Tranflation by the original*
" *Greek; and this is the great teftimony*
" *the text relies upon.*"

Jerome not only *feems* to fay, but *does* pofitively fay, not in this defence only, but in
other parts of his works, that he made his
Tranflation from the *original Greek.* Several
proofs have already (c) been produced to
this point. To thofe let the following paffage

(c) Pages 241, and 242, and their references, viz.
P. 33, 99, and 106.

Newton. fage be fubjoined, from his Epiftle to *Marcella*. " *Latinorum codicum vitiofitatem, quæ* " *ex diverfitate librorum omnium comprobatur,* " *ad* Græcam originem, *unde et ipfi* " *tranflata non denegant, voluiffe revocare.*"

XIX. " *But whilft he*" [Jerome] " *confeffes it*" [the Verfe 1. *John*, v. 7] " *was not in the Latin before,—he fatis-* " *fies us that it has crept into the Latin* " *fince his time.*"

Jerome makes no fuch confeffion. The premifes are not true; *(d)* and muft, therefore, produce an unfound conclufion.

XX. " *And whilft he was accufed by* " *his contemporaries of falfifying the Scrip-* " *tures in inferting it, this accufation alfo* " *confirms, that he altered the public* " *reading.*"

The premifes, here, are as untrue as the former. For *Jerome* never was accufed, by
any

(d) See Pages 104 and 105, where objections, of this kind, have been already confidered, and refuted.

any of his contemporaries, of falfifying the Newton.
Scriptures in inferting this Verfe. On the
contrary, *Auguftine*, who doubted as to fome
of *Jerome*'s corrections of the Old Teftament, expreffes the higheft (I had almoft
faid the moft devout) approbation of *Jerome*'s
New Teftament. (*e*) Nor was fuch a charge
ever brought againft *Jerome*, by any perfon
whomfoever, for more than *twelve hundred*
years after his death. I appeal to all antiquity for the truth of this obfervation.

XXI. " *He*" [Jerome] " *accufes for-*
" *mer Tranflators of falfifying the Scrip-*
" *tures in omitting it*"—[viz. the Verfe
in queftion.]

This objection has (*f*) been already anfwered.

XXII. " *For had the reading been du-*
" *bious before he made it fo, no man would*
" *have charged him with falfification for*
" *following either part.*"

No

(*e*) Page 106, where *Auguftine*'s words are ftated at
large
(*f*) Pages 103 and 104.

NEWTON. No man ever *did* charge *Jerome*, in the sense here meant, with falsification for following either part. *Jerome*, therefore, did *not* make the reading dubious. Nor, moreover, does he even declare it to have been made dubious at all, in his times, except through the error of certain " *unfaithful Translators ;*" who (he says) *had not rendered the Canonical Epistles into the* Latin *language*, " AS THEY " WERE WRITTEN BY THE APOSTLES ." which unfaithfulness had produced ambiguities, and variations of the text, " *particular-* " *ly in that passage of the first Epistle of St.* " John, *where the Unity of the Trinity is set* " *forth.*" (g)

It was the fault of those unfaithful Translators, then, whom *Jerome* reprehends, and not of *Jerome* himself, that the reading of of this Verse was ever rendered, in the smallest degree, dubious, in the *Latin* Church, either in his age, or in any part of the Christian æra, which preceded him.

XXIII. " *They that have been con-* " *versant*

(g) Appendix, No. XIII.

" *verfant in his*" [Jerome's] "*writings,* Newton.

" *obferve a ftrang liberty, which he takes*

" *in afferting things. Many notable in-*

" *ftances of this he has left us in compofing*

" *thofe very fabulous lives of Paul, and*

" *Hilarian*" [Hilarion] " *not to mention*

" *what he has written upon other occa-*

" *fions. Whence Erafmus*"—(p. 503.)

What *Erafmus* fays of the compofitions, here cenfured, is only,—that *Jerome* feems to have *amufed himfelf with writing fuch trifles, merely for the fake of exercifing his genius.* (*h*) He wrote them as *Apologues,* or ftories contrived to teach fome moral, or fpiritual duty ; and not as ftrict details of pofitive facts. They were, therefore, *fabulous ;*

(*h*) " *Videtur et hoc* Hieronymus, *exercitandi ingenii* " *gratia, lufiffe.*" Vol 1 p. 81, F.
In another p'ace he fays, fpeaking of another inftance of this kind of compofition—" *Lufit in hac epiftola Divus* " Hieronymus *artificio fcribendæ Hiftoriæ, et ftilum, jam* " *fcribendi defuetudine torpefcentem, hac exercitatiuncula re-* " *novavit*"
And in the life of *Malchus,* another inftance of this kind, *Erafmus* fays—" Depinxit [Hieronymus] *foli-* " *tarium,*" (meaning this *Paul,* the Hermit) " *depinxit* " *celebrem,*" (meaning *Hilarion*) " *depingit hic,*" (mean- " ing *Malchus*) *captivum, et agitatum. Lufit et in hoc* " *argumento, ingenii exercitandi gratia.*" (Vol. I. p. 80 " and 87.)

NEWTON. *tous*; and were meant, by *Jerome*, to be fabulous: as appears even by the teftimony of *Erafmus*. And fo were the Fables of *Pilpay*, the Apologues of *Æfop*, the two magnificent Epics of *Homer*, and *Jotham*'s parable of the Trees; *(i)* which laft is much more ancient, perhaps, than any other example of this fpecies of compofition, which is now extant.

Thefe prolufions of *Jerome*, then, were, like the other inftances juft mentioned, feigned narrations, defigned to inform, to encourage, to reprove, or to correct. They are—inftruction difguifed under the allegory of an action. They are " *liberties taken*" to fuppofe, rather than to affert, what is " *ftrange*," and unufual; in order to inculcate what is ufeful, and good.

XXIV. " *Whence Erafmus faid of* " *him*," [Jerome] " *that he was in af-* " *firming things, frequently violent, and* " *impudent, and often contrary to him-* " *felf.*"—

Erafmus

(1) *Judges*, IX, 7—20.

Erasmus has spoken thus of *Jerome*; but NEWTON. NOT on account of the lives of *Paul* and *Hilarion*. He applied these expressions to *Jerome*, from another motive, and for another, and a far different, purpose. (*k*) *Erasmus*, when he used these words, was agitated by a dispute, which ruffled his temper, and has added no honors to his name. When his mind was more at ease, he gave a very different description of the same *Jerome*; as the following picture (which, however, is drawn by the hand of a master) will abundantly testify.

" *Cæterum, in optimo Theologiæ ge-*
" *nere, primas*" [scil. laudes] " *tenet Divus*
" *Hieronymus, de* Latinis *loquor : et ita pri-*
" *mas tenet, ut omneis post se longo relinquat*
" *intervallo. Inter tam innumerabiles Theolo-*
" *gos, vix quenquam habeat et ipsa docta*
" Græcia, *qui nostrum æquet* Hieronymum,
" *si modo non unam aliquam laudem, sed uni-*
" *versas ejus dotes simul expendas Tantam*
" *uno in homine reperias secularium, ut vocant,*
" *literarum cognitionem, tantam omnis antiqui-*
" *tatis peritiam, tot linguarum absolutam scien-*
" *tiam, tam admirandam locorum, et histor-*
" *arum,*

(*k*) Annot. in 1 *John*, v. 7.—Edit. 1522.

NEWTON. " *arum, omnium notitiam, tam non vulgarem*
" *mysticorum voluminum eruditionem, tantum*
" *inimitabilis eloquentiæ, tam* EXACTUM UBI-
" QUE JUDICIUM, *tam facrum afflati pec-*
" *toris ardorem, rerum adeo diverfarum tam*
" *digeftam ac præfentem memoriam, tam fæli-*
" *cem juxtà et divitem mixturam; denique,*
" *tanto lepore conditam feveritatem, ut, quem-*
" *admodum per fe facundi, fi cum* Cicerone
" *conferantur, protinus videntur obmutefcere:*
" *ita cæteri doctores, quos citra collationem*
" *fufpicimus, cum* Hieronymo *compofiti, vix*
" *fapere, vix loqui, vix vivere, videantur.*" (*l*)

Again—" *Nullum eft enim argumenti genus,*
" *in quo ille non luferit:* NUSQUAM SUI DIS-
" SIMILIS." (*m*)

And again—" *Multis defuit linguarum pe-*
" *ritia,*

(*l*) Preface to vol. iv of *Jerome's* Works, by *Erafmus,*
Edit *Paris,* A. D. 1546
(*m*) Vita HIERONYMI per *Erafmum,* vol. 1. Ed. *Paris.*
A. D 1516
It would not be credited, perhaps, if it were not here
repeated, that the *Exactum ubique judicium,* the *Nufquam*
fui diffimilis, and the *Omnium concentus virtutum,* of thefe
characters,—and the *Sæpenumero violentus, fæpe varius,*
parumque fibi conftans, of the other,—were written of the
fame *Jerome,* and by the fame *Erafmus!*

" *ritia, nonnullis fidei finceritas, quibufdam* Newton.
" *vitæ integritas :*—Hieronymus, *et unus*
" Hieronymus, *fic omnia præftitit, ut fi ~~non~~*
" *non ad unam aliquam virtutem, fed ad* om-
" nium concentum *et fummam refpicias ·*
" *dicam audaĉter, fed vere, nihil habeat vel*
" *ipfa* Græcia, *quod noftro opponat* Hierony-
" mo."

XXV. " *Yet fince his*" [Jerome's]
" *contemporaries accufed him, it is but*
" *juft that we lay afide the prejudice of*
" *his great name, and hear the caufe im-*
" *partially. Now the witneffes between*
" *them, are partly the ancient Tranflators*
" *of the Scriptures into the various lan-*
" *guages, partly the writers of his own*
" *age, and of the ages next before and*
" *after him, and partly the Scribes, who*
" *copied out the Greek* MSS *of the Scrip-*
" *tures in all ages. And all thefe are*
" *againft him. For by the unanimous*
" *evidence of all thefe, it will appear,*
" *that the teftimony of the* Three in Hea-
" *ven was wanting in the Greek* MSS
" *from whence* Jerome, *or whoever was*
                              " *the*

NEWTON.
" *the Author of that preface to the cano-*
" *nical epiftles, pretends to have bor-*
" *rowed it.*"

It hath been before obferved, that *Je-rome*'s contemporaries have *not* accufed him, as is here alledged. The perfons, therefore, mentioned in the objection, are not wanted, *as witneffes,* becaufe there are no accufers, who require their teftimony. But they fhall, neverthelefs, be examined, in relation to *Jerome,* in like manner as if fuch an ac-cufation had been actually brought : not only for the fake of the very refpectable au-thor of this objection, but for the fake of truth ; which always appears to the greateft advantage, when put the moft feverely to the trial.

Firft, then, it is alledged---(to ftate this objection in parts)---that, " *It appears*
" *by the unanimous evidence of all the*
" *ancient Tranflators of the Scriptures*
" *into the various languages, that the*
" *teftimony of the* Three in Heaven, *was*
" *wanting in the Greek MSS, from*
" *whence*

" *whence Jerome pretends to have bor-* Newton.
" *rowed it.*"

The *evidence* of thefe *ancient Tranflators of the Scriptures into the various languages* is fo fo far from being *unanimous, that the teftimony of the* Three in Heaven *was wanting* in thofe ancient *Greek* MSS, from which even their own refpective Verfions were derived ; that *three* (*n*) out of the whole *five* (as hath been already proved) and *two* of thofe the moft ancient of them, have uniformly contained the teftimony of thefe heavenly witneffes. And the *two,* (*o*) of thefe *five* ancient Verfions, which have *not* exhibited this difputed text, if we admit their evidence to the utmoft, do not eftablifh any part of the propofition advanced in the objection. Thofe two Verfions may give room for prefumptions as to the readings of the particular MSS, from whence *they* themfelves were derived. But they prove nothing as to the MSS, which *Jerome* ufed in his Tranflation ; and from which he

S   not

(*n*) The *Italic,* that of *Jerome,* and the *Armenian.* See pages 53—55, 187, and 196—206.
(*o*) The *Syriac,* and *Coptic.*

NEWTON not only *pretends to have borrowed*, but undoubtedly *did* borrow, the verse in question.

    2. " *The same appears, also, by the*
" *unanimous evidence of all the writers*
" *of Jerome's own age, and of the ages*
" *next before, and after him.*"--

There is NOT ONE Writer, in all those ages, who will justify this assertion. Some of them, indeed, have *not mentioned* this verse (as hath been before remarked) in such parts of their writings as have descended to the present times. But other writers, of the same ages, have cited it in the most pointed terms. The mere *silence* of the former, as to this verse, will not prove that it *was wanting* even in their own *Greek* MSS. Far less will such silence prove, that this verse was wanting in those MSS, by which *Jerome* regulated his translation.

    3. " *The same appears by the unanimous*
" *evidence of all the Scribes, who have*
" *copied out the Greek MSS of the Scrip*
" *tures in all ages.*"

                      How

How a Scribe, who copied out a *Greek* MS Newton. at *Paris,* or at *Rome,* in the *tenth* century, for inſtance, in which the teſtimony of the *Three in Heaven* was, admittedly, wanting, can be a proof that the *Greek* MSS, which *Jerome* uſed in *Paleſtine,* in the *fourth* century, did *not* contain that teſtimony,—is utterly inconceivable. Such aſſertions (for they are not arguments) are too extravagant for a ſerious confutation.

If it ſhall be aſked, *what is become of* Jerome's *MSS,*—let it be conſidered, that he executed his tranſlation of the New Teſtament in a Monaſtery, at *Bethlehem,* near *Jeruſalem;* where he alſo died. When we recollect, how ſoon, after *Jerome's* death, the *Saracens* invaded the Holy Land, and kept its territory under their iron rule for near five hundred years, until their ſtrong holds were retaken, by ſtorm, from them, by the ſoldiers of the *Croiſade,* under the command of *Robert,* Duke of *Normandy,* in the laſt year of the *eleventh* century;—we need not be very doubtful, as to the fate, which befel the MSS of *Jerome.*

XXVI.

XXVI. " *The ancient Interpreters,*
" *which I cite as witnesses against him,*
" *are chiefly the authors of the ancient*
" *vulgar Latin, of the Syriac, and the*
" *Ethiopic Versions.*"—

These three witnesses are, in the first place, only *two*. For the *Ethiopic* is no more than a transcript from the *Syriac*; which reduces them to a single testimony. Of these, thus reduced to *two*, witnesses, the *ancient vulgar Latin*, the most ancient Version in the world, is a witness on the other side of the question. For it hath already (*p*) been proved, that this Version hath constantly, and uniformly, contained the passage, 1. *John*, v. 7.

XXVIII. " *For as he*" [Jerome]
" *tells us, that the Latins omitted the tes-*
" *timony of the* Three in Heaven *in*
" *their Version before his time.*"—

Jerome tells us no such thing. He complains, indeed, of certain unfaithful translators,

(*p*) Page 187.

rors, who had omitted this paſſage of St. NEWTON, *John*; but who might be, and (if we may judge by the vaſt majority of *Latin* MSS, which read the verſe at this day) were, few in number, compared with thoſe which retained it. He makes no complaints, of this kind, againſt the *Latin* Verſions in general; or againſt the public Verſion of that age, the *Old Italic*, in particular. (*q*)

> XXVIII. " *It*" [1. *John*, v. 7.] " *is*
> " *wanting alſo in other ancient Verſions;*
> " *as in the Egyptian Arabic,*" [and] " *in*
> " *the Armenian Verſion, uſed ever ſince*
> " *Chryſoſtom's age, by the Armenian na-*
> " *tions.*"——

This objection is true of the *Coptic*, here called the *Egyptian Arabic*. But it is not true (*r*) of the *Armenian*: for that Verſion hath always read this verſe.

The objections, which follow, as to the

Ruſſian,

(*q*) Pages 103—5.
(*r*) Pages 195—206, where this point hath been diſcuſſed at large.

NEWTON. *Ruffian*, or *Scalavonic*, Bibles, have been confidered already.

XXIX. " *And that it*" [the verfe in " queftion] " *was not written in the an-* " *cient Verfions—Nor in the Greek*"— [viz. original of this Epiftle.]

Every ancient Verfion, which contained this verfe, every ancient Chuich, which received it, and every individual writer, of ancient times at leaft, who quoted it, is a *pofitive* proof againft this objection. To ftate them here at large, would be to recapitulate the whole of the preceding pages. The evidence, oi rather the prefumption, to the contiary, is merely *conjectural*, arifing from *omiffions*. The difference, in degree, between thefe two kinds of evidence, fhall be appreciated hereafter.

XXX. " *But was wholly unknown* " *to the firft Churches.*"—

It was not unknown to the firft *Latin* Churches.

Churches. For their public Verſions, the Newton. *Itala Vetus*, and that of *Jerome*, have conſtantly exhibited this paſſage of St. *John*, from the firſt hour of the exiſtence of that Church, to the preſent moment.

It was not unknown to the firſt *Armenian* Church. For its public Verſion hath (*s*) been proved to have contained this Verſe, from the age of *Chryſoſtom* to the preſent times.

It was not unknown to the *Greek* church. For it hath been proved by the uſe of the ἀποϛολος, that this paſſage was conſtantly read in that church, even in the earlieſt ages of Chriſtianity.

Nor was it, laſtly, unknown to the *African* church. The citation of it, ſo early as A. D. 484, by no leſs than (nearly) *four hundred* Biſhops ; the reliance upon its evidence, by thoſe Biſhops, in oppoſition both to the fraud, and force, of *Huneric*, and *Cyrila* ;

S 4 and

(*s*) Pages 196—206

Newton. and the utter inability of the Tyrant, and his mock-patriarch, to repel its teſtimony, but by violence, and perſecution ;—prove that this paſſage was known, read, and received, in that church, even from the earlieſt æra of its converſion to the Chriſtian faith.

The plain truth, therefore, is, that this verſe was unknown to none of the firſt churches of Chriſtians ; except, perhaps, to the *Syriac*, and the *Coptic*, with their few, and, comparatively unimportant, derivatives.

XXXI. " *In all that vehement, uni-* " *verſal, and laſting, controverſy about* " *the Trinity in* Jerome's *time, and both* " *before and long enough after it, this* " *text of the* Three in Heaven *was never* " *once thought of.*"—

This objection is inaccurate in its *form* (but it is not worth the time to ſtop for inaccuracies only) and untrue in its ſubſtance. The text of the *Three in Heaven* was not only *thought of,* but actually quoted, and inſiſted

fifted upon, not only a little *after* the age of NEWTON.
Jerome, by *Fulgentius*, and *Vigilius*; and in
the fame century with *Jerome*, by the author of the difputation between *Arius*, and
Athanafius, by *Eucherius*, and *Auguftine*, and
by the *African* Bifhops under *Huneric*; but
alfo BEFORE *Jerome's* time, by *Phæbadius*,
and, as it feems, by *Marcus Celedenfis*. And
ALL thefe quotations of this verfe were exprefsly made *in the controverfy about the Trinity*, and in open, and avowed, oppofition to
the *Arians* of thofe ages.

The treatife, now under confideration,
next enumerates feveral ancient writers, who
have omitted to cite this verfe in thofe parts
of their works, which remain to the prefent
times. But the lift is not accurate. For,
of thefe, *Phæbadius*, *Auguftine*, *Athanafius*,
Jerome, *Eucherius*, and *Caffiodorius*, have, in
fome inftances, quoted, and in others plainly referred to, this difputed paffage.

XXXII. " *And therefore if this read-*
" *ing were once out*," [viz. in *Jerome's*
age] " *we are bound in juftice to be-*
" *lieve,*

NEWTON.

" *lieve, that it was out from the begin-*
" *ning ; unless the razing of it out can be*
" *proved by some better argument, than*
" *that of pretence, and clamour.*"—(p.
409.)

It was OUT of some copies, in *Jerome's*
age, and IN others ;—as *Jerome*, himself,
informs us. And this single circumstance
does more than confute the objection,—by
turning it against its author. For, (to use
this illustrious objector's own stile) *if this
reading were once* IN, [VIZ. in *Jerome's* age,—
which *Cyprian's* Bible, as well as *Jerome's*
information, assure us of] *we are bound in
justice to believe that it was in* FROM THE BE-
GINNING ;—*unless the putting of it in, at
some later period, can be proved by some better
argument, than unfair, and violent, constructions.* (t)

XXXIII. " *The* Greeks *received it*
" *not*"

(t) Whenever Mr. *Gibbon* shall find himself disposed
to attempt a refutation of these strictures, the preceding
one is particularly recommended to his notice. It will
require his most serious attention.

I speak thus of the foregoing stricture, without dread-
ing the imputation of vanity. For it is not my own, it
was suggested to me by Dr. HORSLEY.

" *not*" [viz. *Jerome's* reading of 1. *John*, Newton.
v. 7.] " *till this present age, when the*
" Venetians *sent it amongst them in print-*
" *ed books.*"

Was the αποςολος, then, not known to the
Greeks, " until this present age?" Was the
αποςολος " a printed book?" Did *Euthymius
Zygabenus* live only " in this present age?"
Was the treatise, containing the debate
(whether real, or feigned) between *Arius*,
and *Athanasius*, written in " this present
age?" Were any of these works *first* known
to the *Greeks* " in printed books?"—It is irk-
some to see such assertions brought forward;
and to lie under the necessity of repelling
them.

XXXIV. " *It*" [the verse in question]
" *is wanting in the MSS of all languages*
" *but the Latin.*"

It was, perhaps, wanting in those particular *Greek* MSS, from whence the *Syriac*,
and *Coptic*, Versions were translated. But
even that is not certain; because the omission
of

NEWTON. of this paſſage, in thoſe ancient Verſions, might have been, and probably was, the fault of the Tranſlator, or Tranſcriber: who have, or one of them hath, been guilty of much greater miſtakes, (*u*) and omiſſions, than this, in thoſe reſpective Verſions.

This is all that can be granted to this objection For the *Arabic*, *Perſian*, and *Ethiopic*, Verſions are (as hath been before remarked) tranſcripts, only, from the *Syriac*, and *Coptic*. And the *Greek*, and *Armenian*, (as well as the *Latin*) both deny the truth of the objection, as applied to them.

The queſtion of *omiſſions*, in general, will be conſidered hereafter.

XXXV. " *The* Lateran *Council, A. D.*
" 1215, *mentions* Joachim *quoting the*
" *the text in theſe words:* Quoniam in
" *canonica* Johannis *epiſtola* ; Quia Tres
" ſunt, qui teſtimonium dant in cælo,
" Pater, et Verbum, et Spiritus ; et
" hi tres unum ſunt : *ſtatimque ſubjun-*
" *gitur,*

(*u*) Pages 188—196.

" *gitur*, Et tres funt, qui teftimonium Newton.
" dant in terra, Spiritus, aqua, et fan-
" guis, et tres unum funt : *ficut in co-*
" *dicibus quibufdam invenitur. Therefore*
" *this reading*" [1. John, v. 7] " *was*
" *then got but into fome books. For the*
" *words*, Sicut in codicibus quibufdam
" invenitur, *refer as well to the firft*
" *words of* Joachim" [about the three
heavenly witneffes] " *as to the fecond*
" *part*" [about the three witneffes on
earth.] (p. 511.)

Joachim interpreted the final claufe of the
feventh verfe [*Tres unum funt*] to fignify an
unity of confent, only, in thofe heavenly witneffes. And he attempted to juftify that
interpretation, by alledging, that the fame
words [*Tres unum funt*] ftood in fome copies
[*ficut in codicibus quibufdam invenitur*] in the
eighth verfe, as well as in the *feventh* ;—that,
being, there, applied to the *fpirit, water*, and
blood, they *could* impoit an *unity of confent*,
alone, in that verfe ; and that, being fo interpreted in the *eighth*, he had a right to

give

NEWTON. give the fame interpretation to them in the *feventh*, verfe, likewife.

This, Sir, was the argument of *Joachim.*— in which, by the expreffions, *Sicut in codicibus quibufdam invenitur*, he referred, not to the three, *heavenly*, witneffes, but to the *three witneffes on earth*, fingly, and exclufively. And I am happy in being able, further, to alledge the moft refpectable authority againft Sir *Ifaac Newton*, on this head, which is the teftimony of Sir *Ifaac Newton* himfelf: who has, in another part of this treatife, (x) given to the words of *Joachim* a fimilar interpretation.

XXXVI. " Eugenius, *Bifhop of* Car-
" thage, *in the feventh year of* Huneric,
" *anno Chrifti* 484, *in the fummary of*
" *his faith exhibited to the King, cited it*
" *the firft of any man, fo far as I can*
" *find.*"—(p. 512.)

I have no objection to this remark, fave that the fummary of faith, here fpoken of,

19

is defcribed as the Creed of *Eugenius* alone: Newton. —and that he is faid to have been the *firſt* who cited this text. It does not appear to have been the Creed of *Eugenius* alone, in any fenfe; for, although prefented by him to *Huneric*, it does not carry his fignature, but (*y*) that of four other *African* Biſhops: who were moſt probably, from that circumſtance, the perfons deputed, by their brethren, to compofe, and prepare, it. And *Eugenius*, or the perfon, or perfons, who drew up this fummary, was not (or rather were not) the *firſt* who cited this text; becaufe the exprefs citations, and references, of *Tertullian*, *Cyprian*, *Phæbadius*, *Marcus Celedenſis*, *Auguſtine*, and *Eucherius*;—the ufe of the απο϶ολ☉ in the *Greek* Church, the *Synopſis* attributed to *Athanaſius*, and the difputation (real, or feigned) between him and *Arius*; together with the *Old Italic*, and *Armenian*, Verfions, as well as the Verfion of *Jerome*; all of which have recognifed this difputed text:—were, *all*, antecedent to the year 484.

Dr.

(*y*) In pages 44—7, and 111—116, this whole tranfaction is briefly ſtated. The original record is copied in Appendix, No XIV.

NEWTON. Dr. *Benson* (z) has reprefented this identical teftimony of the *African* Church to be
fo very late, in point of time, as not to be
worth *his* notice. Sir *Ifaac Newton* here
places it in the *firft rank* of proof. But—
Non noftrum eft tales componere lites.

XXXVII. " *Of the MSS which have*
" *not the teftimony of the* Three in Hea-
" ven ; *fome have the words* in teria, *in*
" *the eighth verfe,* but the moft *want it.*
" *Of thofe which have the teftimony of*
" *the* Three in Heaven, *fome in the*
" *eighth verfe have* hi Tres Unum funt.
" *Others not. And that teftimony is in*
" *moft books fet before the teftimony of the*
" Three in earth ; *in fome, it is fet af-*
" *ter. So* Erafmus *notes two old books,*
" *in which it is fet after* ; Lucas Bru-
" genfis *a third* ; *and* Heffelius *a fourth* ;
" *and fo* Vigilius Tapfenfis (adverf.
" *Varim.* Cap. v.) *fets it after: which*
" *feems to proceed from hence, that it*
" *was fometimes fo noted in the margin,*
" *that the reader or tranfcriber knew not*
" *whether*

(z) Pages 114—115.

" *whether it were to come before or after.* NEWTON,
" *Now these discords, as they detract*
" *from the authority of the Latin MSS, so*
" *they confirm to us, that the old vulgar*
" *Latin has in these things been tampered*
" *with, and corrected by* Jerome's *ver-*
" *sion.*" (p. 514.)

The discords, which are here complained
of, seem to have been entirely owing to the
oscitancy, and negligence, of transcribers.
Had they originated, in these MSS, from a
desire of correcting them by *Jerome*'s Version,
it seems very difficult to assign a reason, why
these supposed *tamperers* ceased from *tamper-
ing*, until they had rendered their MSS *exact
copies*, in this passage at least (which *ex con-
fesso* they are not) of the Version of *Jerome*.

But, taking the objection as granted, for
the present, and for the sake of argument,——
let it be observed, that, before it can be imputed, as a fault, to any *Latin* MSS, that it
has been corrected by *Jerome*'s Version ;——it
must be proved, that the Version of *Jerome*
is, in itself, erroneous, and of no authority.

T   This

NEWTON. This illustrious objector has. indeed, endeavoured to disparage this Version, as we have already seen ;—by affirming, that *Jerome* was accused by his contemporaries of having altered the public reading, in respect to the passage, in question,—that he wrote the fabulous lives of *Paul*, and *Hilarion*, and that *Erasmus* called him *impudent*. But it hath been already proved, that these intended disparagements of that Version have no solid foundation ; and cannot, therefore, support the inference, which is thus attempted to be built upon them.

XXXVIII. " *The original MSS*" [of R. *Stephens*] " *he*" [Beza] " *does not* " *here*" [in the preface to his annotations] " *pretend to have ; nor could he* " *have them, for they were not* Stephens's " *MSS; but belonged to several libraries* " *in* France, *and* Italy." (p. 516.)

Beza has expressed himself with so little precision, in this preface, on the subject of R. *Stephens*'s original MSS, that it might be doubted whether he had, or had not, the
                                                            use

ufe of thofe MSS, did he not, in other parts Newton. of his works, clear up thofe doubts in the moft fatisfactory manner. Ego *in omnibus noftris vetuftis* libris *inveni :* And—*Sic legitur in omnibus* Græcis *exemplaribus, quæ quidem* mihi inspicere *licuit :*—are his expreffions on other occafions, which are fo plain as to need no comment.

Nor does the fact of *Beza*'s poffeffing thefe original MSS depend on his own affertion, alone, however truly refpectable that may be. For *R. Stephens* has affirmed the fame thing (as hath (*a*) been already remarked) in his poftfcript, or advertifement, fubjoined to *Beza*'s edition of A. D. 1556.

XXXIX. " Stephens *had fifteen MSS*
" *in all, yet all of them did not contain*
" *all the* Greek *Teftament.*" (p. 517.)

R. Stephens has not cited *all* his MSS to all parts of his *Greek* Teftament. But it does not follow, from thence, that all his

T 2

MSS

(*a*) Page 130, note *d*.
Emlyn hath, in fact (however unintentionally) proved this point, in favor of *Beza*. (See page 124, note *x*.)

NEWTON. MSS did not contain all the *Greek Testament.*

    XL. " *Four of them*" [*R. Stephens's* MSS] " *noted* γ, ς, ιβ, ιδ, *had each of* " *them the four gospels only.*"

This affertion is not juft. The MS, noted ιβ, contained the firft epiftle to the *Corinthians.* And that marked ιδ contained, alfo, the Acts of the Apoftles, and the fecond epiftle of St. *Peter.*

    XLI. " *Two noted* β, η, *contained only* " *the Gofpels, and the Acts. One, noted* " ις, *contained the Apocalypfe only. The* " *MS,* ζ, *contained the Epiftles, and Gof-* " *pels;* ι, ια, ιγ, *the Epiftles, and Acts; and* " δ, ς, θ, *the Epiftles, Gofpels, and Acts.*" (p. 518.)

This enumeration abounds with miftakes. Befide the particulars, here mentioned, the MS of *R. Stephens*, marked β, contained the Epiftle to the *Romans;*—ις, the Gofpel of St. *Luke*, the fecond Epiftle to the *Corinthians.*

ans, and the fiıft Epiſtle to *Timothy* ;—ʒ, the Newton.
Acts ;—ί, the Goſpels of St. *Luke*, and St.
John ;—ıα, the Goſpels of St. *Matthew*, and
St. *John*, and the Apocalypſe ;—ıγ, the Goſ-
pels of St. *Matthew*, and St. *John* ;—and ϵ,
the Apocalypſe.

XLII. " *For in the various lections of*
" *the canonical epiſtles, and thoſe to the*
" Theſſalonians, Timothy, Tıtus, *and*
" *the* Hebrews, *are found theſe ſeven*
" *MSS,* δ, ϵ, ʒ, θ, ι, ıα, ıγ, *every where*
" *cited, and no more than theſe.*"

This obſervation is incorrect, like the former. The MSS ıδ, and ıſ, aıe cited by *R.*
Stephens, to theſe, enumerated, parts of the
ſacred Canon, as well as the MSS mentioned
in the objection.

XLIII. " *And this any one may ga-*
" *ther, by noting what MSS the various*
" *lections are cited out of, in every book*
" *of the New Teſtament.*"

He certainly may. It is the very method
T 3 which

NEWTON. which I have purfued; and which has enabled me to correct all the preceding miftakes.

>XLIV. " Stephens, *therefore, did*
> " *collect various lections of the epiftles out*
> " *of only thefe feven MSS,* ð, ε, ζ, θ, ι, ια,
> " ιγ. *And in all thefe feven he found the*
> " *teftimony of the* Three in Heaven *to*
> " *be wanting ; as you may fee noted in*
> " *the margin of his edition.*"

The former claufe of this objection hath been juft difproved. And the latter is utterly groundlefs. The margin of *R. Stephens*'s edition denotes, that the particular words, ευ τω ϐρανω, were-wanting in the *feven* MSS there referred to :—but no more.

The objections, which follow, as to *Erafmus*, have (*b*) been replied to already.

>XLV. " *And fo here, where the tefti-*
> " *mony, of the* Three in Heaven, *is ge-*
> " *nerally wanting in the* Greek *copies,*
> " *they*"

(*b*) Pages 138—149.

" *they*" [the *Complutenſian* Editors] Newton.
" *make a marginal note, to ſecure them-*
" *ſelves from being blamed for printing*
" *it.*"---And that note " *being ſet in*
" *the margin of the* Greek *text, ſhews*
" *that its main deſign is to juſtify the*
" Greek, *by the* Latin *thus rectified and*
" *confirmed. But to us* Aquinas *is no*
" *Apoſtle.*" (p. 520, and 521.)

The marginal note, here referred to, was
evidently deſigned to juſtify the omiſſion of
ᴊτοι οι τρεις εις το εν εισι, in the *eighth* verſe ; and
for no other purpoſe. A ſingle, impartial,
peruſal of the (c) note itſelf, will amply
juſtify this obſervation.

XLVI. " *A third reaſon why I con-*
" *ceive the* Complutenſian Greek *to*
" *have been in this place a tranſlation*
" *from the* Latin, *is, becauſe* Stunica,
" *when, in his objections, he comes to this*
" *text, cites not one* Greek *MS for it a-*
" *gainſt* Eraſmus, *but argues wholly*

T 4   " *from*

<hr>

(c) See Appendix, No XVIII. where this marginal
note is copied at full length

NEWTON. " *from the authority of the* Latin." (p. 522.)

I am ready, Sir, to acknowledge the truth of this objection. And, as far as the conduct of *Stunica* can affect the authenticity of the verse, in question,—I own myself unable satisfactorily to account for it. *But to us* STUNICA (as Sir *Ifaac* properly obferves of *Aquinas*) *is no Apoftle.* Whether the reft of *Stunica's* writings, if they had furvived to the prefent times, would have diffipated thefe doubts, or not,—cannot now be determined. But this may be now, and indeed has (*d*) been already, determined, and, in truth, it is the chief point, which requires determination in the prefent difquifition : viz. that " *the Complutenfian Greek was* NOT " *a tranflation from the Latin,*" as is affumed in the preceding objection.—

XLVII. " *So then the* Complutenfian " *Divines*

(*d*) Pages 184—186.
Thefe Editors pofitively affirm, that they had (*how many* they do not mention) *Greek* MSS, from the *Vatican.* And we are certified, by various authorities, that they had another *Greek* MS from *Rhodes*, commonly called the *Codex Rhodienfis.*

" *Divines did sometimes correct the* Greek NEWTON.
" *by the* Latin, *without the authority of*
" *any* Greek *MS; as appears by their*
" *practice in* Matthew, vi: 13."—(p,
523.)

The marginal note, in *Matthew*, vi: 13,
contains an account, given by the *Complutensian* Editors, of their having omitted the Doxology, in that verse.   And the reason which
they assign for the omission, does them in-
finite honor, as it shews them to have been
conscientiously scrupulous, in not admitting
any thing to stand in the sacred canon,
which had not, in their judgment, an indubitable claim to originality.   Had they entertained any doubts of its authenticity, it
must be presumed that they would have
acted in the same manner with the verse
1. *John*, v. 7.

XLVIII. " *Nor has all the zeal for*
" *this text been able since to discover one,*"
[viz. *Greek* MS which contained the
verse 1. *John*, v. 7.] " *either in* Spain,
" *or any where else.*"

This

NEWTON. This objection will be beſt repelled, perhaps, by a reference to *Wetſtein*; whoſe teſtimony, on *this point*, at leaſt, will not be
conteſted.

Wetſtein, then, in his laſt Edition of the
New Teſtament, affirms (*e*) that he has
availed himſelf of the different readings of
ſixty five Greek MSS (excluſive of four Lectionaries) for that portion of his work, which
contains the canonical Epiſtles. But as *Valla*'s MSS are claſſed with the reſt, by the
numeral 44, as if they were but one MS,
whereas they were ſeven ; the whole number of theſe *Greek* MSS is, properly, *ſeventy-
one.* Of theſe the *lettered* MSS, C, D, E,
and F, do not contain the firſt Epiſtle of
St. *John.* And, of the ſixty-four *numbered*
MSS, that marked 49 is the Goſpel of St.
Mark only ; 52 is the *Codex Rhodienſis*, which
Wetſtein never ſaw, and which, moſt probably, did contain this diſputed paſſage ; 53
does not contain that part of St. *John*'s Epiſ-
ſtle ; 55 is *Jude*, only ; and 56 is no more
than a collection of ſome various readings,
noted

(*e*) *Amſt.* A. D. 1752, vol. ii, p. 449, &c.

noted in the margin of a printed book; and NEWTON. 58 is only a duplicate of 22. Setting thefe afide, there remain, in *Wetftein*'s Lift, *fixty-one* (to which *Griefbach* adds *four* others) *lettered*, and *numbered*, MSS, which fet forth the firft epiftle of St. *John*.

Of thefe fixty-five *Greek* MSS, *Wetftein* admits, that thofe marked 34, 44, 48, 51, 57, and 58, DO EXHIBIT this difputed paffage. But, as *Wetftein* has not taken the *Codex Britannicus* into the account, which *Erafmus* affirms that he collated (*f*) in England; and as *Valla*'s MSS were *feven* in number, and have been fo ftated in the general enumeration, an allowance muft here be made for them, as *for feven*.

But this is not all. In the foregoing lift *Wetftein* has taken the *eight* MSS of *R. Stephens*, which are refpectively marked δ, ε, θ, ι, ια, ιγ, ιε, and ζ, into the number of thofe MSS of the canonical, or catholic, Epiftles, which, [he fays] do *not* exhibit the verfe, in queftion. And he has acted thus, upon the idea, ori-ginally

(*f*) Page 132.

NEWTON. ginally held forth to the world by F. *Le Long*, which (*g*) hath been already proved to be visionary, and vain. Yet, as F. *Le Long* hath proved, that there are, now, such *Greek* MSS of these Epistles, in the Royal Library at *Paris*, which do not contain this disputed passage, the List, which *Wetstein* has thus drawn up, of *Greek* MSS *not* containing this verse, must not be abridged; but instead thereof, the whole number R. *Stephens's Greek* MSS (which were sixteen in all) must be brought to the opposite side of the computation: because they did exhibit this disputed passage.

This mode of calculation, then, will advance the *sixty-five Greek* MSS, herein before brought to account, to EIGHTY-ONE. From whence it, finally, follows, by the very

---

(*g*) Pages 127—138.
Sir *Isaac Newton*, in p. 516 of his treatise, argues, that R. *Stephens* " *never saw the MS marked* β *, but had only various lections* COLLECTED *out of it by his friends in Italy.*" The words of R. *Stephens*, upon which this assumption is built (for there is no other foundation for it) are— " *Exemplar vetustissimum, in* Italia *ab amicis* COLLATUM " It was the *exemplar*, the *book itself*, then, (and not the *lections* out of it) which was (*collected*, or rather) *procured for* R. *Stephens*, by his friends in *Italy*.

very admiffions of *Wetftein*, thus commented Newton.
upon (if thefe reafonings are not, and it
feems that they are not, unjuft) that, of the
whole number of *Greek* MSS, containing the
catholic, or canonical, Epiftles, now known
(by any *fpecial defcription*) ever to have exifted in the world, *thirty-one* out of *eighty-
one*, or (more than) *three* out of *eight*, or
(nearly) ONE HALF of that WHOLE NUM-
BER,—actually did exhibit, or do now exhibit, the verfe 1. *John*, v. 7.

XLIX. " *The differences*" [of *terms*,
in thefe two verfes, in different MSS]
" *are too great to fpring from the bare*
" *errors of Scribes, and arife rather from*
" *the various tranflations of the place,*
" *out of* Latin *into* Greek, *by different*
" *perfons.*"—

This objection confines itfelf to the readings of the *Codex Britannicus*, and the *Complutenfian Polyglott*. But in order to give
all poffible force to the objection, *all* the
readings, which have been mentioned in this
treatife, fhall be here combined together, in
one view.

The

The conteſted paſſage, 1. JOHN, v : 7, 8—as ſtated by, or in,

The COUNCIL *of* LATERAN :	*The* DUBLIN MS :	*The* CODEX BRITANNICUS :
7. Οτι τρεις εισιν οι μαρτυρꙋντες εν τω ꙋρανω, ο πατηρ, λογꙍ, και πνευμα αγιον· και τꙋτοι οι τρεις εν εισιν. [ευθευς τε προςιθησι]	7. Οτι τρεις εισιν οι μαρτυρꙋντες εν τω ꙋρανω, πατηρ, λογꙍ, και πνευμα αγιον· και ꙋτοι οι τρεις εν εισι.	7 Οτι τρεις εισιν οι μαρτυρꙋντες εν τω ꙋρανω, πατηρ, λογꙍ, και πνευμα, και ουτοι οι τρεις εν εισιν.
8. Και τρεις εισιν οι μαρτυρꙋντες εν τη γη, πνευμα, υδωρ, και αιμα· και τρεις εν εισι. [καθως εν τισι κωδηξιν ευρισκηται]	8. Και τρεις εισιν οι μαρτυρꙋντες εν τη γη, πνευμα, υδωρ, και αιμα.	8. Και τρεις εισιν μαρτυρꙋντες εν τη γᴧ, πνευμα, υδωρ, και αιμα.

The COMPLUTENSIAN POLYGLOTT:	ROBERT STEPHENS:	*The* BERLIN MS.

The COMPLUTENSIAN POLYGLOTT:

7. Οτι Τρεις εισιν οι μαρτυ-ρᾶντες εν τω ᾳρανω, ο πατηρ, και ο λογος, και το αἱιον πνευμα· και οι τρεις εις το εν εισι.

8. Και τρεις εισιν οι μαρτυ-ρᾶντες επι της γης το πνευμα, και το υδωρ και αιμα.

ROBERT STEPHENS:

7. Οτι τρεις εισιν οι μαρτυ-ρᾶντες εν τω ᾳρανω, ο πατηρ, ο λογ☉, και το αγιον πνευμα· και ᾳτοι οι τρεις εν εισι.

8. Και τρεις εισιν οι μαρτυ-ρᾳντες εν τη γη, το πνευμα, και το υδωρ, και το αιμα, και οι τρεις εις το εν εισι.

The BERLIN MS.

7. Οτι τρεις εισιν οι μαρτυ-ρᾳντες εν τω ᾳρανω, ο πατηρ, και ο λογ☉, και το αγιον πνευμα· και οι τρεις εις το εν εισιν.

8. Και τρεις εισιν οι μαρτυ-ρᾳντες επι της γης, το πνευμα, και το υδωρ, και το αιμα.

NEWTON.   Upon the face of this collection of the *Greek* readings of this contested passage, compared with the *Latin* copies, the following observations offer themselves to the mind.

1. The *Latin* copies, universally, read *Spiritus* SANCTUS [the *Holy* Spirit] in the *seventh* verse; which epithet is not found in the *Codex Britannicus*.

2. The same *Latin* copies, universally, read *Tres* UNUM *sunt* [*Three* ARE *one*] in the conclusion of the *seventh* verse. But the *Complutensian Polyglott*, and the *Berlin* MS, read τρεις εις το εν εισι, which is equivalent to *Tres* IN *unum sunt*, or *These three* AGREE IN *one*.

3. The *Latin* copies have, universally, the concluding clause of the *eighth* verse. It stands thus (with so few exceptions as not to merit any notice) in those copies, IN *unum sunt*, or *These three* AGREE IN *one*. But the *Dublin* MS, the *Codex Britannicus*, the Edition of *Complutum*, and the *Berlin* MS, do not contain this concluding clause, under

any

any terms, or mode of expreſſion, whatſo- NEWTON.
ever.

Now theſe differences, from their *nature*,
cannot be imputed to any tranſlators, with
any reaſonable degree of probability. For, if
theſe expreſſions (nay whole clauſes) were
loſt by any Tranſlators,—they muſt have ſo
loſt them by *incapacity*, or by *inadvertence*.
Now no tranſlator can be ſuppoſed to have
been ſo INCAPABLE, as not to know how
to render theſe *omitted* expreſſions, and
clauſes, from the *Latin*, into the *Greek*,
language. And the omiſſions ſeem to be
too large, and to contain too many words,
to permit a well grounded idea of their
having been loſt, through INADVERTENCE,
by a *tranſlator*; whoſe office, *verbum de verbo
reddere*, requires him to yield an inceſſant
attention to his original, and to give to his
tranſlation frequent, and painful, reviſals,
leſt he ſhould injure, or betray, the meaning
of his author.

It ſeems, therefore, to be almoſt an impoſſibility, that theſe aberrations ſhould have

U   ariſen

NEWTON. arifen from any (*fuppofed*,—for there is no proof that there *ever were* any fuch) tranflators. From whence it feems to follow, that they have arifen from the other caufe, ftated in the objection,—namely, the *bare errors of Tranfcribers*, whofe object hath always been to hurry through their tafk, as faft as poffible, without much regard to any thing, beyond the reward expected at the clofe of it.

L. " Erafmus *tells us, that he never* " *faw it*" [the verfe, 1. *John*, v: 7.] " *in any* Greek *MS*; *and, by confequence*, " *not in that corrected one*" [the *Codex Britannicus*] " *which fell into his hands.*" —(p. 528.)

Erafmus did, in the earlier part of his controverfy on this fubject, affirm, that he had, at *that time*, never feen any Greek MS, which contained this difputed paffage. But he admits, in another place, that he *(g)* did afterwards

---

(g) Pages 139—149.
The charge, here infinuated, of this MS having been corrected by the *Latin*, has been confidered in the pages juft referred to.

afterwards find this verſe in the *Codex Bri-* Newton.
tannicus; which HE COLLATED *in England.*

LI. " *He that ſhall hereafter meet*
" *with it*" [this diſputed text] " *in any*"
[*Greek*] " *book, ought firſt, before he in-*
" *ſiſt upon the authority of that book, to*
" *examine, whether it has not been cor-*
" *rected by the* Latin, *and whether it be*
" *ancienter than the* Lateran *Council; for*
" *if it be liable to either of theſe two ex-*
" *ceptions, it can ſignify nothing to pro-*
" *duce it.*"

This concluſion,—although, in general,
juſt,—is liable to many exceptions. One of
them, at leaſt, ought here to be mentioned :
which is,—that, where any *Greek* MS NOW
exiſts, which was, probably, or even confeſſedly, copied, or written, SINCE the thirteenth century (the æra of the *Lateran*
Council)—ſuch MS is not to take its eſti-
mation, *ſtrictly,* from the *time, when* it was
ſo copied; but from ſome higher æra, which
gave date to *that* Copy, *from which* it was
ſo tranſcribed.

But

NEWTON. But, Sir, I am contented to take the con‑
clufion in its *ſtrictest* terms, as to ſeveral
parts of the evidence, herein before adduced
to the originality of this verſe. For I find
myſelf, even in that ſituation, at liberty to
affirm, that the απος ολ©,—the *Confeſſion of
Faith* of the *Greek* Church,—the Diſputa‑
tion, and the *Synopſis*, of *Athanaſius*,—the
Greek MSS of *Walafrid Strabo*, and of *Je‑
rome*,—the quotation of *Euthymius Zygabe‑
nus*,—and the authority of the Council of
Epheſus, in A. D. 431, upon which the *Ar‑
menian* Verſion was framed, and adjuſted,—
(*b*) form an accumulation of GREEK teſti‑
monies, the authority of which cannot be
denied, even upon the terms of the objec‑
tion itſelf. For there is no color of reaſon,
to affert that ANY of them have been " *cor‑
" rected by the Latin.*" And there is no
ground, to ſuppoſe, that they are not, ALL,
more ancient, in point of date, than the *La‑
teran* Council.

This moſt reſpectable objector, laſtly,
ſtates his own paraphraſe of this paſſage, in
order

(*b*) Pages 22—24, 48—50, 100—103, and 196—264.

order to fhew that the *fenfe* of St. *John*, Newton.
without the teftimony of the *Three in Hea-*
ven, is (to ufe his own words) " *plain, and*
" *ftrong ; but if you infert that teftimony, you*
" *fpoil it.*"

This *fenfe*, or *internal evidence*, of the paffage, will be confidered hereafter : in which
confideration, I truft, the very oppofite conclufion will appear. At the fame time I
moft freely admit, in common with this illuftrious objector, (*i*) that I " *have that ho-*
" *nor for St.* John, *as to believe that he wrote*
" *good fenfe ; and, therefore,*" do moft implicitly " *take that fenfe to be* his, *which is*"
[or which, at leaft, appears to me to be]
" *the beft.*"

And here, Sir, I wifh to take my leave of
the objections, urged by this great ornament
of human nature, this " *firft, and chiefeft, of*
the race of men :"—from whom it will detract little, that he cherifhed an erroneous
opinion as to this difputed paffage ; his errors
being more than redeemed by his candor,

U 3 his

(i) Page 530.

NEWTON. his miftakes by his unaffected magnanimi-
ty.—His own declaration, ftated in the outfet of thefe obfervations, affords the faireft
reafon, the moft available pretenfions, to
conclude, that, if Sir *Ifaac Newton* had been
apprifed of ALL the *pofitive* evidence, which
has been alledged, in the preceding pages,
on behalf of the authenticity of this text (a
great part of which was utterly unknown to
him) : he would not have caft the weight of
his name into that fcale, which (as it feems,
he would then have confeffed) OUGHT NOT
to preponderate in the prefent queftion.

It feems neceffary, now, to attend to M.
Griefbach, and Mr. *Bowyer*, according to
the plan heretofore laid down. But as the
objections, infifted upon by thefe Writers,
ftand on foundations very fimilar to thofe of
Dr. *Benfon*, and Sir *Ifaac Newton*, which
have been already difcuffed ; they will,
fortunately, require no more than a very
brief confideration.

And firft, for M. *Griefbach*.

I. " R.

I. " R. Stephens *confulted, indeed,* Griesbach. " *fome*" [Greek] " *MSS, but they were* " *few;* viz. *in the Gofpels,* ten; *in the* " *Acts, and Epiftles,* eight; *and* two *in* " *the Apocalypfe.*" (*k*)

This is but an indifferent fpecimen of the *accuracy* of M. *Griefbach.* In the Gofpels, *R. Stephens* confulted fourteen MSS, at leaft, inftead of *ten*, as here alledged; in the Acts, ten, at leaft, inftead of *eight*; in the Epiftles, twelve, at leaft, inftead of *eight*; and in the Apocalypfe, four, at leaft, inftead of *two.*

The margins of *R. Stephens*'s Edition prove *(l)* thefe allegations, beyond all contradiction. And there is no room to conclude, either from *R. Stephens*'s preface, or from any mode of found argumentation, that thefe particular MSS, thus cited, were

U 4 all

(*k*) Vol. ii, Preface, page 25.
(*l*) To the Gofpels *R Stephens* has cited the MSS β, γ, δ, ε, ζ, η, θ, ι, ϛ, ια, ιβ, ιγ, ιδ, and ιϛ.
To the Acts, β, δ, ε, ζ, η, θ, ι, ια, ιγ, and ιϛ.
To the Epiftles, β, δ, ε, ζ, θ, ι, ια, ιβ, ιγ, ιδ, ιε, and ιϛ.
And to the Apocalypfe, ε, ια, ιε, and ιϛ.

GRIESBACH. *all* the MSS, of *R. Stephens*, which contained thofe feveral portions of Scripture. *Fourteen* MSS, only, are directly CITED, by him, to the Gofpels; but that circumftance does not prove, that the whole *fixteen* did not contain the Gofpels. *Twelve* MSS, only, are directly CITED to the Epiftles; but that circumftance does not prove, that the Epiftles were not exhibited in all the *fixteen* MSS, poffeffed by *R. Stephens*.

The Divines of the Univerfity of *Louvaine*, who were contemporaries with *R. Stephens*, pofitively affirm, in their Bible, publifhed A. D. 1574, that ALL the MSS of *R. Stephens* did contain (*m*) not only the Epiftle of St. *John*, but *this difputed paffage* alfo. And this teftimony, at leaft, proves the *general belief*, and reputation, of that age, and time, to be fo; and, added to the evidence of *R. Stephens's* own marginal references, on this verfe, form a body of proof, which no cavils, or conjectures, of modern times,—which nothing but the production

of

(*m*) " *Inter* OMNES Stephani *ne* UNUS *eft, qui diffideat*"— are the expreffions of thefe Divines, on the fubject, now under confideration.

of *R. Stephens*'s MSS themselves,—can ever GRIESBACH. difcredit, or deftroy.

II. " *And thefe MSS were not collated*
" *by* R. Stephens *himfelf, but by* Henry,
" *his Son, a boy of eighteen years of age.*"

It appears, from *Mattaire*, as well as from other proofs, that *Henry Stephens*, under the tuition of his Father, acquired, very early, a compleat knowledge of the *Greek* language. Thus capacitated for the employment, it is no wonder that the father required, or that the fon afforded, his *affiftance* in thefe laborious collations. But that *R. Stephens*'s MSS were " NOT *collated by R. Stephens*," at all ; but that the tafk of collation was devolved on *Henry*, his Son, fingly, and exclufively,—as is afferted in the preceding objection ;—is not to be admitted for a moment ;—becaufe there is no pretence *for* the affertion, and becaufe reafon, propriety, and probability, are uniformly *againft* it.

III. " *There are very many good, and*
" *valuable, readings, in* R. Stephens's
" *MSS*

GRIESBACH.   *" MSS, which are not inserted in the*
" margin of his Book."

When M. *Griesbach* shall be able to produce these original MSS, he may be at
liberty, perhaps, to bring this accusation
against *R. Stephens.* It is, at present, as
groundless, and improbable, as it is uncan-
did, and injurious.

IV. *" R. Stephens has very often*
" closely followed the footsteps of Eras-
" mus, or some other Editor, in opposition
" to the faith, and authority, of all his
" MSS: and the boasts, which he makes
" in his preface, as to his very great care,
" and diligence, in collating his MSS, and
" his faithfulness in settling his text, are
" empty and false." (n)

The answer to the last, preceding, objection, will suffice for this also. It merits no
further attention.

Thus far for M. *Griesbach*'s Preface to
his second volume.

In

(n) Preface, p. 26.

In his differtation (o) upon this contefted GRIESBACH. text, he affirms that it exifts in no *Greek* MS, except that of *Dublin*, which, he fays, is the *Codex Britannicus* of *Erafmus*—that *Valla's Latin*, as well as his *Greek*, MSS did not contain this verfe—that it firft appeared, in *Greek*, in the Acts of the Council of *Lateran*—that it was not read in the ancient, *Armenian* Verfion, (which he afferts on the bare authority of *Sandius)*—that the Preface to the canonical Epiftles is not *Jerome's*, —that *Eucherius*, (p) *Jerome*, and *Augufline*, have not quoted the verfe—that *Fulgentius* ufes the word *confitetur*—that the confeffion of faith of *Eugenius*, and the *African* Bifhops under *Huneric*, has no fubfcription, or fignature (whereas it is figned by no lefs than *four* Bifhops)—and that *Vigilius* was the firft who explicitly quoted this difputed paffage. It is fufficient to have barely mentioned thefe objections: not only becaufe they

are

(o) Pages 225—226.
(p) The proofs, which he brings, as to *Eucherius*, are, that *Flacius* publifhed an edition of the *Formula*, in which he left out this paffage, and that *Eucherius* has not quoted it in other parts of his works.

GRIESBACH. are, in general, brought forward without even the decency of an attempt to support them; but becaufe they have been already replied to, and, as it is truſted, overthrown, without a ſingle exception, in the preceding pages.

The objections, which follow, ſeem to require a more particular conſideration.

> V. " *It is now beyond a doubt, that*
> " R. Stephens *had no more MSS of the*
> " *catholic Epiſtles than ſeven*; *and that*
> " *none of theſe contained any part of this*
> " *diſputed paſſage.*" (p. 226.)

It is truly aſtoniſhing, to ſee ſo many men of learning, *Le Long*, (taking them in order of time) *Emlyn, La Croze*, Sir *Iſaac Newton*, Dr. *Benſon*, and M. *Grieſbach* (not to mention any other modern Writers in *Germany*) follow each other ſo implicitly in ſo groſs an error. Thoſe *Greek* MSS, which now ſubſiſt in the Royal Library, at *Paris*, have been already proved not to be thoſe, of *R. Stephens.* And yet this is the ſuppoſition, up-

on which this charge, and all fimilar char- Griesbach.
ges, againſt *R. Stephens*, are founded.—But
R. Stephens can bear them all. Such accuſations tarniſh not his well-earned honors.
They prove nothing—but the precipitancy
of his accuſers.

VI. " *The* obelus, *which is rightly*
" *fixed in* R. Stephens's Latin *editions,*
" *is found out of its proper place in his*
" Greek" [Edition of A. D. 1550.]

In printing his *Latin* (as well as his *Greek*)
Teſtaments, when *R. Stephens* did not find
certain words, or ſentences, in ſome of his
MSS, which ſtood in the reſt,—he marked,
in his text, the words, ſo omitted in theſe
MSS, with an *obelus,* and crotchet; refer-
ing, in his margin, to the particular MSS,
in which thoſe words were ſo wanting. He
acted thus in his *Latin* Edition of A. D.
1539. He placed this paſſage entire in the
text; he then fixed his obelus, and crotchet,
ſo as to comprehend, within them, all the
words of this diſputed paſſage, from *in cælo*
to *in terra,* incluſively; and laſtly, inſerted
in

Griesbach. in his margin the *insignia* of *four* only, of his *Latin* MSS: Thus signifying to his readers, that the words so included within his obelus, and crotchet, were not, indeed, contained in *those four* MSS,—but that they were for that very reason (*q*) contained in *all the rest.*

Let *R. Stephens*, then, by his *Latin* Testament of A. D. 1539, determine the dispute about his *Greek* Testament of A. D. 1550. His sentence, in respect of these two Testaments, will stand thus:

    In all my Latin *MSS from whence I compiled my* Latin *Edition of A. D.* 1539, *the whole of the disputed passage,* John, v : 7, *and* 8, *is read, except in* four *MSS only; in which* four, *the words from* in cælo *to* in terra *(inclusive) alone are wanting :—*

    In all my Greek *MSS from whence I compiled my* Greek *Edition of A. D.* 1550, *the whole of the same disputed passage is also*

(*q*) Exceptio probat regulam, in non exceptis.

alfo read, except in feven *only; in which* GRIESBACH.
feven *the words,* εν τω ϭϱανω, *alone are
wanting.*

This is the plain language of *R. Stephens*'s
crotchets, in both his *Latin,* and *Greek,*
Teftaments. And this is, alfo, as to the
Greek, what hath been uniformly contended
for, throughout the preceding pages. The
collation, and comparifon, of *R. Stephens*'s
Latin Edition (*r*) with his *Greek* one, feem
only to prove, that his conduct hath been
uniformly fincere, in both. His, admitted,
integrity as to the *Latin* Teftament, is a
warranty, a pledge, for the like integrity in
his *Greek* Teftament. And the defenders of
the authenticity of this verfe, of St. *John,*
ought not to wifh for a more favorable ar-
bitration, in the debate, as to the *intentions* of
R. Stephens in placing his crotchets, than
this expofition of them by *Stephens* himfelf.

VII. " *What learned men have long*
" *feen*" [as to the MS of *Berlin*] " *I*
" *have*

(*r*) He printed feveral Editions of both But thefe
two, principal, Editions alone are here ftated, for the
fake of argument.

GRIESBACH.   " *have found to be most certain, on a strict*
     " *examination of the MS itself, and on a*
     " *comparison of it in part with that Edi-*
     " *tion ; namely, that it is nothing but a*
     " *transcript from the Bible of* Complu-
     " tum." (p. 226.)

In addition to the arguments which I ventured to urge against this objection, in some
(s) of the preceding pages, I have just been
obliged, and honored, by M. I. F. ZOELLNER,
of *Berlin*, with a very particular description
of this MS : by which it appears, (as I have
before contended) that it is NOT a transcript
from the Bible of *Complutum*.

  " *Gratissimum sane mihi fuisset, vir plur.*
  " *reverende, si literas Tuas ad* GIBBONEM
  " *legere potuissem, quo melius ea Tecum com-*
  " *municarem, quæ præcipue scire Tua interest.*
  " *Libris autem* Anglicanis *plerumque serò ad*
  " *nos venientibus, hanc quoque discussionem eru-*
  " *ditam* BEROLINI *frustra quæsivi. Sed ut*
  " *nihilominus Tibi officium meum probem, quæ*
           " *ad*

(s) Pages 159—171.

" *ad lucem difquifitionibus Tuis affundendam* GRIESBACH,
" *valere opinor, breviter ea commemorabo.*

" *Quod, quidem, ad antiquitatem Codicis*
" RAVIANI *attinet, vereor ut fufficiat, fi*
" *meam tantùm fententiam Tecum communicare*
" *velim. Sunt enim tam multa in* Germania
" *recentiffimis temporibus, hac de re, a viris*
" *eruditiffimis difputata, ut meum non fit inter*
" *criticos tantos tantas componere lites.*

" *Quod* La Crozius *fimpliciter dicit, fcribam*
" *indoctum etiam mendas typographicas ex-*
" *preffiffe, ut omnino conftet, &c,—id quidem*
" *nimis feftinanter ab illo dictum eft. Codex*
" Ravianus *a textu* Complutenfium INNU-
" MERIS LOCIS *difcrepat.*"

And, after affigning many, and, as it
feems, unanfwerable, reafons for his opinion,
and judgement, he fubjoins this very probable conclufion.—" *Quæ cum ita fint, haud ab-*
" *fonum foret, fi cui placeret, codicem noftrum*
" *apographum effe,* NON *è* Complutenfibus,
" *fed ex* ALIO *codice manufcripto, quem Edi-*

X
" *tores*

Griesbach. " *tores* Complutenfes *potiffimùm fecuti funt,*
" *concinnatum.*" (*t*)

VIII. " *This verfe was not read*" [or
quoted] " *at the Council of Nice.*"––(p.
227,) and is, therefore, fpurious.

This hath been often faid :––but, as it
feems, without fufficient grounds. For how
is this affumption to be proved ? Not by the
Acts of this Council. For they are Decrees
only, and Ordinances, and fet forth no
texts of Scripture, whatever, refpecting the
nature, the attributes, (*u*) or even the exiftence, of the Deity. Nor can it be proved
by the *(Nicene)* Creed of this Council.
For that, although infifting ftrongly on the
divinity of *Jefus Chrift*, does not contain a
fingle citation from Scripture. Nor is this
affumption to be proved from thofe pretended difputes of Bifhops, and others, at that
Council. For thefe are mere fables, compofed by *Gelafius Cyzicenfis*, (*x*) fome centuries

(*t*) Appendix, No. XXIII, where this letter is given
more at large

(*u*) The only texts, cited in them, refer to Eunuchs,
and ufury *Harduin in loco.*

(*x* *P* 1, Art, *Gelafius.*

ries after that Council was held, as is now GRIESBACH.
univerfally admitted. The *Nicene* Fathers,
therefore, are filent, as to this contefted verfe,
in their *Acts*, and *Creed*; but that filence is a
thing the moft remote in nature from a
proof, that it did *not* then fubfift in their
Greek MSS; or that it was not even quoted
at the council of *Nice*.

Whenever it fhall be affirmed, then, that
the Acts, and Creed, of the *Nicene* Fathers
have not mentioned the verfe, 1. *John*, v: 7,
and that it is, therefore, fpurious :——it
would, as it feems, be no very unapt *corol-
lary*, to fuch a propofition, to fay—*Nor have
they mentioned the baptifmal inftitution*,—therefore that is fpurious : *Nor that paffage in St.
John's Gofpel, I, and my father, are one*,—
therefore that is fpurious : *Nor any part either of that Gofpel, or of his Epiftles*,—therefore they are fpurious : *Nor yet any one paffage, from any one part of the Bible, refpecting
the nature of the God-head*,—therefore, in
fine, thofe paffages are all fpurious !————The
inference is either valid in all its parts, or
it is valid in none. But, in truth, it is utterly invalid. It has no foundnefs in it. It

proves

Griesbach, proves too much, and therefore proves nothing.

M. *Griesbach* proceeds to remark, (*y*) that *Latin* MSS, written before the *tenth* century, do not contain this disputed passage;—that the MSS of the Vulgate had it not, at the time when *Jerome*'s preface was written;—that some copies have the preface, and yet do not read the verse; and that, in others, it is not placed in the body of the text, but in the margin.

I shall content myself, with just remarking, in reply to these observations, that the *second*, and *third*, of them have been answered (*z*) already. The *first* should be answered now, if the learned professor had sufficiently ascertained his own meaning. The last of them will receive its answer hereafter.

IX. " *The preface of* Jerome *is not* " *found in any MS, written before the* " *time of* Charles *the* Bald, *in the ninth* " *century.*" (p. 235.)

Admitting

(*y*) Page 228.
(*z*) Pages 97—104, and 241—266.

If this allegation were true (which, how- Griesbach.
ever, (*a*) is not the cafe) it would not prove
that this preface was not written by *Jerome.*
A confiderable fpace of time muft elapfe, after
the writing of this pieface in *Afia,* befoie
the *Latins* of *Europe,* in general, could know
(by the flow, and expenfive, method of
propagating books then in ufe) that fuch a
preface even exifted. And, when the fact
became, in fome meafure, known, the MSS,
prior to that time, could not receive it ; for
it was too large a piece of compofition to be
interlined, or written *in the margin.* As it
was no pait of the facred Canon, many
would refufe to infeit it, even in the MSS
written *after* the knowledge of it became
general. Thofe Chriftians, who favored
the *Arian, Semi-Arian, Sabellian,* or even
the *Eunomian,* and *Eutychian,* fyftems, would
certainly deny it a place in their books.
And thus it is poffible, that fome few MSS
(for they cannot be many) written in, or
before, the *ninth* century, may now be produced, in which this pieface is not found.
But this circumftance (as befoie obferved)
is

(*a*) M. SIMON, *Hift. du Texte,* p 208 *Hift des Ver-*
fions, p 105.—MARIIANiY, Proleg. Vol. I. Op *Hieron.*
Dr. BURNIT, Letter 1.

is far from proving the preface *to be spurious* :—especially when it is further considered, that, IN *the ninth century*, this preface was publicly admitted to be the work of *Jerome* ; as appears by the *Glossa ordinaria* of *Walafrid Strabo*, which hath been already called (*a*) in evidence to this point, in the preceding pages.

────────────

And now, Sir, I beg to be dismissed from M. GRIESBACH,—in order that I may, lastly, attend to Mr. BOWYER, as was originally proposed.—And his objections are, chiefly, these which follow.

BOWYER.
I. " *St*. Cyprian *does not quote the* " *verse*, totidem verbis, *as the text is* " *now read, though Bishop* Pearson " (*Not. ad* Cyprian. de Unitate Ec- " clesiæ, *p*. 109) *rather too strongly af-* " *serts* Cyprianum citasse ante Hiero- " nymi tempora. The *words of* Cy- " prian *are*—Et hi tres IN unum funt "

X 3 *Cyprian*

(*a*) Page 110—Note *I*.
See also *Bengelius*, Edit. *Tubingæ*, A. D. 1734, pa. 763.

Cyprian DOES quote the verfe *totidem* BOWYER. *verbis,* (as far as his words are meant to be a quotation) and Bifhop *Pearfon*'s affertion is NOT too ftrong. *Cyprian*'s woids are NOT " Et hi tres IN unum funt," but " Et hi tres (*b*) unum funt," an exact Tranfcript of the *Latin* Text of St. *John.*

II. " *And in another place,* Cyprian
" *(Epif. ad* P. Julianum, *p.* 223, *Ed.*
" Pearfon (Quæro cujus Dei, *&c.*—
" Cum tres unum funt. *It is certain*
" *St.* Cyprian *does not cite it in teims*
" *from the text, nor yet, in both places,*
" *agreeably to himfelf.*"

The Epiftle, here referred to, is *Ad Ju-baianum,* not *Julianum.* In the former in-ftance, which has been confidered under the laft, preceding, objection, *Cyprian* cites the claufe *in direct terms* from the Text of St. *John.* The latter inftance is rather an al-lufion, or a reference, (*c*) than a direct quotation.

III. " *He*

(*b*) Page 37, and Appendix, No. III.
(*c*) Appendix, No. IV.

Bowyer.   III. " *He does not say in either, the*
" *Father, the Word, and the Holy Ghost :*
" *but in the former, the Father, Son,*
" *and Holy Ghost ; and in the latter,*
" *the Creator, Christ, and the Holy*
" *Ghost.*"

Cyprian only meant to *quote*, directly, the
concluding clause of the verse, " Et hi tres
unum sunt." And this he has literally done
in the former of these examples.

IV. " *The Montanists, soon* after *this*
" *time, generally interpreted the Spirit,*
" *Water, and the Blood, in the* eighth
" *verse, to denote, in their mystical sense,*
" *the Father, Son, and Holy Ghost.*"

The Heresy of *Montanus* began long *before* (not *after*) the time of *Cyprian*. What
the *Montanists* interpreted of the eighth verse
is of no consequence, unless it could be
proved that the seventh verse did not exist
in the times of the *Montanists*.

V. " *If so, it will be no hard thing*
X 4   " *to*

" *to suppose* Cyprian *to do the same.*" Bowyer.

If *to suppose* would have been *to succeed*, the question would have been decided long since. But if *Cyprian* had really done as this objection *supposes*, his quotation would have been " Et hi tres *in* unum sunt," according to the invariable *(d)* tenor of the *eighth* verse; which it is not. Mr. *Bowyer* has, indeed, endeavoured to give color to this objection, by affirming, as we have just seen, that *Cyprian* did quote " *in* unum." But the affirmation is invalid; and the inference, is, therefore, inadmissible.

VI. " *It*" [the verse in question] " *first appeared to the public in* Greek, *in* " *the* Complutensian *Edition, upon the* " *authority of* Thomas Aquinas, *whose* " *note is printed in the margin of the* " Greek."

If Mr. *Bowyer* here means that the verse first appeared to the public in *printed Greek*,

(d) The exceptions to this description are so very few, as not to merit notice.

Bowyer. in the *Complutensian* Edition, the affertion may be juft The *Complutenfian* was not, however, the *firft*, printed, *Greek*, Teftament which appeared to the public ; for the firft Edition of *Erafmus* was publifhed long before the *Complutenfian*, viz. in A. D. 1516.

But the verfe, in queftion, did *not* appear, in the *Greek* of the *Complutenfian* Edition, upon the authority of *Aquinas*, in any refpect ; the marginal note, here (*e*) mentioned by Mr. *Bowyer*, having no fuch import, and being capable of no fuch conftruction.

And here, Sir, I take my leave of Mr. *Bowyer* :—who has, indeed, urged feveral other objections againft the originality of this verfe. But they have been already confidered, in fome part, or parts, of the preceding pages.

I am, Sir,

&c.

(*e*) Appendix, No. XVIII.

L E T T E R   V.

SIR,

I HAVE now replied to all thofe *objections*, which it feemed neceffary for me to ex-amine in detail.—And I am encouraged to hope, that (in having been thus enabled to detach thofe incumbrances from it,) the whole queftion, as to the authenticity of this contefted paffage, may be, henceforth, difcuffed in a lefs defultoiy manner. The fubject appears to be now compreffed within a fmall compafs ; and may now, therefore, as it feems, be quickly determined by a difcerning mind.

UPON A FULL CONSIDERATION, then, of the whole queftion (fetting afide thofe objections which have been alieady iefuted)

the

the only impeachments of this verfe, which claim the ferious deliberation of an unprejudiced mind, feem to be comprifed in thefe thiee, following, particulars: namely,

1. Its not being found in thofe parts of the works of many *Greek*, and of fome few *Latin*, Fathers; which have defcended to the piefent age:

2. Its not being found in any of the *Greek* MSS of the Scriptuies, which are now extent. And

3. The (fuppofed) injury done to the context of the Apoftle, by the admiffion of the text in queftion.

As to the firft of thefe objections,—it undoubtedly feems, on a primary view, a ftiange circumftance, that this verfe fhould not be found in thofe parts of the works of ceitain ancient *Chriftian* Fathers, which have remained to the piefent age. And this circumftance appeais the more peculiarly ftrange, when it is confidered, that many of
thefe

thefe Fathers wrote upon fubjects, which feemed to call for a citation of this verfe; as the Divinity of *Jefus Chrift*, and of the *Holy Spirit*; or that awful fubject, which involves them both in itfelf, the Trinity of perfons in the Godhead.

But, in anfwer to this objection, it ought to be obferved, in the firft place, that, at leaft, fome of thefe Fathers, perhaps all of them, conceived the words of this verfe to indicate an *unity of confent*, only, and not an *unity of nature*, in thefe *three*, heavenly, *Witneffes*. We know, that many learned men have given this expofition to the verfe; for their works, particularly thofe of *Calvin*, and *Beza*, prove it to us. Upon this *hypothefis* (and it feems very far from being a forced, or an extravagant, idea) every difficulty vanifhes at once. Thofe pious *Chriftian* Fathers, whofe citations of this verfe have, fortunately, furvived to the prefent age, have quoted it in affirmation of the Divinity of the fecond, and third, Perfons in the Holy Trinity; becaufe they interpreted the verfe, as holding forth a proof of fuch Divinity.

Thofe

Thofe ancient Fathers, equally pious, perhaps, and equally fincere, whofe private
judgement reftricted their interpretation of
this text to an *unity of confent*, alone, would
not cite it, at all, in their Treatifes upon
thofe myfterious fubjects : becaufe, in their
apprehenfion, it did not eftablifh the doctrines, for which they contended. The
former clafs of thefe Fathers, would *fpeak* ;
becaufe they had no doubts as to the expofition of the verfe, but were convinced. The
latter would *be filent* ; becaufe they had their
doubts as to its interpretation, and were
perplexed. But, had not the verfe *exifted*,
at all, in their Bibles, it cannot even be
imagined that thefe laft-mentioned Fathers
would have contented themfelves with *filence* only. They would certainly have en-
quired of thofe, who thus quoted the verfe,
—*Why do you impofe fuch words upon us, as
parts of Holy Writ ? They do not exift in our
Bibles. Shew us, whence they are derived!*
But they have urged no fuch queftions, have
expreffed no fuch doubts, at any time, in
any part of their writings.

The

The *fact*, that some of these ancient Fathers have, and that others have not, quoted
this verse, is undoubtedly true. It is admitted by all. And this method of accounting for the ambiguity is, at least, obvious, and easy, as well as candid. It does
not suppose Men wilfully to betray the
truth, which Dr. *Benson* more than supposes
Robert Stephens, *Theodore Beza*, and the *Complutensian* Editors, to have done. It only
presumes Men formerly to have been, as
they now are, of different opinions in dif-
putable matters. It involves itself in no
painful perplexities. It offers no violence to
the plain dictates of common sense : and is,
therefore, most likely to be the truth.

When this argument is still further extended to the *opponents* of those Doctrines, in
support of which this verse hath been thus
alledged, it seems to become insuperable.
Throughout the vast series of *one thousand
four hundred* years, which intervened between the days of *Praxeas*, and the age of
Erasmus, not a single Author, whether *Pa-
tripassian*, *Cerinthian*, *Ebionite*, Arian, *Ma-
cedonian*,

cedonian, or *Sabellian*, whether of the *Greek* or *Latin*, whether of the Eastern, or Western, Church,—whether in *Asia*, *Africa*, or *Europe*,—hath ever taxed the various quotations of this verse, which have been set forth in the preceding pages, with interpolation, or forgery. Such silence *speaks*, most emphatically *speaks*, in favour of the verse. Had it, in any of these ages, been even suspected as supposititious, those adversaries (especially the *Arians*) would not have been silent only.—They would have exclaimed aloud, vehemently, and without ceasing ; they would have filled the *Christian* world with their invectives against those who quoted it : they would have charged them with absolute falsehood, with impiety, with blasphemy.

Thus it seems, that the circumstance of this verse *not having been quoted* by some ancient Fathers (as it has been by others) may be candidly, and satisfactorily, accounted for ; without suffering any impeachment to rest upon the authenticity of the verse, and without seeking any refuge for it, in such

parts

parts of the works of thofe Fathers, as are
now loft. But, fuppofing for a moment,
and for the fake of argument, that no ra-
tional account could be given of thefe omiffions; what would their weight be, in the
fcale of found judgment? All thefe *omiffions*
could amount, only, to a fort of *negative*
evidence. They might perplex the mind,
indeed, and lay it under difficulties; but
they could do no moie. If there weie No
pofitive evidence, that other Writeis, of
thofe ages, had quoted the verfe, thefe
omiffions, indeed, ought to turn the ballance againft the authenticity of this Text.
But there is fuch evidence. It is ample, it
is various, it is particular;—and it has been
particularly ftated. Thefe omiffions, therefore, cannot make what is in itfelf, and in
its own nature, only a difficulty, or a *nega-*
tive prefumption, become a *pofitive proof*, to
deftroy a fact well eftablifhed. It is impoffible for Writers of this age pofitively to
pronounce, on what grounds, or for what
reafons, certain *Greek*, or *Latin*, Authors,
who wrote more than a thoufand years ago,
have omitted to quote this text. This,

however,

however, may be said,—that such omissions are, at the most, only negative evidence. But *negative* evidence, although multiplied infinitely, will still be no more than *negative*. And the slightest *positive* testimony (which, however, is, in the present case, not slight, but most powerful, most convincing) will, at all times, and on all occasions, totally overballance, and destroy it.

The SECOND of these objections is,—That *the verse, in question, is not found in any of the* Greek *MSS of the Scriptures, which are now extant*. But to this objection let it be answered,

First, that the assertion is not strictly true. "*Apparent rari nantes in gurgite vasto.*" The MSS of *Dublin*, and *Berlin*, at least,—(and, as it seems by the admissions of *Wetstein*, *three* others)—yet remain to justify this observation.

But if it should be granted, for the present, that the verse, in question, is found in none of the very few *Greek* MSS, which are

now

now extant,—does it thence follow, that it was not found in many which formerly did exift, but are now perifhed? What may have been an omiffion in one MS, is no proof of interpolation in another. Such a conclu-clufion, at all times weak in itfelf, is, in the prefent cafe, overthrown by irrefiftible evidence. *Robert Stephens* points to this verfe in his MSS; *Theodore Beza* confirms his teftimony: and the *(f)* mifreprefentations of Father *Le Long*, on this great queftion, have been, in the preceding part of thefe letters, compleatly refuted. *Laurentius Valla* had feven *Greek* MSS for the ufe of his Commentary; he fets forth the very terms in which thofe MSS read this verfe: and the miftakes *(g)* of Dr. *Mill*, on this fubject, have been rectified. The Divines, of the Univerfity *(h)* of *Louvaine*, affirm that this

Y 2

verfe

(f) Pages 127—138.

(g) Notes on Pages 18, and 144.

(h) An Edition of the New Teftament was publifhed, by them, in A. D 1574, in which they fpeak of this contefted verfe, in the following terms.

" *The reading of this text is fupported by very many* Latin " *copies, and alfo by two* Greek *copies, produced by* Erafmus, " *one in* England, *the other in* Spain. *The* King's Bible " *agrees with the* Spanifh *MS in this paffage, as well as in* " *every other.* WE HAVE, OURSELVES, SEEN SEVERAL

verse existed in several ancient *Greek* MSS of
their times and their affirmation has never
been disproved. *Erasmus* confesses ONE
such MS; although, in truth, he ought to
have acknowledged EIGHT. *Walafrid Strabo* directs his readers, in all cases of difficulty, to resort to the *Greek* copies; which im-
plies that to have been his own practice:—
and this contested passage hath always stood
in his *Glossa ordinaria*. The ancient *Armenian* Version was rendered from the *Greek*
of the Council of *Ephesus*; and that Version
hath constantly exhibited this disputed text.
Jerome declares, that the *Greek* MSS of his
times read the verse; for he makes his appeal, in behalf of his Version, to the authority of the *Greek* text: and this passage hath
always existed in his Version. The απο϶ολος
contained the Epistles themselves, in the
original *Greek*, read in the *Greek* Churches
as early as (perhaps much earlier than) the
fourth, or fifth, century; and this απο϶ολος
has always exhibited this verse. And *Tertullian*, who quotes this verse in the second
century,

" OTHERS LIKE THESE. This verse is also found in
" ALL Stephens's *MSS; save that the words*, in Heaven,
" *are wanting in seven of them*,"

century, appeals to the " *authentico Græco*," the " *ipsæ literæ Apoftolorum*," the *Auto-graphs*, the very originals written by the A-poftles themfelves, which were extant in his times. Above all, the old *Italic* Verfion, which is believed to have been made in the firft century, and was read publicly among the Aflemblies of *Chriftians* for feveral cen-turies afterwards, has always had this paf-fage. Now, the Compilers of this very an-cient Verfion muft, either, have furrepti-tioufly introduced this verfe into their Tran-flation; or they muft have found it in the *Greek* Original, from whence they tranflated. But the former alternative feems impoffible to be adopted. For if it fhall even be grant-ed that this Verfion was not made until the *fecond* century; it is decifively certain, from the authority of *Tertullian*, which has juft been referred to, and of *Ignatius*, *(i)* that the *original Epiftles* of the Apoftles were then extant, to detect the daring impiety of in-ferting a forged, a falfe, text in the facred Volumes, if any fuch had been committed. But if this Verfion were executed in the *firft*

Y 3   century,

(i) See page 40—Note *q*.

century, which we have every reaſon to believe, St. *John* himſelf was then alive, to
ſtrike the bold impoſtors dead (as St. *Peter*,
(*k*) and St. *John*, together, had before puniſh-
ed *Ananias*, and *Sapphira*) for " *agreeing to-*
" *gether to tempt the Spirit of the Lord, and*
" *lying unto the Holy Ghoſt.*"—The former
alternative, therefore, being abſurd, and in-
admiſſible, the latter is at once ſubſtantiated :
namely, that the Tranſlators of the old *Italic* Verſion found this verſe in the original
Greek ; and therefore, that this *Italic* Verſion
holds the place, not of a *Greek* Copy only,
but of the very *Autograph* itſelf, the original
Epiſtle written by the pen of St. *John*.

Let it be further obſerved, on this head,
that ſome, tolerably ſatisfactory, account
may yet be given (although none can rea-
ſonably be required) why ſome of theſe ancient *Greek* MSS, now in debate, would probably (I had almoſt ſaid *neceſſarily*) be loſt
to the preſent times. The MSS of *Laurentius Valla* ; thoſe which were ſent into *Spain*,
from the *Vatican* Library, for the uſe of the
Complutenſian

(*k*) *Acts* of the Apoſtles, v, 1—11.

Complutenfian Editors; thofe which were in the poffeffion of *Robert Stephens*, of *Theodore Beza*, and of the Univerfity of *Louvaine*; exifted at a time when the Art of Printing, then recently invented, was beginning to extend itfelf to the *Greek* Teftament. Efteemed, as thefe written Copies, or MSS, muft be before the invention of Printing, the Books, multiplied by that invaluable Art, were fo much more compendioufly corrected, (a fingle revifion ferving for a thoufand Copies) were fo much lefs expenfive, fo much more eafy to be obtained, and fo much more convenient for ufe, that the value, *at that time*, of MSS muft be fo exceedingly depreciated at once, as almoft to fink into nothing. All thefe early Editors, when their MSS had ferved the purpofe of fettling the text of their refpective Editions, would confider them as defunct, in fome degree, and neglect them accordingly. This muft be the cafe, in general, for a long feafon after the printed Copies began to fpread themfelves over the *Chriftian* world. It was not until more modern times, when a tafte for critical enquiries of this kind arofe,

that

that thefe MSS (or rather the remnants of them) have been fo much fought for, and fo highly valued. In this interval of neg-lect, the MSS of *L. Valla*, and of the *Com-plutenfian* Editors; the MSS feen by the Divines of *Louvaine*; the MSS of *Robert Stephens*, and, by confequence, of *Theodore Beza* :—have perifhed   Had it not been for a fortunate (*l*) adventure of *Erafmus*, the MS of *L. Valla* had, in all probability, been ut-terly loft.   Had it not been for *Maffeius*, it can hardly be imagined that the *Complexiones* of *Caffiodorius* would ever have feen the light.   But we need not travel into *Italy* for inftances to illuftrate this argument.   Our own country exhibits an example fufficiently conclufive.   There was not a Cathedral, a Parifh-Church, a Monaftery, Nunnery, or Chantry, (not to bring private families into the account) within this kingdom, which may not be fuppofed to have poffeffed, at the æra of the invention of Printing, one MS Copy of the Scriptures, in the *Latin* lan-guage, at leaft.   And yet, where are thofe

MSS

(*l*) " FORTE in caffes meos incidit præda," &c, (Appendix, No. XV.)

MSS now ?—Out of the many THOUSANDS, which then exifted, it may be doubted whether there is a fingle *hundred* (there may, perhaps, be a folitary fcore, or two) which can now be produced. Let us hear, then, no more of the improbability of loft MSS, or of queftions framed on the idea of fuch an improbability. If the MSS of *Dublin*, and *Berlin*, had been annihilated fome centuries fince, and if it could be now fatisfactorily proved, that there did not fubfift, at this hour, a fingle *Greek* MS, which exhibited the verfe, in queftion: yet ftill the teftimonies of its *former* exiftence, which have been already produced, would greatly over-ballance any prefumption which might arife from fuch a circumftance; would controul, would fubdue, would govern, every unprejudiced mind.

Thefe reflections on the lofs of thofe ancient *Greek* MSS, which contained this verfe, will derive additional ftrength, perhaps, from a recollection of fimilar deftructions, which have befallen other monuments of ecclefiaftical, as well as prophane, learning; for

for which no adequate account can, human-ly, be given. If the demand be made, *What is become of thofe ancient* Greek *MSS, which contained this verfe; and why are they, in general, loft, rather than thofe which did not contain it?* It may, in return, be afked, what is become of the loft Books of *Livy?* What of the reft of the Hiftory of *Polybius?* Why hath the whole of *Claudian*'s Poem, on the *Gildonic* War, perifhed, the firft Book only excepted? Why hath *Origen*'s Confutation of *Celfus* furvived to our times; although the work itfelf is loft, which *Origen* fo confuted? Why have we a part, only, of the *Chronicon* of *Eufebius*; and that fcarcely the hundredth part, if *Jofeph Scaliger* may be credited? Why have we *Tacitus* only in part? And why have THOSE PARTICULAR PARTS, of all thefe MSS, been loft, RATHER THAN THE OTHERS which have, fortunate-ly, come down to our hands? Such queftions as thefe may be infinitely multiplied, whe-ther they relate to the records of things fa-cred, or profane, in general, or to thofe, now loft, *Greek* MSS of the New Teftament, in particular, which contained this verfe of

St.

St. *John*; but they will prove nothing, and, therefore, will deserve no attention. Whether these particular MSS, last mentioned, have perished by the slowly, yet surely, destructive efforts of Time; or by accident, negligence, or fraud: it matters not to enquire. Although " dead," they " yet speak" to us, in those faithful transcripts, and quotations, which are stated in the preceding Letters. And their testimony will be rejected only by prejudice; because it cannot be so rejected, but by a violation of all those rules of reasoning, and acting, by which men govern themselves on all other occasions.

The THIRD, and last, of these objections, is—*the supposed injury done to the context of the Apostle, by the admission of the verse in question.*

But this objection seems to have still less foundation than either of those, which preceded it. Before this Epistle was written, the two, opposite, Heresies of the *Cerinthians*, and the *Docetæ*, had arisen, to the great disturbance of the Christian Church. The *Docetæ* denied the INCARNATION of *Christ*;

refusing

refusing to admit that he was ever cloathed with human flesh, or ever took our nature upon him. The *Cerinthians*, on the contrary, denied his DIVINITY; affirming that *Jesus Christ* had no other *than* the human. Against such errors as these it was highly needful to protest, and to contend for the faith once delivered to the Saints: and St. *John* (*m*) alone, probably, then remained, of the sacred College of Apostles, to undertake the work with the authority of an inspired writer. In a few of the first verses of his Gospel he asserts the God-head of the WORD, the Almighty, and Eternal WORD, in confutation of the errors of *Cerinthus.* " *In* " *the beginning was the Word, and the Word* " *was with God, and the Word was God.* " *The same was, in the beginning, with God.* " *All things were made by him; and in him* " *was life.*" And in a succeeding verse he stops to affirm the incarnation of *Christ*, with a plainness, and precision, equally fatal to the opposite error of the *Docetæ.* " *And* " *the Word was* MADE FLESH, *and dwelt* " *among*

(*m*) Dr. *Townson's* Discourses on the Gospels. Ed. 1778, p. 204—5.

" *among us.*" He condemns the *Docetæ* alſo, in the *exordium* of this Epiſtle. " *That* " *which was from the beginning, which we* " *have* HEARD, *which we have* SEEN " WITH OUR EYES, *and our* HANDS HAVE " HANDLED, *of the* WORD *of life : declare* " *we unto you.*" He confounds the *Cerin-thians* in the cloſe of it. " *And we know* " *that the Son of God is come, and hath given* " *us an underſtanding that we may know him* " *that is true ; and we are in him that is* " *true, even in his Son Jeſus Chriſt :* THIS " *is the* TRUE GOD, *and eternal life.*"

Theſe ſeparate condemnations are found united together, and are urged in conjunc-tion, in that paſſage of this Epiſtle, which is the object of this preſent diſquiſition, and in a few words antecedent, and ſubſequent, to it. The text ſtands, literally, thus :

" *This is the victory that overcometh the* " *world ; even our faith. Who is he that* " *overcometh the world, but he that believeth* " *that Jeſus is the Son of God ? This is he* " *that came by Water, and Blood, even Jeſus* Chriſt,

" *Chriſt, not by Water only, but by Water and*
" *Blood. And it is the Spirit that beareth*
" *witneſs, becauſe the Spirit is truth. For*
" *there are three that bear record in Heaven ;*
" *the Father, the Word, and the Holy Ghoſt .*
" *and theſe three are one. And there are three*
" *that bear witneſs in earth ; the Spirit, the*
" *Water, and the Blood: and theſe three agree*
" *in one. If we receive the witneſs of Men,*
" *the witneſs of God is greater ; for this is*
" *the witneſs of God, which he hath teſtified*
" *of his Son.*"

And theſe words may, in the ſenſe juſt
ſtated, be thus paraphraſed.

" It is this conviction, which giveth us
" that *victory which overcometh the world,*
" which riſes ſuperior to its terrors, as well
" as to its temptations, *even our faith that*
" *Jeſus is the Son of,* a partaker of the ſame
" nature with, *God.* But *this Jeſus* is not
" a partaker of the divine nature, only ; for,
" when he *came* on earth, he took our hu-
" man nature alſo upon him, as appeared
" by the *Water, and Blood,* which flowed
" from

" from his fide, when pierced by the Spear,
" upon the Crofs. Thefe two truths, di-
" rectly oppofite to both your errors, ye
" *Cerinthians*, and ye *Docetæ*, are eftablifh-
" ed by the moft powerful proofs. *For*
" *there are three in Heaven, that bear record*
" to the DIVINE nature of Chrift: namely,
" *the Father*, who declared by his own voice
" from Heaven, This is my beloved Son,
" in whom I am well pleafed ; *the Word*,
" who continually affirmed of himfelf, that
" he was the predicted Meffiah, that he had
" exifted before Abraham, that he was the
" true Chrift, the Son of God ; *and the Holy*
" *Ghoft*, who defcended, in bodily prefence,
" like a Dove, upon his head, at his Bap-
" tifm, and fat in cloven tongues, like as of
" fire, upon the heads of his Apoftles after
" his refurrection. *And thefe three are one*
" in nature, or, at leaft, in unity of tefti-
" mony, proving againft you, ye *Cerinthians*,
" the DIVINITY of Jefus Chrift. *And*
" *there are* (moreover) *three which bear wit-*
" *nefs on earth*, againft you, ye *Docetæ* ; *and*
" *thefe three agree in one*, as to the reality of
" Chrift's taking our HUMAN natuie upon
" him :

" him : namely, *the Spirit,* (*n*) Soul, or
                                " Life,

(*n*) The last words of the first Martyr, St. *Stephen,*
were, Κυριε Ιησου, δεξαι το πνευμα μου. Which are
rendered, in our Translation, as to the word πνευμα, by
the same expression, *spirit,* as in this passage, and in the
same sense. " Lord Jesus, receive my *spirit.*" (*Acts,*
vii. 59.)

To which the following examples may not improperly, perhaps, be added.

Luke XXIII: 46—εις χειρας σα παρα- } *Into thy hands I*
        θησομαι το πνευμα } *commend my*
        μɤ— } SPIRIT.

——viii: 55—Και επεςρεψε το πνευ- } *And her* SPIRIT
        μα αυτης— } *came again, and*
         } *she arose.*

Matt. xxvii: 50—αφηκε το πνευμα— } *yielded up* [*the*
         } *ghost, or*] *his*
         } SPIRIT.

John XIX: 30—κλινας την κεφαλην, } *He bowed his head,*
        παρεδωκε το πνευ } *and gave up* [*the*
        μα— } *ghost, or*] *his*
         } SPIRIT.

I have herein endeavoured to keep the paraphrase of
Erasmus in view : but the elegance, and force, of his
Latin, are not, easily, to be transfused into another
language.

" *Tres sunt enim in cœlo, qui testimonium præbent Christo,*
" *pater, sermo, et spiritus sanctus.* PATER, *qui semel,*
" *atque iterum, voce cœlitùs emissà, palàm testatus est hunc*
" *esse filium suum, egregiè charum, in quo nihil offenderet*
" SERMO, *qui tot miraculis editis, qui moriens, ac resurgens,*
" *declaravit se verum esse Christum, Deum pariter atque*
" *hominem, Dei & hominum conciliatorem* SPIRITUS
" SANCTUS, *qui in baptizati caput descendit, qui post resur-*
" *rectionem delapsus est in discipulos. Atque horum trium*
" *summus est consensus. Pater est autor, Filius nuntius,*
" *Spiritus suggestor.*

" *Tria sunt item in terris, quæ attestantur Christum:*

" Life, *(Spiritus humanus)* which he breath-
" ed forth upon the Crofs, when he gave
" up the Ghoft; and *the Water, and the*
" *Blood,* which flowed from his fide (as
" was before obferved) when they looked
" on him whom they pierced. Thefe, ye
" *Cerinthians,* thefe, ye *Docetæ,* are the
" teftimonies which overthrow both your
" errors: proving *Jefus Chrift* to have a di-
" vine, as well as a human, nature; to be
" God as well as man. *If ye receive the*
" *witnefs of Men, the witnefs of God is*
" *greater: for this is the witnefs of God,*
" *which he hath teftified of his Son.*"

If this comment, and paraphrafe, be juft,
the context of the Apoftle is fo far from re-
ceiving any injury, by the retention of the
verfe, in queftion; that it would lofe all its

Z

genuine

" *Spiritus huma* ius, *quem pofuit in crucem; et aqua, et fan-*
" *guis, qui fluxit è latere mortui. Et hi tres teftes confen-*
" *tiunt.*'
    (PARAPHRASEON *Erafmi* in Nov. Teft Tom. ii.
      Page 347, Edit. *Bafil* A. D 1541)
   This paraphrafe was publifhed by *Erafmus,* about nine-
teen years after his re-admiffion of the verfe, 1. *John,*
v. 7, into the facred page. It feems impoffible to read it,
without believing, that *Erafmus* was, at *that time,* at leaft,
fully convinced of the *authenticity* of this text.

genuine fpirit, would become unapt, and
feeble in its application, and therefore could
hardly be faid to fubfift, without it.

Indeed, the exiftence of the feventh verfe
appears to be effential to the context, under
any interpretation whatfoever, which may
be annexed to this part of the Epiftle of St.
John. In whatever point of view we place
thefe fix, fucceffive, verfes, the expreffions,
" *Witnefs of God,*" in the ninth verfe, can
find no due antecedent in any of them, can,
indeed, bear no proper reference to any
preceding paffage of the whole Chapter,
fave to the feventh verfe. So that if this
verfe (the verfe in queftion) fhould be ex-
punged from the Epiftle, it feems that the
other muft, neceffarily, be involved in the
like profcription.

If, Sir, it fhall be further required, that
fome probable account be given of the abfence of the text, now in debate, from fome
of the ancient MSS of this Epiftle of St.
John,—I feel no repugnance in believing, I
fee no abfurdity in concluding, that this
verfe

verfe was thus, *partially*, loft in fome period
of that interval, which elapfed between the
death of St. *John*, in A. D. 101, and the revifion of the New Teftament by *Jerome*, a-
bout A. D. 384. Whether this defalcation
happened by accident, or fraud: Whether
fome hafty, and heedlefs Scribe, having juft
inferted the οι μαρτυρουντες of the *feventh* verfe
in his copy, fuffered his eye, in its next
glance from his Tranfcript to the Original,
to fix itfelf on the fame words, οι μαρτυρουντες,
which alfo occur in the *eighth* verfe; and,
being fatisfied with the identity of the expreffion, travelled onwards through his tafk,
without perceiving the error into which he
had fallen: OR, Whether, in the violent
contefts which arofe within this period, between the opponents of *Arius*, and his abet-
tors, the *Arian* Writers purpofely left out
of their own tranfcripts the words, which
ftood, in the (*o*) Original, between thofe
two *Greek* Participles, and which are the
very words now in difpute, hoping that their
Copies might, in time, be followed as origi-

Z 2   nals,

(*o*) In fome erroneous Copics, the words εν τη γη, are
alfo omitted in the eighth verfe But that feems to have
been the cafe with a few of them, only.

nals, and divide, at leaſt, if not govern, the *Chriſtian* world :—is not now very important to enquire, becauſe it is not poſſible to determine the fact, with precifion, at this diftance of time. But, as *Arianiſm*, during a confiderable part of this interval, fat upon the throne of the *Cæſars* ; as the Emperors *Conſtantius*, and *Valens*, in particular, had their *Arian* Archbiſhops, and Biſhops, who, for a long time, poſſeſſed the fupreme eccle- fiaſtical power, and baniſhed their opponents : it is, perhaps, not utterly impoſſible to con- ceive, that fome of the warmeſt of the fol- lowers of *Arius* ſhould confpire, at that time, to devife fome fubdolous means of baniſhing this obnoxious verſe, along with its fup- porters. Far be it, however, from the pre- fent age, abfolutely to affirm that this latter was the real truth of the cafe. Either caufe is equal to the effect ; and each is, at leaſt, *poſſible*. For, as one, fingle, *miſtaken*, Copy might, with perfect purity of intention in the feveral fucceſſive Copyiſts, generate all the erroneous MSS of this kind, which have ever yet been produced : So the *Arians*, on

the

the other hand, are not fo free (*p*) from imputations of the oppofite nature, as to be entitled to demand, from an impartial Hiftori-
an, a certification of their innocence. And
when a fingle erroneous Tranfcript, of this
kind, had been once made, whether through
intention, or inadvertence, within any part
of the interval herein before mentioned; it
would certainly propagate its own errors,
for fome time unchecked, and uncorrected,
on account of the various, and continued,
perfecutions of the *Chriftians*, which prevailed through the greateft part of that period: and oftentimes prevented them from
meeting together but by ftealth, " *ante lu-*
" *cem*," and in too much terror, and tre-
pidation, to think, at fuch meetings, of
comparing their MSS with each other. But
when the rage of perfecution began (*q*) to

Z 3 abate,

(*p*) The *Arians* are exprefsly accufed of having mutilated the Scriptures during *this, their reign*. (*Ambrofe,
De Fide*, Lib ii C. 15, p 494 —And Lib. v. C. xvi,
p. 586 —Alfo *Epif Claffis* 1. pa. 795.)

And *Socrates* (*Hift Eccl.* vii, 32—and *Tripart.* xii, 4.)
directly charges them with having garbled this very Epiftle
of St. *John*, for the purpofe of detaching, if poffible, the
Divinity of *Chrift* from his *human* nature. See alfo *Wit-
fius*, vol. ii. Exercitat. 3, pa. 113. Edit. *Herborne
Naffavior* A D. 1712.

(*q*) Thefe impediments were not compleatly removed,

abate, and when the different affemblies of *Chriftians* had leifure to communicate together, and to confult, in fecurity, their ori-
ginals, or fuch authentic Tranfcripts thereof
as held, with them, the place of Originals
—then the abfence of this verfe was difcovered, and the omiffions of it were, in fome
degree, rectified. Private perfons corrected
their erroneous MSS, in the moft compendious, as well as leaft expenfive, method:
namely, by interlining the omitted verfe in
the text, or by adding it in the *margin* (r) of
their Copies of this Epiftle. The public
Bibles, the old *Italic* (and afterwards the
Vulgate of *Jerome*) of the *Latins*, the Verfion

until the *fixth* Century, for *Arianifm* was not compleatly fubdued until that time.

(r) The Adverfaries of this verfe have founded, on
this latter circumftance, their idea of a *marginal glofs*, or
comment But, furely, nothing can be more affected,
or abfurd When the poffeffor of a MS of this Epiftle
had difcovered the omiffion of this verfe, in his copy,
how is it to be fuppofed that he would act ? He would
not *re-copy the whole of his MS*, beginning with this omiffion, for that expedient would be too troublefome, or
too expenfive He muft, of neceffity, correct his erroneous MS, either by an *interlineation* (which, however,
would be impracticable in fome MSS) or by inferting the
omiffion *in its margin*. And this feems to be the true,
the obvious, and the only, reafon why fome MSS have
interlined, and others have exhibited in their margins,
this verfe of St. *John*.

fion of the *Armenians*, and the απος0λος of the *Greeks*, needed no correction, as to the text in queftion, and confequently received none. And this verfe hath ever fince maintained its place in every (ancient) public Verfion of this Epiftle, wherefoever the name of *Chrift* hath been profeffed, except in the *Syriac*, (s) and the *Coptic*: both of which, however, have been proved to be fo very incorrect, fo very full of omiffions of other verfes, as to render their omiffion of this paffage not to be even a matter of any furprife.

THUS, Sir, I have travelled through the tafk, which I firft prefcribed to myfelf, of ftating, and replying to, the chief objections, which have been urged againft the originality of the verfe 1. *John*, v: 7. The undertaking hath been, occafionally, rendered arduous by actual difficulties, caft in its way by the adverfaries of this verfe. But it hath been, much more frequently, made difguftful, by their fophiftical (as it feems) perverfions of the truth. The labor, and activity, which

Z 4 were

<hr>

(s) The *Arabic*, *Ethiopic*, and *Perfic*, are no more than Copies of thefe Verfions, and, therefore, not entitled to a fpecial enumeration in this place. (See page 193.)

were requisite to encounter the former, have borne no comparison with the patience, and forbearance, which became neceffary to endure the latter. But, whether originating in truth or fallacy, whether holding forth real, or feigned, perplexities, thofe objections have been (fuch of them, at leaft, as appeared deferving of notice) all fairly ftated, and fully confidered. I have not fuppreffed, I have not fhrunk back from, even one of them. And now, Sir, let me intreat you to eftimate for me, for yourfelf, for the public, the real value of fuch objections, when compared with the anfwers which they have received. Left, however, you fhould, through modefty, (our language will not convey the full import of the *Latin* word, *pudor*) decline the unpleafing office—I muft, of neceffity take it upon myfelf. The employment may, in fome fenfe, be affumed improperly; but it fhall be difcharged impartially.

THE RESULT, then, FROM THE WHOLE, is,—that THE VERSE, in queftion, SEEMS, BEYOND ALL DEGREE OF SERIOUS DOUBT, TO HAVE STOOD IN

THIS

THIS EPISTLE, WHEN IT ORIGINALLY
PROCEEDED FROM THE PEN OF ST. JOHN.
In the *Latin*, or Weſtern, Church, the ſuf-
frages of *Tertullian*, and *Cyprian*, of *Marcus
Celedenſis*, and *Phœbadius*, in its favor, aided
by the early, the ſolemn, the public, appeal
to its authority, by the *African* (*t*) Biſhops
under *Huneric*; the Preface, Bible, and *con-
ſcripta ſides*, of *Jerome*; the frequent, and direct, citations of the verſe by *Eucherius*, *Auguſtine*, *Fulgentius*, *Vigilius*, and *Caſſiodorius* :
—theſe, ſupported, as to the *Greek*, or Eaſtern,
Churches, by the Dialogue between *Arius*,
and *Athanaſius*, as well as by the *Synopſis* of
this Epiſtle,—by the *Armenian* Verſion,
which was framed from *Greek* MSS ; by the
very early, and conſtant, uſe of the ἀποϛολ☉ in
the ſame *Greek* Church (an uſage which ſeems
to be deducible even from the Apoſtles (*u*)

them-

(*t*) The authority of *Victor Vitenſis*, as a hiſtorian, will
not be reſiſted by Mr *Gibbon*, when he turns to pages 337,
342, 343, 348, 393, and 442, of the third Volume of
his own Hiſtory.

It is remarkable, that theſe *African* Biſhops, in their
public Confeſſion of Faith, ſtile the diſbelief of a Trinity
of perſons in the Godhead, " *quandam novitatem*," a NEW
OPINION, and that this deſcription was given in A. D.
484. (Appendix, No. V.)

(*u*) *Fabricius*, treating of this ἀποϛολος, affirms—" E-

themselves) and by its *public Confeſſion of Faith* :----ALL THESE evidences, ariſing within the limit of the *ſixth* century, (to paſs over the immenſe accumulation of teſtimony which has been produced ſubſequent to that æra) offering themſelves to the teſt of the judgement, combined in one point of view, unchecked by a ſingle negation, unrebuked by any *poſitive* contradiction, unreſiſted by any the ſmalleſt, *direct*, impeachment (*w*) of the authenticity of the verſe, throughout all the annals of all antiquity :—ALL THESE CIRCUMSTANCES ſeize the mind, as it were, by violence, and compel it to acknowledge the verity, the original exiſtence, of the verſe in queſtion. For, *although* it undoubtedly

---

" *piſtolarum hujuſmodi lectionem non eſſe Novatorum inven-* " *tum, ſed* AB APOSTOLIS IPSIS *ad nos tranſmiſſam* " And he quotes, on this ſubject, *Clement* Conſtit ib. 11. Cap. 57—*Jacobus* in Liturgia—and *Juſtin Mar*. Apolog. 2.

(*Fabricius*, Bibl. *Græc.* vol V, Diſſ. 1. p. 3'.—Edit *Hamb*. A. D. 1712)

(*w*) *Omiſſors* of the verſe, in ancient MSS, or by ancient writers, are neither *poſitive contradictions*, nor *direct impeachments*, of its authenticity. They are *food for conjecture*, and no more. But CONJECTURE has no weight, whatſoever, in any caſe, or under any circumſtances, when put into the balance againſt the evidence of POSITIVE FACTS.

doubtedly appears ftrange, on a firft confideration of the fubject, that feveral ancient
Greek, and *Latin*, Fathers have not quoted,
or commented upon, this verfe, in thofe
parts of their works, which have defcended
to the prefent age; *although* it appears, on a
primary view, ftill more ftrange, that thofe
numerous *Greek* MSS (not *Latin*, for a vaft
majority of thefe have ALWAYS read the
verfe) which formerly exhibited this paffage
of St. *John*, fhould be NOW in general (not
totally) loft, rather than thofe few, which
did not contain it : Yet both thefe objections,
when aggravated to the utmoft, are but *prefumptions*, amount to no more than *negative*
evidence ; and they have been already, as it
fhould feem, compleatly, and fatisfactorily,
explained, and avoided,—or accounted for,
and defeated. And from whetherfoever of
the fources, which have been heretofore
affigned, the partial occultation of this verfe,
antecedent to the times of *Jerome*, proceeded, that temporary obfcuration was difperfed
at once, and the verfe was fummoned forth
to fhine in its proper fphere, by his Preface,
and Verfion ; which are confirmed, and ef-

tablifhed

tablifhed (if they could be faid to need any confirmation, or eftablifhment) by the Revifion of *Charlemagne*.   And this verfe hath EVER SINCE (if we may now defcend to modern times) not only maintained its place in EVERY public Verfion, which hath been in ufe fince the days of *Jerome*; (*x*) but it hath alfo been EVER SINCE uniformly quoted, and referred to, by individual Writers, of the firft eminence for learning, and integrity, in *Afia*, and in *Africa*, as well as in *Europe*, without the leaft queftion, without the fmalleft interruption : EXCEPT the invafion of *Erafmus*, which, however, was foon repelled, and of which he lived to repent, and be afhamed, (*y*) unlefs his own Paraphrafe, on this verfe, be the compleateft piece of literary hypocrify, now fubfifting ;— and EXCEPT the affaults of fome more modern objectors, which neverthelefs, it is hoped, and trufted, have been repulfed, in the preceding Differtation, in a manner (although unequal to the fubject, yet) fufficiently

(*x*) The exceptions of the *Syriac*, and the *Coptic*, with their Tranfcripts, have already been made, and accounted for, in pages 188—196.

(*y*) Page 336, Note *n*.

ciently adequate to the ferious, the compleat, conviction of every unprejudiced enquirer after truth.

I beg leave to clofe thefe reflections with a quotation from a work, which, by its peculiar felicity in combining metaphyfical learning with the Scriptural fcheme of *Revelation*, has ennobled the one, whilft it has illuftrated the other; (z) which admonifhes, " *That, in queftions of difficulty, or fuch as are* " *thought fo, where more fatisfactory evidence* " *cannot be had, or is not feen; if the refult of* " *examination be, that there appears, upon the* " *whole, any, the loweft, prefumption on one* " *fide, and none on the other, or a greater pre-* " *fumption on one fide, although in the loweft* " *degree greater; this determines the queftion,* " EVEN IN MATTERS OF SPECULATION: " *and in matters of practice, will lay us under* " *an abfolute, and formal, obligation, in point* " *of prudence, and of intereft, to act upon that* " *prefumption, or low probability, although it* " *be fo low, as to leave the mind in very great* " *doubt, which is the truth.*" At the fame time,

(z) *Butler*'s Analogy, Introduction, *ad initium.*

time, however, I do not mean to seek any
shelter for the authenticity of this verse, under the *strict* terms of this quotation, but
will venture to claim a much higher protection for it, than the *literal* expressions of
the quotation will support ; by affirming,
that the *result of examination*, in the present
disquisition, is, that, upon the whole, a
VERY STRONG POSITIVE PROOF appears
on one side, and nothing but a VERY LOW
PRESUMPTION on the other ; and, therefore,
that the question is determined, even when
viewed as a MATTER OF SPECULATION:
but when considered as a MATTER OF
PRACTICE (and surely there is no speculation, as to the nature of the Deity, which
will not, in some degree, at least, influence
our *practice*) we shall find ourselves laid under an ABSOLUTE, AND FORMAL, OBLIGA-
TION, IN POINT OF PRUDENCE, AND OF
INTEREST, to act upon such a speculation ;
and the more emphatically so, because the
evidence, in the present case, does NOT appear to be SO LOW, AS TO LEAVE THE
MIND IN ANY (reasonable) DOUBT, WHICH
IS THE TRUTH.

Having

Having now, Sir, difcuffed the general queftion as to the originality of this verfe, I fhould beg to take my leave of you, did it not feem, in fome refpects, requifite that this intercourfe fhould be continued yet a few moments longer.

And firft, let me fubmit to your confideration a few remarks on the general defign of your feveral publications, as far as they difclofe it to your readers. But, as this is not the direct object of this Differtation,—I will be brief, yet plain.

You have, Sir, throughout the whole of your publications, feemed to fnatch, with avidity, at every occafion, apt, or unapt, of leffening the power of *Chriftianity* over the human mind. You have not, indeed, attempted to produce this effect by open impeachments of the external evidences of its truth (for thofe would have been fpeedily confuted) or by direct charges againft the internal purity of its doctrines (for thofe would have confuted themfelves) : but you have endeavoured to effectuate your purpofe

by

by indirect machinations. You have, art-
fully enough, suggested ambiguous insinua-
tions, where you durst not hazard a positive
accusation. You have labored to raise a
sneer, where you durst not risk an argument.
When such passages, as these, occur to your
readers——

"*Rome* submitted to the *Yoke* of the
" Gospel——"(*a*)

" Some advocates would disgrace Chris-
" tianity, *if Christianity could be disgraced.*"
——(*b*)

" If I had designed to investigate the
" Jewish Antiquities, reason, as well as
" faith, must have directed my enquiries to
" the sacred *Books*, which, *even as human*
" *productions*, would deserve to be studied as
" ONE" (I cannot help Mr. *Gibbon's* bad
English) " of the most curious, and original,
" Monuments of the East."——(*c*)

" *Apollonius*,

(*a*) History, vol. iii, p. 77.
(*b*) Vindication, ad init.
(*c*) Vindication, p. 20.
The *Parenthesis*, in this quotation, will find its prece-
dent in Mr. *Gibbon's* Vindication.

" *Apollonius*, of *Tyana*, was born about
" the fame time as *Jefus Chrift*. His life
" (that of the former) is related in fo fabu-
" lous a manner, by his fanatic *Difciples*,
" that we are at a lofs to difcover, whether
" he was a Sage, or an Impoftor."---(*d*)

" This prohibitory Law" (viz. of *Theodo-*
fius, when he abolifhed the fanguinary, as
well as idolatrous, worfhip of the *Greek*, and
Roman, pagans) " was expreffed in the
" moft abfolute, and comprehenfive, terms.
" *It is our will and pleafure* (favs the (*e*)
" Emperor) *that none of our fubjects fhall*
" *prefume, in any city, or in any place, to*
" *worfhip an inanimate Idol by the facrifice of*
" *a guiltlefs Victim.* The *Act of facrificing*,
" and the practice of divination by the *en-*
" *trails of the Victim*, are declared High
" Treafon againft the State. The rites of
" Pagan fuperftition, which might feem
A a " lefs

(*d*) The *regular confufion* of this fentence befpeaks defign " Mais j' ai d'abord vu qu' il en vouloit à *Jefus*
" *brift*, fou le character de *Mahomet* " (*Lord Chefter-
field* to *Crebillon*, refpecting *Voltaire*'s Tragedy of *Ma-*
homet)

(*e*) Hiftory, vol. iii, p. 89.

" lefs bloody and attrocious, are abolifhed,
" *as* highly injurious to the truth, and ho-
" nour, of religion ; and the HARMLESS
" CLAIMS of the domeftic Genius, of the
" houfehold Gods, are included in this *ri-*
" *gorous profcription* Such was the *perfe-*
" *curing Spirit* of the laws of *Theodofius,*
" which were repeatedly enforced by his
" Sons, and Grandfons, with the loud,
" and unanimous, applaufe of the Chriftian
" world."

" Neither the violence of Antiochus, nor
" the arts of Herod, nor the example of the
" circumjacent nations, could ever perfuade
" the Jews to affociate, *with the inftitutions*
" *of Mofes,* the *elegant Mythology of the*
" *Greeks.*" (*f*)

When fuch paffages as thefe occur to your
readers, the interpretation, which was moft
intended, although leaft exprefled, cannot
lie hid even from the commoneft apprehenfion.

But

(*f*) Hiftory, C. XV, p. 451.

But, Sir, paffing over other enquiries, Why are you not confiftent with your-felf? After having, in the former part of thefe extracts, thus endeavoured, how-ever vainly, to overturn the Syftem of Reve-lation by ridicule, by indecent farcafms le-velled at it, and at its divine Author; after having thus attempted, however feebly, to fupport the caufe of Deifm;--why do you, at once, carry over your faithlefs colors to the Hofts of Heathenifm,—and Idolatry? What was the principal inftitution of *Mofes* (if you are refolved to attribute thofe infti-tutions to *Mofes, alone)* upon which all the reft depended? It was—" *Hear, O Ifrael,*
" *the Lord thy God is one God. Thou fhalt*
" *have none other Gods but Him. Him only*
" *fhalt thou worfhip, and him only fhalt thou*
" *ferve.*" But what was " the elegant My-
" thology of the *Greeks* ?" It was—*Gods many, and Lords many.* And do you, then, Sir, really wifh to cenfure the *Jews*, be-caufe they would not affociate, with the worfhip of the God of *Abraham*, of the great I AM, " *Him, befide whom there is no*
" *God; the Lord, who is God in Heaven a-*

A a 2 " *bove,*

" *bove, and in the earth beneath,—and there*
" *is none else ; the Lord, who prepared the*
" *light, and the sun,—who set all the borders*
" *of the earth, who made summer and winter ;*
" *before whom the nations are as the drop of a*
" *bucket, and are counted as the small dust of*
" *the ballance ; who holdeth the sea in the*
" *palm of his hand ; and taketh up the isles as*
" *a very little thing :"*—Do you, serioufly,
condemn the *Jews*, becaufe they would not,
in the days of *Antiochus*, and *Herod* (for before that time they had but too often, and
too fatally, tried the experiment) defile the
adoration of this fole God of the Univerfe,
with the worfhip of the adulterous, and in-
ceftuous, *Jupiter*,—the paffionate, and re-
vengeful, *Juno*,—*Venus*, the ftrumpet, and
Mercury, the pickpocket ? I forbear to purfue you through the inferior *Godlings*, the
Pan and *Priapus*, the (g) *Laverna*, and *Cloa-
cina*, of this " elegant Mythology." Nothing exhibits human reafon in a more hu-
miliating light, than to take a view of its
mythological Reveries, when unaided by
divine

(g) —————" Pulchra *Laverna*,
" Da mihi fallere."— HOR,

divine Revelation. If the moſt inventive mind ſhould ſtudy foɩ abſurdity, what could it deviſe more ludicrous on the one hand, or moɩe abominable on the other, than the worſhip of Calves, and Serpents,—Monkies, and Onions? It may be granted, that part, at leaſt, of ˌheſe ADORABLE EXISTENCES belong, pɩoperly, to the *elegant Mythology* of the *Egyptians* But aɩe the Serpents, and Monkies, of the Boɩdeɩers upon the *Nile,* more prepoſterous, aɔ objeᵭs of worſhip, than *Gods and Goddeſſes,* (*h*) *ɩn Hell*—than *Dog-Gods, Hoɩſe-Gods, Fɩſh-Gods, and Goat-Gods?* And yet this hideous hoſt, this beaſt-ly herd, this contemptible (*ɩ*) " *crew,* de-" baſed with eveɩy human weakneſs, and " polluted with every human vice," are, ɩn your opinion, it ſeems, fit compeers, as ob-

A a 3 jeᵭs

(*h*) *Pluto, Pɩoſerpɩne, Ceɩberus, Pegaſus, Triton, Pan,* and the *Satyɩs,* &c

(*ɩ*) Sermons by THE (where meɩɩt ɩs pre-eminently conſpɩcuous, *epɩthets* are needleſs) PRELATE, to whom this diſſertation ɩs humbly ɩnſcribed. (4th Edɩt.)

A certaɩn ſelf-delegated, anonymous, *Cɩɩtɩc* (I mean ɩn the *Englɩſh,* not the *Greek,* ſenſe of the word) hath cen-ſured the expreſſɩon, *cɩew,* here quoted, as low and mean. If ɩt hath any fault, ɩt ɩs that of not beɩng low and mean enough. It ɩs much too good for the ſubjeᵭ, provided a more contemptuous expreſſion could eɩther have been ᵃdopted, or ɩnvented.

jects of worfhip, with the felf-exiftent, om-
nipotent, and eternal God: and the *Jews*
are, as you inform us, guilty of inexcufable
obftinacy, in refufing to place, on the throne
of Heaven, this *elegant Mythology*, and to
yield to BOTH a like adoration!

This then, Sir, it feems, is your Syftem
(if any thing fo mutable, now *Deiftical*, now
Pagan, can merit the name of a Syftem) of
Theology. And your plan of morality is the
amiable offspring (*k*) of fo engaging a parent.
It expofes itfelf to your readers, occafionally,
and, as it were, in momentary glances, in
the preceding parts of your Hiftory; but it
feems to look out at full upon them in the
following paffage (*l*).

" The Sifter of Valentinian was educated
" in the Palace at Ravenna; and as her
" marriage might be productive of fome
" danger to the State, fhe was raifed, by
" the title of Augufta, above the hopes
" of the moft prefumptuous *fubject*. But
" the

(*k*) " *O Matre pulchra Filia pulchrior !*" HOR.
(*l*) Hiftory, vol. III, p. 404.

" the fair Honoria had no fooner attained
" the fixteenth year of her age, than fhe de-
" tefted the importunate greatnefs, which
" muft *forever* (*m*) exclude her from the
" comforts of honourable love : in the midft
" of vain, and unfatisfactory, pomp, Ho-
" noria fighed, yielded to the impulfe of
" natuie, and threw herfelf into the arms
" of her Chamberlain, Eugenius. Her
" guilt, and fhame (fuch is the abfurd lan-
" guage of imperious man) were foon be-
" trayed by the appearances of pregnancy :
" but the difgrace of the royal family was
" publifhed to the world by the impru-
" dence of the Emprefs Placidia; who dif-
" mifled her daughter, after a ftrict, and
" fhameful, confinement, to a remote exile
" at Conftantinople."

To the conduct of *Honoria*, then, in thus
foregoing every confideration that was due
to her rank, and ftation ; in thus betraying
her own perfonal honor, and, at fo early an

A a 4

age,

(*m*) Why, FORFVER ? She was only raifed, by the
title of *Augufta*, above the " honorable love" of *fubjects*.
Foreign Princes, of any country, might (as indeed *Attila*
afterwards did) afk her in marriage.

age, breaking through all the bashful re-
straints of virgin modesty; in thus equally
disregarding the laws of God, and man, and
prostituting herself to one of her domestics,
merely because the dignity of her title (the
only poor apology held out for her) placed
her above the *subjects* of her Brother, the
Emperor : to such a conduct neither *guilt*,
nor *shame*, is, in your opinion, to be imputed;
for such imputations, in such a case, you affirm to be " *absurd language.*" It is even
proper, in your judgement, that other *Honorias*, of distinguished birth, and high race,
of the present, and of future ages, should be
instructed to act, or at least to reason, in this
manner : for, if they should become your
readers, they are here told, that to apply the
expressions of *guilt*, and *shame*, to such a conduct, would be only " *the absurd language of*
" *imperious* MAN." It is, it seems, a suffi-
cient justification for those present, or future,
Honorias, when they have thus played the
strumpet with (pardon, Sir, the inadver-
tency—" *when they have thus yielded to the*
" *impulse of nature, and thrown themselves*
" *into the arms of*") their Footmen, or their

Chamberlains,

Chamberlains, to fay, that they were " *in*
" *their fixteenth year*," and that they " *figh-*
" *ed.*"---And the indignation, and affliction,
of a Royal parent, anxious to interrupt fo
offenfive a commerce, and to prevent the introduction of any more fpurious iffue into
the imperial Houfe of the *Cæfars*, by fepa-
rating her daughter from the object of her
libidinous, and criminal, attachment,—
ought, it feems, to be reprobated as " *a ftrict,*
" *and fhameful, confinement*," ending in a
" *remote exile!*" Surely, Sir, the honeft blufh
of ingenuous fhame hath long fince forfaken
your cheek. Are thefe the grave inftructions
of the Hiftoric Mation, combining truth
with majefty; or are they the meretricious
artifices of an abandoned Procurefs, pleading,
in her choiceft terms, the caufe of proftitu-
tion? I intreat your aid, Sir, to affift me in
folving the difficulties which you have thus
thrown around me. If left to my own
guidance, I can find but one way of extri-
cating myfelf from them: which is,—to
fuppofe that, in Mr. *Gibbon*, the School-boy
is not yet loft in the Man; that, although
when he *was a child*, it was allowable for
him

him (even by the fuffrage of an Apoftle) to *think as a child*, and to *fpeak as a child*, yet that, *when he became a man*, he could not *put away childifh things*, but even now *underftands as a child*, and believes in the fenfelefs, and idolatrous, Polytheifm of the ancients. In this point of view, Mr. *Gibbon* is, indeed, entitled to claim one merit, that of being confiftent with himfelf. Beyond all doubt, a writer teaches fuch morals, as thefe, with the moft perfect confiftency, who announces his partiality for a *Theology*, which reprefents them as the PRACTICE of its Deities; who openly declares, that the " *claims*" of fome of thofe Deities are " *harmlefs*" at leaft, (although they are claims of *divinity* in themfelves, and of *worfhip* from men) and who feems to lament, in terms not very ambiguous, or obfcure, that " *the elegant mythology*," which contains them, is no longer the eftablifhed religion of the world !

If, Sir, this delineation, the outlines of which have been fketched by your own hand, be a juft reprefentation of your mind, your Creed is already known : and the prefent

fent age may, future ages moſt certainly
will, be at no loſs to form their judgment
of you accordingly. If it be not juſt, if
either your own text, or my comment, hath
wronged you,---do juſtice to yourſelf. You
have the remedy in your own power. Favor
the public with your ſyſtems of Theology,
and Morals. Delineate them at full length.
Deſcribe them at large. Stand forth in the
open field. The world is weary of ſeeing
you fight ſo long in ambuſh. Walk no
more forth with your Stiletto in the Twi-
light. Seek your adverſary honorably, with
your naked ſword, in the face of day. Aſ-
pire to the credit of *Toland*, and *Tindal*,---of
Chubb, and *Morgan*,---of *Vanini*, and *Spinoza*,
by a direct attempt to break this " *Yoke of*
" *the Goſpel.*" Take to yourſelf the honors
of *Rouſſeau*, at leaſt, and give us the Creed
of YOUR *Savoya·d* Curate alſo. Aſſume the
diſtinction of *Voltaire*, and favor us with
YOUR *Dictionnaire Philoſophique Portatif.*
Diſtinguiſh the grounds of your oppoſition
to *Chr'anity*, with plainneſs, and perſpicu-
ity. Leave your readers no longer at liberty
to confound, in you, modern Deiſm with
ancient

ancient Polytheifm, or either of them with Atheifm. If any of thefe *Baals* be God with you,---tell us which of them you wor-fhip. Your friends expect from you fome plan of unbelief, which may, at leaft, *appear* to be tolerably regular, and confiftent, or they will foon defpair (*n*) of being able, in any degree, to enter upon your defence. The impartial public demand it from you; or the perfuafion, already entertained by many, will foon become univerfal, that you conceived a decent *modicum* of infidelity, no matter how prepared, to be neceffary to give *fafhion* to a work, pompous, yet not fubftan-tial,

---

(*n*) One of the moft (perhaps *the moft*) truly refpectable of them feems already to have loft the very hope of your defence, in defpair.

Think not my verfe means blindly to engage
In rafh defence of thy profaner page !
Though keen her fpirit, her attachment fond,
Bafe fervice cannot fuit with Friendfhip's bond ;
Too firm from duty's facred path to turn,
She breathes an honeft figh of deep concern,
And pities Genius, when his wild career
Gives faith a wound, or innocence a tear.
Humility herfelf, divinely mild,
Sublime Religion's meek, and modeft child,
Like the dumb fon of *Cræfus*, in the ftrife,
When force affail'd his Father's facred life,
Breaks filence, and, with filial duty warm,
Bids thee revere his Parent's hallow'd form.

Hayley's Effay on Hiftory, Epiftle iii, *ad finem.*

tial,—fpecious, yet not fatisfactory,—labored, yet not accurate. And *Chriftianity* calls you to the teft, dares you to the onfet; it being her fupreme wifh, her only *prayer,* where fhe hath any enemies, that fhe may, like the *Grecian* Warrior, fo well defcribed by the *Grecian* Bard, be permitted to *confront her Adverfaries in open day.* She challenges your ftricteft fcrutiny. She loveth not " *darknefs rather than light, becaufe her deeds* " *are evil*;" fhe " *hateth not the light, left* " *her works fhould be reproved:*" but fhe " *doeth the truth,*" and therefore wifheth to come " *to the light, that her deeds may be* " *made manifeft, that they are wrought in* " GOD !" (*o*)

But, Sir, your Hiftory, *in general,* is not my principal concern. I leave that fubject to the impartial Tribunal of future times, which will do it ample juftice. A *particular* part, only, of your work is my propei object. Let me, then, ceafe from purfuing this digreffion any longer. Let me return, for a few moments, to my original defign,

and

(*o*) *John,* iii. 19—21.

and then conclude this long, perhaps to you tedious, addrefs.

In addition to the NOTE, in page 545 of your third Volume, which has caufed you the trouble of thefe letters, you declare, in the body of the correfpondent pages, and in their Notes, with Dr. *Benfon*, that this *text, which afferts the unity of the* THREE *in Heaven, is condemned by the* UNIVERSAL SILENCE *of the orthodox fathers, ancient verfions, and authentic MSS*; and *that the* TWO *MSS of* Dublin, *and* Berlin, *are unworthy to form* AN *exception.* You then refer to Mr. *Emlyn's* works, and infinuate, rather than affirm (for your expreffions are conftrained, and obfcure) that this text owes its prefent exiftence to *an allegorical interpretation, in the form, perhaps, of a marginal Note, invading the text of the* Latin *Bibles, which were renewed and correfted, in a dark period of ten centuries.* You affirm, with Sir *Ifaac Newton,* that this verfe *was* FIRST *alledged by the Catholic Bifhops, whom* Hunneric *fummoned to the Conference of* Carthage. And from *your own* Treafures you produce a confident affertion,

that

that *Gennadius*, Patriarch of *Conſtantinople*, *was ſo much amazed at the extraordinary com-poſition* (the Creed of *Athanaſius*, commonly ſo called) *that he frankly pronounced it to be the work of a drunken Man ·* in ſupport of which remark, you refer to the *Dogmata Theologica* of *Petavius*. (*p*)

Theſe,

(*p*) " *The famous Creed, which ſo clearly expounds the myſte-*
" *ries of the Trinity, and the Incarnation, is deduced, with ſtrong*
" *probability, from this* African *ſchool.* [113] *Even the Scrip-*
" *tures themſelves were profaned by their raſh, and ſacrilegious,*
" *hands. The memorable text, which aſſerts the unity of the*
" Three who bear witneſs in Heaven, [114] *is condemned*
" *by the univerſal ſilence of the orthodox fathers, ancient ver-*
" *ſions, and authentic MSS.* [115] *It was firſt alledged by the*
" *Catholic biſhops whom* Hunneric *ſummoned to the conference*
" *of* Carthage. *An allegorical interpretation, in the form,*

" [113] *The P* Queſnel *ſtarted this opinion, which has been favourably*
" *received. But the three following truths, however ſurpriſing they may*
" *ſeem, are now univerſally acknowledged* (Gerard Voſſius, tom. vi. p.
" 516—522 Tillemont, Mem Eccleſ tom viii. p. 667—671)
" 1 *St* Athanaſius *is not the author of the Creed which is ſo frequently*
" *read in our Churches.* 2. *It does not appear to have exiſted, within a*
" *century after his death* 3 *It was originally compoſed in the* Latin *tongue,*
" *and conſequently in the* Weſtern *provinces* Gennadius, *patriarch of*
" Conſtantinople, *was ſo much amazed by this extraordinary compoſition,*
" *that he frankly pronounced it to be the work of a drunken man.* Petav.
" Dogmat Theologica, tom ii l vii. c 8. p. 687 "
" [114] 1. John, v 7 S e Simon, *Hiſt Crit* &c *and the elabora*
" Prolegomena *and annotations of Dr* Mill, *and* Wetſtein, *to their editio*
" *of the* Greek Teſtament *In* 1689, *the Papiſt* Simon *ſtrove to be free*
" *in* 1707 *the Proteſtant,* Mill, *wiſhed to be a ſlave, in* 1751, *the Armi-*
" *nian* Wetſtein *uſed the liberty of his times, and of his ſect* "
" [115] *Of all the MSS now extant, above* 80 *in number, ſome of which*
" *are more than* 1200 *years old* (Wetſtein, ad loc) *The orthodox copies of*
" *the* Vatican, *of the* Complutenſian *editors, and of* R Stephens, *are*
" *become inviſible, and the two MSS of* Dublin, *and* Berlin, *are unworthy*
" *to form an exception* See Emlyn s *works,* vol ii p 227—255 269—
" 293 *and M* de Miſſy s *four ingenious letters, in* tom. viii *and* ix *of*
" *the* Journal Britannique,"

Thefe, Sir, are your affertions. And it feems that they ought not to pafs without fome (but they fhall be brier) animadverfions.

In the firft place, then, let it be obferved, that by having thus adopted the objections, juft ftated, you are now become refponfible for them as your own. If this adoption were, originally, no more than the refult of a curfory, and imperfect, examination of the fubject, and if any part of the preceding letters (in which, I truft, thofe objections have been proved to be *in general* FALSE, and *univerfally* INCONCLUSIVE) fhall have been fortunate enough to convince you of your error; you will, without doubt, as the beft reparation in your power, haften to efface the ftigma, with which you have endeavoured to brand this text, by cancelling

thofe

" *perhaps, of a marginal note, invaded the text of the* Latin
" *Bibles, which were renewed, and corrected, in a dark*
" *period of ten centuries. After the invention of Printing,*
" *the editors of the* Greek *Teftament yielded to their own*
" *prejudices, or thofe of the times, and the pious fraud,*
" *which was embraced with equal zeal at* Rome, *and at*
" Geneva, *has been infinitely multiplied in every country,*
" *and every language of modern* Europe." (p. 543—4.)

thofe pages which contain it. Such a proceeding would do juftice to the text, and
honor to yourfelf. But if upon a patient,
and attentive, review of the fubject, you
fhall fee no reafon to reverfe your former
fentence, fhall ftill pronounce the verfe, in
queftion, to be fpurious ;—it will be highly
incumbent upon you to demonftrate, to the
world, the incompetency of the facts ftated,
and the infufficiency of the arguments urged, in the preceding letters, in fupport of
its authenticity. Attempt this confutation,
then, without delay. Silence will be a proof
of confcious impotence. And attempt it
with candor, and ferioufnefs. Tinfelled
phrafes, and empty farcafms, will have no
effect, but to double the load which now lies
heavy upon you. I prefs not, however, this
caution through private, or perfonal, confiderations. It is a matter of no fmall indif-
ference to the Writer of thefe pages, whether (to ufeyour own language) you *falute
him* (q) *with gentle courtefy, or ftern defiance.*
Your facts, if you fhall produce any to explain the queftion, fhall be received with

B b

compla-

_____

(q) Vindication—Edit, A. D. 1779.

complacence. Your arguments, if you shall
urge any to illuminate the subject, shall be
weighed with candor, and coolness. But
your cavils, if you shall practise any, shall
be checked with steadiness; and your info-
lence, if you shall affect any, shall be repelled
with disdain.

Let me in the next place, Sir, but still
more briefly, remark, on these Extracts, that
they convey no very favorable idea of your
impartiality, as a Historian. You have, in
them, brought forward Mr. *Emlyn*, on the
subject of this verse, because he is your fellow-advocate. And you have consigned even
the name of Mr. *Martin*, his respectable antagonist, to deep silence,—*no friendly* Note
to tell where his work lies,—because his opinions were directly adverse to yours, and because he has overthrown many of *Emlyn's*
misrepresentations. But, Sir, is this the
part of an impartial Historian? To state
authorities, and to urge arguments, on *one
side* of a question, alone, is but barely tolera-
ble in a hired Advocate. A Historian, who
acts in this manner, is——but his description

tion will be beft given in your own words.
" WHATEVER SUBJECT *he has chofen,*
" WHATEVER PERSONS *he introduces, he*
" *owes to himfelf, to the prefent age, and to*
" *pofterity, a juft and perfect delineation of*
" ALL *that may be praifed, of* ALL *that may*
" *be excufed, and of* ALL *that muft be cenfured.*
" *If he* FAILS *in the difcharge of his important*
" *office, he partially* VIOLATES THE SA-
" CRED OBLIGATIONS OF TRUTH." *(r)*

But, Sir, this is not all. Let me, in the
third, and laft, place, remark, that the extracts, in queftion, fupply the moft palpable
proof of your partiality, and prejudice, in
refpect to the great queftion of the authenticity of this verfe of St. *John.* They fhew
you to be capable even of *forging* authorities
in a matter, which bears no more than a
collateral, or rather an implied, relation to
it. You have *wilfully* (for your reference is
too exact to allow you fhelter under any
fuppofed *inadvertence*) mifreprefented both
Petavius, and *Gennadius,* in the laft of thofe
extracts. Your own words have been al-

B b 2 ready

(r) Vindication—Edit. 1779, p. 139.

ready fet forth. The words of *Petavius* may be thus tranflated.

"It is certain, that the Creed, which
"paffes under the name of *Athanafius*, was
"not only read, but had in great authority,
"by the *Greek*, as well as by the *Latin*,
"Church. In this Creed are thefe expref-
"fions, as is known to all: *The Holy Ghoft*
"*is of the Father, and of the Son, neither*
"*made, nor created, nor begotten, but pro-*
"*ceeding.* Which plain, and weighty, tef-
"timony was fo offenfive to the *Greeks*, that
"they carried up their frantic, and foolifh,
"rage even to *Athanafius* himfelf; which
"*Gennadius* RELATES, and LAMENTS.
"*They fear not* (fays he) *to affirm that A-*
"thanafius *was a drunkard, and that he was*
"*drunk when he wrote this paffage:* a
"SENSELESS, and RIDICULOUS, CALUM-
"NY, which merits *filent contempt*, rather
"than a *ferious confutation.*" (s)

What

(s) "Symbolum dico quod vulgo *Athanafii* dicitur—
"Certè fub *Athanafii* nomine, non modo ab *noftris*, fed
"a *Græcis* etiam, et legitur, et in magnam auctoritatem
"affumitur. Eft autem in eo ita fcriptum, quod igno-
"rat nemo *Spiritus fanctus a Patre, et Filio, non factus,*
"*nec creatus, nec genitus, fed procedens.* Quod tam grave,

What fay you, Sir, to this quotation?
May it not be fufpected, that by fondly
ftudying Dr. *Benfon*, you have imbibed no
fmall portion of his fpirit? You have, in
your Hiftory, confidently placed this affertion, as to the expreffions of *Gennadius*, a-
mong certain *truths*, which you affirm to be
now univerfally acknowledged. But you will
not repeat the affertion. Let me befeech
you to compare the real expreffions of *Gennadius*, with your own account of them ; and
then to inform the world how far *your account* is diftant from a DIRECT FALSEHOOD.
Is it not practicable for you to utter truth,
even whilft you have its facred name in your
mouth? Surely, Sir, " this feemeth to argue
" a bad caufe, or a bad confcience, or (*t*)

B b 3   " both."

" ac difertum, teftimonium *Græculos* fic offendit, ut in
" *Athanafium* ipfum ftolidè debacchati fint QUOD RE-
" FERT, ac DEPLORAT, *Gennadius* *Non verentur*, in-
" quit, *dicere fanctum Athanafium ebriofum fuiffe, et, cum
" ifta fcriberet, vino plenum* STULTA, *et* INEPTA,
" CALUMNIA, rifuque potius, et contemptu, quàm
" feria expoftulatione digna."
    (*Petav.* Dogm Theol. vol. 11 lib. vi. c. 8. p. 687.)
    For the words of *Gennadius*, himfelf, to which *Peta-
vius* here refers, fee Appendix, No XXIV.
    (*t*) The Tranflators' Preface to the Bible of *James*
1 —a performance, which feems not to be fo generally
known, as it deferves.

" both." Is there any phyfical, or moral, impoffibility, for thofe who deny the authenticity of this verfe, to quote fairly, to argue candidly, and to fpeak truly ? *Is there any reafon in nature for* SUCH *hard hearts?* Thofe *reafons*, fuch as they are, can only be found (but they may be there plentifully found) in pride, and prejudice. If a falfe tenet, or opinion, is to be defended, *at all events*, to what auxiliaries muft it look for affiftance ? Not to truth ;—for fhe is all fair, and artlefs, uniform, and confiftent, fimple, and fincere. It muft feek the treacherous aid of cavils, and equivocations ; it muft practife the foul (*u*) arts of fophiftry, and deceit, of fimulation, and diffimulation : by felecting a part only, and ftating them as the whole, of an Author's words ; by afcribing to him expreffions which he never uttered, and meanings which he never meant ; by fuppreffing what is known to be true, and infinuating, if not afferting, what is known to be falfe. This defcription feems to apply, with all its energy, to Dr. *Benfon.*

It

(*u*) *Rien n'eft beau que le vrai, le vrai feul eft aimable.*
BOILEAU.

It is very far, Sir, from being inapplicable
to yourſelf.

IN FINE,—The defence of this *Text of
the three* (heavenly) *Witneſſes*, which you
affirm to have been *profanely* introduced into
the ſcriptures, by raſh, and ſacrilegious hands,
hath been thus attempted with, at leaſt, up-
right intentions, and a ſerious perſuaſion of
its originality, the reſult of much patient,
and, as I believe, impartial, inveſtigation.
This defence, fixing its foundation upon the
impeachments alledged againſt the text, in
a part of your Hiſtory, hath, almoſt neceffarily, produced a counter-charge againſt
yourſelf. This general defence, on the one
hand, and this particular accuſation, on the
other, are now, both, laid before the tribunal
of an impartial, and diſcerning, Public. You
are called upon to traverſe, or to acknowledge,—to reſiſt, or to ſubmit. If you *refuſe
to plead*, the charge will be taken as con-
feſſed. And the definitive judgment may,
in ſuch a caſe, perhaps, with no very great
impropriety, be framed out of ſome part, at
leaſt, of theſe, your own (*x*) words—

" *If*

(*x*) *Gibbn's* Vindication—Edit. A. D 1779. p. 7.

" *If I am indeed* INCAPABLE OF UNDER-
" STANDING WHAT I READ, *I can no*
" *longer claim a place among thofe Writers,*
" *who merit the efteem, and the confidence of*
" *the Public.* If I am CAPABLE OF WIL-
" FULLY PERVERTING WHAT I UNDER-
" STAND, *I no longer deferve to live in the*
" *fociety of thofe men, who confider a ftrict and*
" *inviolable adherence to* TRUTH, *as the foun-*
" *dation of every thing that is virtuous or ho-*
" *nourable in human nature.*"

I am, Sir,

&c.

APPENDIX.

No. I.

*E*GO *et Pater unum fumus.* Hic ergo jam gra-
dum volunt figere ftulti, immò cœci, qui non
videant, primô, *Ego, et Pater,* duorum effe fignifi-
cationem; dehinc in noviffimo, *fumus,* non ex u-
nius effe perfona, quod pluralitèr dictum eft; tum
quod, *unum* fumus, non *unus* fumus. Si enim dixiffet, unus fumus, potuiffet adjuvare fententiam il-
lorum. Unus enim fingularis numeri fignificatio
videtur. Adhuc cum duo, mafculini generis.
Unum dicit, *neutrali verbo, quod non pertinet ad fingularitatem, fed ad unitatem,* ad fimilitudinem, ad
conjunctionem, ad dilectionem Patris qui Filium
diligit, et ad obfequium Filii, qui voluntati Patris
obfequitur. *Unum fumus,* dicens, *Ego et Pater,* oftendit effe *quos æquat* et jungit (*Tertullianus* adverfus *Praxeam,* Cap. XXII, ad finem.)

No. II.

Poft *Philippum,* et totam fubftantiam quæftionis
iftius, quem in finem Evangelii perfeverant in
eodem genere fermonis, quo Pater et Filius in fua

A   proprietate

proprietate diftinguuntur, Paracletum quoque a
Patre fe poftulaturum, quum afcendiffet ad Patrem,
et miffurum repromittit, et quidem alium, fed jam
præmifimus quomodo alium. Cæterùm, *de meo
fumet*, inquit, ficut ipfe de Patris *Ita connexus Patris in Filio, et Filii in Paracleto, tres efficit cohæren-
tes*, alterum ex altero, *qui tres unum funt*, *non unus*,
QUOMODO *dictum eft*, *Ego et Pater unum fumus*, ad
fubftantiæ unitatem, non ad numeri fingularitatem.
(Idem, Cap. xxv, ad initium.)

No. III.

Dicit Dominus; *Ego et Pater unum fumus*. Et
iterum de Patre et Filio et Spiritu fancto fcriptum
eft *Et hi tres unum funt* Et quifquam credit
hanc unitatem, de divina firmitate venientem, fa-
cramentis cæleftibus cohærentem, fcindi in Ecclefia poffe, et voluntatum collidentium divortio fepa-
rari? Hanc unitatem qui non tenet, Dei legem non
tenet; non tenet Patris, et Filii, fidem, et veritatem non tenet ad falutem. (*Cyprianus*, De *Unitate
Ecclefiæ*, Edit. *Oxon.* p. 109.)

No IV.

Si peccatorum remiffam confecutus eft, et fanc-
tificatus eft, et templum Dei factus eft, quæfo
cujus Dei? fi *Creatoris*, non potuit, qui in eum
non credidit · fi *Chrifti*, nec hujus fieri poteft templum, qui negat Deum Chriftum · fi *Spiritus fancti*,

cum

cum tres unum sint, quomodo Spiritus fanctus placatus effe ei poteft, qui aut Patris, aut Filii, inimicus eft? (Epiftola ad *Jubaianum*, lxxiii, circa mediam partem, p. 203.)

No. V.

Phæbadius, Agenni Galliarum Epifcopus, edidit contra *Arianos* librum. Dicuntur et ejus effe alia opufcula, quæ necdum legi. Vivit ufque hodie, decrepitâ fenectute. (*Hieronym.* Catal. Scriptor. Eccl. p. 125.)

No. VI.

Ad Trinitatem in Joannis Epiftola: *Tres funt qui teftimonium dant in cælo, Pater, Verbum, et Spiritus fanctus; et tres funt qui teftimonium dant in terra, fpiritus, aqua, et fanguis.* (*Eucherius*, C. xi. Sec. 3.)

No. VII.

Ergo quamvis in fuperioribus exemplis Scripturarum tacita fint nomina perfonarum; tamen unitum nomen divinitatis per omnia tibi eft in his demonftratum: ficut et in hoc exemplo veritatis, in quo nomina perfonarum evidentêi funt oftenfa, et unitum nomen divinitatis claufê eft declaratum, Dicente *Johanne* Evangelifta in epiftola fua, *Tres funt qui teftimonium dicunt in cælo, Pater, et Verbum, et Spiritus, et in Jefu Chrifto unum funt;* non tamen unus eft, quia non eft in his una perfona. (*Vigilius*, Liber primus, p. 775.)

No.

No. VIII.

Jam audifti fuperius Evangeliftam *Johannem* in Epiftola fua tam abfolutè teftantem, *Tres funt qui teftimonium dant in cælo, Pater, Verbum, et Spiritus fanctus, et in Chrifto Jefu unum funt.* Utique fine dubio in Trinitate divinitatis per omnia unum funt, & in nominibus perfonarum tres funt. (*Vigil.* Lib. primus, ad calcem, p. 776.)

Sed et Spiritus Sanctus in Patre, et in Filio, et in fe, confiftens eft, ficut *Johannes* Evangelifta in epiftola fua tam abfolute teftatur, *Et tres unum funt.* (Lib. v. p. 786.)

Cur, *Tres unum funt, Johannem* Evangeliftam dixiffe legitis, fi diverfas naturas in perfonis effe accipitis? *(And a little afterwards)* Rogo quomodo *tres unum funt*, fi diverfa in utrifque eft natura divinitatis? (Lib. vii. p. 789.)

Unde et *Johannes* in Epiftola fua ait, *Tres funt qui teftimonium dicunt in cælo, Pater, Verbum, et Spiritus.* et in Chrifto Jefu *unum funt*, non tamen unus eft, quia non eft eorum una perfona. (Lib. x p. 793.)

No. IX.

Beatus *Johannes* Apoftolus teftatur dicens, *Tres funt qui teftimonium perhibent in cælo, Pater, Verbum,* &

& Spiritus, & hi tres unum sunt. Quod etiam beatissimus Martyr, *Cyprianus*, in Epistola *De Unitate Ecclesiæ*, confitetur; dicens, Qui pacem *Christi*, et concordiam rumpit, adversus *Christum* facit; qui alibi præter Ecclesiam colligit, *Christi* Ecclesiam spargit —Atque, ut unam ecclesiam unius Dei esse monstraret, HÆC confestim TESTIMONIA de Scripturis inseruit: Dicit Dom'nus, *Ego et Pater, unum sumus*. Et iterum de *Patre, Filio, et Spiritu Sancto* scriptum est, *Et hi tres unum sunt*. (*Fulgentius*, Responsio contra *Arianos*.)

No. X.

Sæculo eodem (viz circiter A. D. 550) *Cassiodorus*, vel *Cassiodorius* potiùs, Patricius *Romanus*, vixit, Monachisque sibi subjectis delectum antiquissimorum, et correctissimorum Scripturæ sacræ codicum commendavit, et in eorum usum exemplaria, ope contextûs *Græci*, emendavit, auctorque extitit, ut in locis dubiis duos, tresve, antiquos, et emendatos, codices consulerent. Tanto studio is ferebatur in recognoscendum sacrum contextum, ut, operâ reliquos libros emendandi Notariis suis relictâ, ipse sacrorum librorum curam in se reciperet. Testatur porro se de *Orthographiâ* ideo commentatum esse, ut accuratam sacrorum librorum descriptionem proveheret. (*Wolfii* Cur. Phil. p. 305—6.)

A 3 EXTRACTS

EXTRACTS from the Introduction, &c. of MAFFEIUS, to the *Complexiones* of CASSIODORIUS.

Membraneus Liber, in quo infigne hoc antiquitatis monumentum unice perennavit, eximiæ, ac venerandæ, vetuftatis notas præ fe fert omnes; adeo ut videri poffit ab ipfius *Caffiodorii* ætate non ita multum abeffe.—[Ejus titulus] " CASSIODORII " SENATORIS COMPLEXIONES IN EPISTOLAS, ET " ACTA APOSTOLORUM, ET APOCALYPSIM."

Ex *Caffiodoriano* hoc opere conflat non in *Africanis* tantum, (quod patet ex *Eugenio, Fulgentio, Vigilio, Victore, Facundo, Cypriano* quoque, ut videtur) fed in antiquiffimis, et emendatioribus, Ecclefiæ *Romanæ* codicibus, verficulum illum fcriptum fuiffe. Cum enim tanto ftudio Monachis fuis in Div. Lect. id præceperit, ut præftantiffimis, et GRÆCI *etiam textus collatione* repurgatis, codicibus uterentur, utque in ambiguis locis duorum, vel trium, *prifcorum emendatorumque codicum* auctoritas inquireretur,—ipfum imprimis idem præftitiffe, quis ambigat ?

Clamant ifti, Scripturæ verficulum, quo Sanctiffima *Trias* perfpicuè docetur, S. *Johannis,* Ep. i. C. 5, in prifcis codicibus ut plurimum non reperiri,

periri, et ab antiquis Patribus lectum non esse, *Africanis* quibusdam exceptis. At docet vos *Cassiodorii* interpretatio lectum ab ipso fuisse, quo constat et in *Romanis* exemplaribus exstitisse Quibusnam autem? Nimirum *selectissimis,* et *qui jam tum haberentur antiqui.*

Qui vero *Vulgatæ,* seu *Hieronymianæ,* Versioni eam περικοπην olim intrusam putant, deditionem tandem faciant, atque arma submittant, necesse est. Evidentèr enim patet, ex quamplurimis harum *Complexionum* locis, *Cassiodorium* alia Versione a *Hieronymiana* usum esse, et nihilominus eam περικοπην legit.

———— Quæ in hac explanatione vel affert *Cassiodorius* hemistichia, vel designat a *Vulgata antiqua,* sive ab *Italica,* verè deprompta esse, id apud me fermè evincit, quod illa Versio probatissima, inter cæteras, a doctissimis Veterum haberetur. Quapropter adhibitam procul dubio arbitror ab erudito Scriptore, sacrorumque librorum scrutatore eximio, eoque magis, quo vetustiores Scripturæ codices perquirere solitus erat, et collatos cum GRÆCO TEXTU, quem cælestia testimonia præ se tulisse, cum Scriptorum auctoritas, tum optimi qui supersint MSS Libri, testantur. (pag 42, &c)

Extract

Extract from the Preface of *Caffiodorius*.

Sed quamvis omnis Scriptura divina superna luce resplendeat, et in ea virtus Spiritus sancti evidenter irradiet, in Psalterio tamen, et Prophetis, et Epistolis Apostolorum, studium maximum laboris impendi, quoniam mihi visi sunt profundiores abyssos commovere, et quasi arcem totius Scripturæ divinæ, atque altitudinem gloriosissimam continere. Quos ego cunctos NOVEM CODICES auctoritatis divinæ (ut senex potui) sub COLLATIONE PRISCORUM CODICUM, amicis ante me legentibus, sedula lectione transivi. Ubi me multum laboraffe, Domino adjuvante, profiteor; quatenus nec eloquentiæ modificatæ deeffem, nec libros facros temeraria præsumptione lacerarem.

The Words of *Caffiodorius*, in loco.

Sic autem diligimus eum, cum mandata ejus facimus, quæ juftis mentibus gravia non videntur, fed potius vincunt fæculum, quando in illum credunt, qui condidit mundum. Cui rei teftificantur in terra tria myfteria, *aqua, fanguis, et fpiritus,* quæ in *paffione Domini* leguntur impleta · IN CÆLO, autem, PATER, ET FILIUS, ET SPIRITUS SANCTUS, ET HI TRES UNUS EST DEUS.

No.

No. XI.

The Notes of *Theodore Beza* on the Verfes
I. *John*, v. 7, 8.

VII. *Nam tres funt*, &c. οτι τρεις, Hic verficulus omnino mihi retinendus videtur. Explicat enim manifeftè quod de fex teftibus dixerat, tres feorfim cœlo, tres terræ tribuens. Non legit, tamen, *Syrus*, nec Vetus *Latinus* interpres, nec *Nazianzenus* (oratione 5. de Theologia) nec *Athanafius*, nec *Didymus*, nec *Chryfoftomus*, nec *Hilarius*, nec *Cyrillus*, nec *Auguftinus*, nec *Beda* ; fed legit *Hieronymus*, legit *Erafmus* in *Britannico* codice, & exftat in *Complutenfi* editione, & in nonnullis *Stephani* veteribus libris. Non convenit tamen in omnibus inter iftos codices. Nam *Britannicus* legit fine articulis πατηρ, λογος, και πνευμα. In NOSTRIS vero leguntur articuli, & propterea etiam additum erat *fancti* epitheton Spiritui, ut ab eo diftinguatur cujus fit mentio in fequenti verficulo, quique in terra collocatur. ¶ *In cælo*, εν τω ϰρανω. Hoc deeft in feptem vetuftis codicibus, fed tamen omnino videtur retinendum, ut tribus in terra teftibus ifta ex adverfo refpondeant. ¶ *Sermo*, ὁ λογ©. Cur filius Dei dicatur λογ©, expofuimus *Joan.* I. I. At enim dices, Nemo in fua caufa idoneus eft teftis. Hunc nodum ifte Chriftus explicat *Joan.* viii, 13, & deinceps qui locus iftum mirè illuftrat, ut et alii multi

multi apud hunc noſtrum Evangeliſtam, in quibus ſœpe fit iſtius teſtificationis mentio. ¶ *Et hi tres unum ſunt,* και ετοι οι τρεις εν εισι. Id eſt, ità prorſus conſentiunt, ac ſi unus teſtis eſſent, uti reveie unum ſunt, ſi εσιαν ſpectes Sed de illâ (ut mihi quidem videtur) non agitur hoc in loco: quod et Gloſſa ipſa interlinearis, quam vocant, agnoſcit Sed & *Complutenſis* editio legit εις το εν εισι, *ad unum ſunt,* id eſt, in unum conveniunt, uti legitur in ſequenti membro.

VIII *In terra,* επι της γης. *Syrus* interpres, & plurimi ex vetuſtioribus, tum *Græcis,* tum *Latinis,* iſtud non habent quod, tamen, in *Græcis* ɴoſtris codicibus, & apud veterem *Latinum* interpretem legitur; & ſanè videtur retinendum, niſi proximè antecedens verſiculus expungatur. ¶ *Et hi ties in unum conſentiunt,* και οι τρεις εις το εν εισιν. *Compluteiſis* editio hæc non legit hoc in loco, quæ tamen mihi videntur prorſus retinenda, ut intelligamus hæc omni teſtimonia penitus conſentiie; & ad unum, et eundem, illum ſcopum tendere.

No XII.

The Preface of Robert Stephens to his Edition of the *Greek* Teſtament of A D 1550.

Robertus Stephanus Typographus regius, Sacrarum literarum ſtudioſis, S.

Superioribus diebus, Chriſtiane lector, Novum Domini noſtri JESU CHRISTI Teſtamentum,

qua,

qua, dictante Spiritu fanto, fcriptum fuit lingua, cum vetuftiffimis *fedecim* fcriptis exemplaribus, quanta maxima potuimus cura, et diligentia, collatum, minore forma, minutioribufque Regiis characteribus, tibi excudimus! Idem nunc iterum et tertio, cum iifdem collatum, majoribus vero etiam Regiis typis excufum, tibi offerimus; iis praefixis (nequid defyderes) infertifve, aut in calce pofitis, quæ ufquam in fcriptis, aut excufis leguntur codicibus. quæ omnia, augufta alterius forma capere non potuerat. Ad hæc, in margine interiori varias codicum lectiones addidimus: quarum unicuique numeri *Græci* nota fubjuncta eft, quæ nomen exemplaris, unde fumpta eft, indicet. aut exemplarium nomina, quum plures funt numeri.

Iis nanque placuit, primo, fecundo, ad fextum-decimum ufque, nomina imponere. ut primo, *Complutenfem* editionem intelligas, quæ olim ad antiquiffima exemplaria fuit excufa : cui certè cum noftris mirus erat in plurimis confenfus. Secundo, exemplar vetuftiffimum, in *Italia* ab amicis collatum. Tertio, quarto, quinto, fexto, feptimo, octavo, decimo, & quinto-decimo, ea quæ ex bibliotheca Regis habuimus. Cætera funt ea quæ undique corrogare licuit. Cujus, quidem, vetuftiorum codicum colla* *iis, doctiffimos *Hebræorum* authores habemus.   *os* poft reductum è *Babylo-*

nia

nia populum Dei, quum facros veteris Teftamenti libros difcrepare verbis aliquando, aut apicibus, etiam comperiffent, diverfam in margine lectionem adnotaffe, teftantur hodie libri ad exemplaria fcripta excufi. Capitum, præterea, juxta *Græcos* divifionem, in interiori margine numeris *Græcis* notavimus, quibus refpondent in Evangeliis κεφαλαια in fuperiore, & inferiore, paginarum parte . in Epiftolis, vero, ipfa κελαφαια fingulis Epiftolis præfixa. *Latinorum* autem capita numeris & ipfa *Græcis*, in margine exteriori fignificavimus . ipfofque *Latinos* fequuti, breviora capita in quatuor, longiora in feptem, partes diftribuimus · literis alphabeticis majufculis partes illas in eodem margine fignantes. Ubi etiam, et *Latinorum* more, notavimus locum, vel ex Evangelifta aliquo, vel ex Apoftolicis fcriptis, qui cum præfenti loco aut idem fit prorfus, aut non parum abfimilis · aut qui certe, cum ipfo collatus, lucem aliquam afferre poffe videatur: adjecta litera majufcula, quæ capitis eam partem indicet, in qua quæri locus ille debeat. Locos ex Veteri teftamento aut ad verbum, aut eodem fenfu citatos, magna cura fignavimus. Nec tamen omifimus *Eufebii Cæfarienfis* canones, fed iis quoque in interiori margine locum dedimus, ut *Græcis* etiam fatisfieret. Sed ne numerum quidem ϛιχων, prefertim quum is in noftris prope omnibus codicibus invenietur, in calce cujufque Evangelii, & Epiftolæ. Quam rationem

recenfendi

recenfendi ςιχ8ς, & apud nonnullos piophanos
fcriptores videre eft.

Hæc verò omnia, ut te alacriorem ad facrofancti
Novi Teftamenti *Servatoris* noftri, DEI, lectionem
redderemus, nobis effe fufcepta exiftimato. Noftris
igitur utere, & fruere laboribus, dum ad tandiu
delyderata *Juftini*, philofophi, & martyris, accin-
gimur opeia. Vale.

No XIII.

Incipit Prologus feptem Epiftolarum Canonicarum.

Non idem ordo eft apud *Græcos*, qui integrè fa-
piunt, et fidem rectam lectantui, epiftolarum feptem, quæ *Canonicæ* nuncupantur, qui in *Latinis*
codicibus invenitur. Quòd quia *Petrus* primus
eft in numero Apoftolorum, primæ funt etiam ejus
epiftolæ in oidine cæteiaium. Sed ficut Evan-
geliftas dudum ad veritatis lineam correximus, ita
has proprio ordini, Deo nos juvante, reddidimus.
Eft enim prima earum una *Jacobi*; *Petri* duæ;
Johannis tres, et *Judæ* una. Quæ fi ut ab eis di-
geftæ funt, ita quoque ab interpretibus fideliter
in *Latinum* verterentui eloquium, nec ambiguita-
tem legentibus facerent, nec fermonum fefe varietas impugnaret; illo piæcipue loco ubi de unitate
Trinitatis in prima *Johannis* epiftola pofitum legi-
mus. In qua etiam ab infidelibus tranflatoribus
multùm

multùm erratum esse a fidei veritate comperimus; trium tantùm vocabula, hoc est, aquæ, sanguinis, et spiritus, in sua editione ponentes, et Patris, Verbique, ac Spiritus testimonium omittentes, in quo maximè et fides Catholica roboratur, et Patris, ac Filii, ac Spiritus sancti una divinitatis substantia comprobatur. In cæteris vero Epistolis, quantum a nostra aliorum distet editio, lectoris prudentiæ derelinquo.

Sed tu, virgo Christi, *Eustochium*, dum a me impensius Scripturæ veritatem inquiris, meam quodammodo senectutem invidorum dentibus corrodendam exponis, qui me falsarium, corruptoremque sacrarum Scripturarum, pronunciant. Sed ego, in tali opere, nec æmulorum meorum invidentiam pertimesco, nec sanctæ Scripturæ veritatem poscentibus denegabo.

(*Hieronymi* divina Bibliotheca, per *Martianay*, Edit. *Parisiis*, A. D. 1693, page 1667—9.

No. XIV.

Extracts from VICTOR VITENSIS, De Persecutione Vandalica.

(Note. This History is comprised in three Books, containing fifty-three pages in folio.)

The

The Edict of *Huneric* mentioned in page 24.

REX HUNERICUS *Vandalorum* & *Alanorum*, univerfis Epifcopis *Omoufianis*.

Non femel, fed fæpius, conftat effe prohibitum, ut in fortibus Vandalorum facerdotes veftri conventus minime celebrarent, ne fua feductione animas fubverterent Chriftianas. Quam rem fpernentes, plurimi reperti funt contra interdictum Miffas in fortibus Vandalorum egiffe, afferentes fe integram regulam Chriftianæ fidei tenere Et quia in Provinciis a Deo nobis conceffis fcandalum effe nolumus, ideo Dei providentia cum confenfu fanctorum Epifcoporum noftrorum hoc nos ftatuiffe cognofcite, ut ad diem Kalendarum Februariarum proxime futurarum, amiffa omni excufatione formidinis, omnes *Carthaginem* veniatis, ut de ratione fidei cum noftris venerabilibus Epifcopis poffitis inire conflictum, et de fidei OMOUSIANORUM, *quam defenditis*, de DIVINIS SCRIPTURIS *proprie approbetis*, quo poffit agnofci fi integram fidem teneatis. Hujus autem Edicti tenorem, univerfis Epifcopis tuis per univerfam *Africam* conftitutis, direximus

Data fub die XIII Kal. *Jun.* Anno VII *Hunerici*.

Appropinquabat jam futurus dies ille calumniofus Kalendarum Februariarum, ab eodem ftatutus.

tus. Conveniunt non folùm univerfæ Africæ, verùm etiam infulaium multarum Epifcopi, afflictione, et mæroie, confecti. Fit filentium diebus multis, quoufque peritos quofque et doctiffimos viros exinde fepararet, calumniis appofitis enecandos. Nam unum ex ipfo choro Doctoium, nomine LÆTUM, ftrenuum, atque doctiffimum viium, poft diutuinos caiceris fqualores, incendio concremavit, æftimans tali exemplo timorem incutiens reliquos elifuium. Tandem venitur ad difputationis conflictum, ad locum fcilicet quem delegerant adverfarii. Evitantes igitur noftri vocifeiationis tumultus, ne foitè poftmodum Ariani dicerent quod eos noftroium oppreffit multitudo, eligunt de fe noftii qui pro omnibus refpondeient, decem. Collocat fibi Cyrila cum fuis fatellitibus in loco excelfo fuperbiffimum thionum, aftantibus noftiis. Dixeruntque noftri epifcopi. Illa eft femper grata collocatio, ubi fuperba non dominatur poteftatis elatio: fed ex confenfu communi venitui, ut cognitoiibus decernentibus, partibus agentibus, quod verum eft agnofcatur. Nunc, autem, qui eiit cognitor, qui examinator, vel libra juftitiæ aut bene prolata confirmet, aut prave affumpta refellat? Et cum talia et alia dicerentur, notarius regis refpondit: *Patiarcha Cyrila*, dixit, *legatur nobis*. Quo concedente iftud fibi nomen Cyrila affumpfit. Et exinde ftrepitum concitantes, calumniari adverfaiii cœperunt. Et quia hoc

noftii

nostri petierant, ut saltem si examinare non licebat, prudenti multitudini vel expectare liceret, jubentur universi filii catholicæ ecclesiæ, qui adeiant, centenis fustibus tundi. Tunc clamare cœpit beatus Eugenius: Videat Deus vim quam patimui, cognoscat afflictionem persecutionum quam à persecutoribus sustinemus. Conversique nostri, Cyrilæ dixerunt: Propone quod disponis. Cyrila dixit · Nescio latine. Nostri episcopi dixerunt: Semper te latine esse locutum manifesto novimus, modo excusare non debes, præsertim quia tu hujus rei incendium suscitasti. Et videns catholicos episcopos ad conflictum magis fuisse paratos, omnino audientiam diversis cavillationibus declinavit. Quod ante nostri providentes, libellum de fide conscripserant, satis decenter sufficienterque conscriptum, dicentes: Si nostram fidem cognoscere desideratis, hæc est veritas quam tenemus.

PROFESSIO FIDEI CATHOLICÆ.

Regali imperio, fidei catholicæ, quam tenemus, præcipimur reddere rationem · ideoque aggredimur, pro nostrarum virium mediocritate, divino fulti adjutorio, quod credimus & prædicamus, breviter intimare. Primum igitur de unitate substantiæ Patris & Filii, quod Græci ὁμοούσιον dicunt, exponendum nobis esse cognoscimus. Patrem ergo, & Filium, & Spiritum sanctum, ita in unitate

B   deitatis

deitatis profitemur, ut & Patrem in fuæ proprietate perfonæ fubfiftere, & Filium nihilominus in
propria extare perfona, atque Spiritum fanctum
perfonæ fuæ proprietatem retinere, fideli confeffi-
one fateamur · non eumdem afferentes Patrem quem
Filium, neque Filium confitentes qui Pater fit,
aut Spiritus fanctus . neque ita Spiritum fanctum
accipimus, ut aut Pater fit, aut Filius . fed ingenitum
Patrem, & de Patre genitum Filium, & de Patre et
Filio procedentem fpiritum fanctum, unius credimus
effe fubftantiæ vel effentiæ . quia ingeniti Patris,
et geniti Filii, & procedentis Spiritus fancti, una
eft deitas, tres vero perfonarum proprietates.   Et
quia contra hanc catholicam, vel apoftolicam fidem
exorta hærefis NOVITATEM QUAMDAM, induxerat,
afferens Filium non de Patris fubftantia genitum,
fed ex nullis extantibus, id eft ex nihilo, fubftitiffe . ad hanc impietatis profeffionem, quæ contra
fidem emerferat, refellendam, & penitus abolen-
dam, ομασια fermo Græcus pofitus eft, quod inter-
pretatur unius fubftantiæ, vel effentiæ, fignificans
Filium non ex nullis extantibus, nec ex alia fubftantia, fed de Patre, natum effe.   Qui ergo putat
omoufion auferendum, ex nihilo vult afferere Filium
extitiffe.   Sed fi ex nihilo non eft, ex Patre fine
dubio eft, & recte *omoufios*, id eft, unius cum Patre
fubftantiæ, Filius eft.   Ex Patre autem effe, id eft,
unius cum Patre fubftantiæ, his teftimonis approba-
tur, Apoftolo dicente . Qui cum fit fplendor gloriæ,
& figura fubftantiæ ejus, gerens quoque omnia verbo

bo virtutis suæ. Et ipse iterum Deus Pater, in-
credulorum perfidiam objurgans, qui prædicantis
per Prophetas Filii vocem in sua substantia manen-
tem, audire noluerunt, dixit. Non audierunt vocem substantiæ. Quam vocem substantiæ cum
tam terribili intestatione increpans, ad eumdem
Prophetam loquitur, dicens : Super montes accipi-
te planctum, & super semitas deserti luctum, quia
defecerunt, eò quod non sint homines · non audierunt
vocem substantiæ, à volatibus cœli usque ad peco-
ra. Et rursum eos, qui à professione unius substantiæ declinantes, in eadem fidei substantia stare
noluerunt, increpat, dicens. Si stetissent in substantia mea, avertissem utique eos à via sua mala,
& à pessimis · cogitationibus suis. Et iterum non
extra substantiam Patris Filium confitendum, sed
eadem fideliter mentis oculis contuendum, aper-
tissime declaratur, dum dicit Propheta : Quis ste-
tit in substantia Domini, & vidit verbum ejus ?
Patris ergo substantiam Filium esse, Propheticis
jam olim designatum est oraculis, dicente Salomo-
ne. Substantiam enim, & dulcedinem tuam, quam
in filios habes, ostendebas, quam in figura, & imagine, panis cœlestis, populo Israel cœlitùs apparet profluxisse : Quod ipse Dominus in Evangelio
exposuit, dicens. Non Moyses dedit vobis panem
de cœlo, sed Pater meus dat vobis panem de cælo :
se utique panem esse designans, cum dicit, Ego sum
panis vivus, qui de cœlo descendi : de quo etiam

Propheta

Propheta David dicit . Panem Angelorum man-
ducavit homo.   Namque ut adhuc evidentius Patris & Filii fubftantiæ unitas, & divinitatis æqua-
litas, oftendatur, ipfe in evangelio dicit . Ego &
Pater unum fumus   Quod non ad unitatem tan-
tummodo voluntatis, fed ad unam refertur eamdemque fubftantiam, quia non dixit, Ego & Pater unum volumus, fed unum fumus.   Ex eo enim
quod funt, non ex eo tantum quod volunt, paternæ
unitatis declaratur affertio.   Item Joannes Evangelifta dicit, Propterea quærebant eum Judæi interficere, quia non folum folvebat fabbatum, fed &
Patrem fuum dicebat Deum, æqualem fe faciens
Deo.   Quod utique non ad Judæos eft penitus
referendum, quia Evangelifta veraciter dixit de Filio, quia æqualem fe faciebat Deo.   Item in Evangelio fcriptum eft , Quæcunque Pater facit, eadem & Filius facit, fimiliter & ficut Pater fufci-
tat mortuos, & vivificat, ita & Filius quos vult
vivificat   Item, ut homines honorificent Filium,
ficut honorificant Patrem.   Æqualis enim honor
non nifi æqualibus exhibetur.   Item ibi Filius ad
Patrem dicit, Omnia mea tua funt, & tua mea
Item   Philippe, qui me videt, videt & Patrem
Quomodo tu dicis, Oftende nobis Patrem ? Hoc
non dixiffet, nifi Patri per omnia fuiffet æqualis.
Item ipfe Dominus dixit : Creditis in Deum, &
in me credite.   Et adhuc ut unitatem æqualitat
demonftraret, ait: Nemo novit Filium nifi Pater,

                                            neque

neque Patrem quis novit nisi Filius, & cui volue-
rit Filius ievelare · Et ficut Filius cui vult revelat
Patrem, ita & Pater revelat Filium . ficut ipfe
Petro ait, confitenti eum Chriftum Filium Dei vivi :
Beatus es, inquit, Simon Barjona, quia caro &
fanguis non ievelavit tibi, fed Pater meus qui in
cœlis eft. Et iterum Filius dicit : Nemo venit ad
Patrem, nifi per me, & nemo venit ad me, nifi Pater
qui mifit me, attraxerit eum. Unde claret æqualitatem Patris & Filii ad fe invicem ciedentes addu-
ceie. Item dicit . Si cognoviffetis me, & Patiem
meum utique cognoviffetis, & à modo noftis eum,
& vidiftis eum. Veium quia duas in Filio
profitemur effe naturas, id eft, Deum veium, &
hominem verum, corpus & animam habentem,
quicquid eigo excellenti fublimitatis potentia de
eo refeiunt fcriptuiæ, admirandæ ejus divinitati
tiibuendum fentimus & quicquid infra honorem
cœleftis potentiæ de eodem hu milius enarratur,
non Verbo Dei, fed homini ieputamus affumpto.

Secundum divinitatem eigo eft, quod fuperius
diximus, ubi ait : Ego & Pater unum fumus Et
Qui videt me, videt & Patrem. Et Omnia quæcunque Patei facit, eadem Filius fimiliter · Vel cætera quæ fuperius continentur. Illa veio quæ de eo
fecundum hominem referuntur, ifta funt · Patei ma-
joi me eft. Et · Non veni facere voluntatem meam,
fed voluntatem ejus qui mifit me Et Pater, fi fieii

poteft,

poteſt, tranſeat à me calix iſte　vel cum de cruce
dicit. Deus, Deus meus, quare me dereliquiſti? Et
iterum ex perſona Filii Propheta dicit. De ventre
matris meæ Deus meus es tu: Vel cum minor an-
gelis indicatur, & quàm plura his ſimilia, quæ
ſtudio brevitatis non inſeruimus. Filius ergo Dei,
nullis conditionem neceſſitatibus obſtrictus, ſed
libera divinitatis potentia, ita, quæ noſtra ſunt,
mirabili pietate aſſumpſit, ut à ſuis, quæ divina
ſunt, omnino non deſtiterit: quia divinitas nec
augmentum admittit, nec patitur detrimentum.
Unde gratias agimus Domino noſtro Jeſu Chriſto,
qui propter nos, & propter noſtram ſalutem, de
cœlo deſcendit, ſua paſſione nos redemit, ſua mor-
te vivificavit, ſua aſcentione glorificavit: Qui ſe-
dens ad dexteram Patris, venturus eſt judicare vi-
vos, et mortuos · juſtis æternæ vitæ præmium lar-
giturus, impiis atque incredulis merita ſupplicia
redditurus.

Profitemur itaque Patrem de ſeipſo, hoc eſt de
eo quod ipſe eſt, ſempiterne atque ineffabiliter Filium genuiſſe, non extrinſecùs, non ex nihilo, non
ex alia genuiſſe materia, ſed ex Deo natum eſſe:
et qui de Deo natus eſt, non aliud eſt quàm id
quod Pater eſt, et idcirco unius ſubſtantiæ eſt,
quia veritas nativitatis diverſitatem non admittit
generis　Nam ſi alterius à Patre ſubſtantiæ eſt,
aut verus Filius non eſt, aut (quod nefas eſt dicere)

degener

degener natus eft. Eft enim verus Filius, ficut Joannes ait. Ut fimus in vero Filio ejus. Non eft etiam degener, quia Deus verus de Deo natus eft vero : ficut idem Joannes Evangelifta exequitur, dicens : Hic eft verus Deus, & vita æterna. Et ipfe Dominus in Evangelio. Ego fum, inquit, via, veritas, & vita. Ergo fi aliunde fubftantiam non habet, de Patre habet. Si de Patre habet, unius fubftantiæ cum Patre eft. Sed fi unius fubftantiæ non eft, ergo non de Patre, fed aliunde eft : quoniam unde eft, inde fubftantiam habeat neceffe eft. Omnia enim ex nihilo, Fillius vero de Patre. De duobus eligat quifque quod velit : aut det ei fubftantiam de Patre, aut fateatur ex nihilo fubftitiffe. Sed Propheticum forfitan objicitur teftimonium. Generationem ejus quis enarrabit ? Cum ego non dixerim, Enarra mihi modum vel qualitatem, divinæ generationis, et tanti fecreti archanum humanis verbis enuntia, quoniam unde natus fit, non quem ad modum natus fit, requifivi. Divina enim generatio inenarrabilis eft, non ignorabilis. Nam ufque adeo non eft ignorabilis, id eft, non ignoratur unde fit, ut & Pater de ipfo genuiffe, & Filius de Patre fe natum fæpiffime proteftetur. Quod nullus omnino ambigit Chriftianus, ficut in Evangelio demonftratur, ipfo Filio dicente : Qui autem non credit, jam judicatus eft, quia non credidit in nomine unigeniti Filii Dei. Item Joannes Evangelifta dicit · Et

vidimus

vidimus gloriam ejus, gloriam quafi unigeniti à Patre.

Ergo profeffionem noftram brevi fermone concludimus. Si vere de Patre natus eft, unius fubftantiæ eft, & verus Filius eft. Sed fi unius fubftantiæ non eft, nec verus Filius eft. Et fi verus Filius non eft, nec verus Deus eft : aut fi verus Deus eft, & tamen de patris fubftantiæ non eft, ingenitus ergo & ipfe eft. Sed quia ingenitus non eft, factura ergo eft, ut putatur aliunde fubfiftens, fi de Patris fubftantiæ non eft. Sed abfit hoc ita credere Nos enim unius fubftantiæ cum Patre filium profitemur, deteftantes Sabellianam hære-fim, quæ ita Sanctam Trinitatem confundit, ut eumdem dicat effe Patrem quem Filium, eumdemque credat effe Spiritum fanctum, non fervans tres in unitate perfonas.

Sed forfitan objicitur, cum ingenitus Pater fit, genitus Filius, non fieri poffe unam eamdemque effe fubftantiam geniti, atque ingeniti, cum utique, fi ficut ingenitus Pater eft, ingenitus effet & Filius, tunc magis diverfa poffet effe fubftantia, quia unufquifque à feipfo fubfiftens, communem fubftantiam cum altero non haberet. Cum vero ingenitus Pater de feipfo, id eft, de eo quod ipfe eft, fi quid illud eft aut dici poteft, (immò quia ut eft dici omnino non poteft) Filium generavit, apparet

ret unam effe gignentis, genitique, fubftantiam : quia Deum de Deo, lumen de lumine, Filium effe veraciter profitemur Nam lucem effe Patrem, Joannes apoftolus teftis eft, dicens. Quia Deus lux eft, & tenebræ in eo non funt ullæ. Item de Filio ait. Et vita erat lux hominum, & lux in tenebris lucet, & tenebræ eam non comprehenderunt. Et infra : Erat lumen verum, quod illuminat omnem hominem venientem in hunc mundum. Unde apparet Patrem, & Filium, unius effe fubftantiæ, dum lucis, & luminis, diverfa non poteft effe fubftantia, ejus fcilicet quæ de fe gignit, & quæ de gignente exiftit.

Denique ne aliquis inter Patrem, & Filium, diverfitatem naturalis luminis introducat, ideo apoftolus de eodem Filio dicit : Qui cum fit fplendor gloriæ, & figura fubftantiæ ejus. In quo evidentius & coæternus Patri, & infeparabilis à Patre, & unius cum eo effe fubftantiæ, perdocetur: dum luci fplendor eft femper coæternus, dum fplendor a luce nunquam feparatus eft, dum fplendor à luce, natura fubftantiæ, nunquam poteft effe diverfus. Qui enim fplendor lucis eft, idem & Dei Patris virtus eft. Sempiternus ergo propter virtutis æternitatem, infeparabilis propter claritudinis unitatem. Et hoc eft quod nos fideliter profitemur, Filium de Patris fubftantia natum· ficut ipfe Pater Deus apertiffimum perhibet teftimonium. Qui ut de fua ineffabilis naturæ fubftantia proprium Filium genuiffe monftraret,

ad

ad inftruendam fragilitatis noftræ imperitiam, ut
nos ex vifibilibus ad invifibilia erigeret, terrenæ
nativitatis vocabulum ad divinæ generationis trax-
it exemplum, dicens: Ex utero ante luciferum
genui te. Quid clarius, quid luculentius, effari
divinitas dignaretur ? Quibus indiciis, quibus
exiftentium rerum exemplis, proprietatem generationis potuit intimare, quam ut, per uteri appel-
lationem, proprietatem genetricis oftenderet ? Non
quia corporeis compofitus eft membris, aut aliqui-
bus artuum lineamentis diftinctus; fed quia nos
aliter veritatem divinæ generationis, auditu mentis,
percipere non poffemus, nifi humani uteri provo-
caremur vocabulo, ut ambigi ultra non poffet
de Dei fubftantia natum effe, quem conftat ex Patris utero exftitiffe. Credentes ergo Deum Patrem
de fua fubftantia impaffibiliter Filium generaffe,
non dicimus ipfam fubftantiam aut divifam effe
in Filio, aut diminutionem pertuliffe in Patre ·
et per hoc paffionis potuiffe vicio fubjacere. Abfit
enim à nobis, ut talia vel opinemur, vel cogitemus,
de Deo: quia nos perfectum Patrem, perfectum
Filium, fine fui diminutione, fine aliqua derivati-
one, fine omni, omnino, paffionis infirmitate, genuiffe fideliter profitemur. Nam qui objicit Deo,
quod fi de feipfo genuit, divifionis vicium pertulit: poteft dicere, quia et laborem fenfit quando
univerfa condidit, et ob hoc, die feptima ab omni fuo opere requievit. Sed nec in generando de
fcipfo

feipfo paffionem, vel diminutionem, aliquam fenfit, nec in condendo univerfa fatigationem aliquam pertulit. Namque ut evidentius nobis divinæ generationis impaffibilitas infinuaretur, Deum ex Deo, lumen ex lumine, filium profitendum accepimus. Si ergo in efficientia vifibilis, ac mundani, luminis tale aliquid invenitur, ut lumine ex lumine fumpto, et per quamdam generationis nativitatem exorto, ipfa luminis origo, quæ ex fe lumen aliud dedit, nec minui, nec ullum omnino detrimentum miniftrati ex fe luminis perpeti contingat. quanto rectius, et melius, de divini et ineffabilis luminis natura credendum eft, quæ ex feipfa lumen generans, minui omnino non potuit? Unde æqualis eft Patri Filius, non natus ex tempore, fed gignenti coæternus ficut fplendor, ab igne genitus, gignenti manifeftatur æqualis.

Hæc de Patris et Filii æqualitate, vel de fubftantiæ unitate (quantum brevitatis ratio finit) dixiffe fufficiat. fupereft ut de Spiritu fancto, quem Patri, ac Filio, confubftantivum credimus, coæqualem, et coæternum, dicamus, et teftimoniis approbemus. Licèt enim hæc veneranda Trinitas perfonis, ac nominibus, diftincta fit, non tamen ob hoc à fe, atque à fua æternitate, difcrepare credenda eft, fed manens ante fæcula, divinitatis in Patre et Filio et Spiritu fancto, vere ac proprie creditur, nec dividi noftris interpretationibus poteft,

nec

nec rurfus verfa in unam perfonam Trinitas ipfa confundi. Hæc fides plena, hæc noftra creduli‑ tas eft. Idcirco Deos nec æftimari patimur, nec vocari, fed unum Deum in prædictis perfonis, ac nominibus, confitemur. Inenarrabilis enim divi‑ nitas, non ut concludi, aut apprehendi, velut vo‑ cabulis poffet, intra nomina, perfonafque, fe præ‑ ftitit. fed ut id, quod erat, effe nofceretur, intelli‑ gentiam fui ex parte, quam capere humanæ men‑ tis auguftiæ prævalebant, credentibus dedit, Pro‑ pheta dicente · Nifi credideritis, non intelligetis. Una eft ergo Trinitatis deitas, et in hujus vocabu‑ li appellatione, fignificatio eft unius fubftantiæ, non unius perfonæ. Ad quam rem fidelibus compro‑ bandam in teftimonium fui divinitas ipfa multis, et creberrimis, conteftationibus femper affuit. Li‑ ceat ergo ob brevitatis compendia, ex multis pau‑ ca proferre, quoniam veræ probatio majeftatis, ta‑ metfi habet pluralitatem teftimoniorum, pluroli‑ tate tamen non indiget, quoniam credenti pauca fufficiunt.

Primum igitur de Veteris teftamenti libris, poft etiam novi, Patrem, et Filium, et Spiritum fanctum, unius docebimus effe fubftantiæ, libro Genefis fic inchoante: In principio fecit Deus cœlum, et ter‑ ram. Terra autem erat invifibilis, et incompofita, et tenebræ erant fuper abyffum, et fpiritus Dei fe‑ rebatur fuper aquas. Ille principium, qui Judæis,

quis

quis effet interrogantibus, dixit · Principium qui
et loquor vobis. Superferebatur fpiritus Dei fuper aquas, utpote creator virtute potentiæ fuæ con-
tinens creaturam, ut, ex his viva omnia productu-
rus, ipfe rudibus elementis ignis proprii fomenta
præftaret, et jam tunc mysterio emicante baptif-
matis, virtutem fanctificationis liquoris natura per-
ciperet, primaque ad vitam corpora animata pro-
duceret. David pro inde afpirante. Verbo Domini cœli firmati funt, et fpiritu oris ejus omnis virtus
eorum. Vide quam plena fit brevitas, et quam
clare in facramentum unitatis recurit. Patrem in
Domino, in verbi fignificatione Filium ponens,
Spiritum fanctum altiffimi ex ore nuncupavit. Et
ne vocis editio acciperetur in Verbo, cœlos per eum
afferit effe firmatos. Ne autem flatus in Spiritu
reputetur, cœleftis in eo virtutis plenitudinem de-
monftravit. Nam ubi virtus, ibi neceffe eft perfona fubfiftens Ubi omnis non ablata à Patre,
et Filio, fed confummata fignificatur in Spiritu
fanclo, non ut folus habeat quod in Patre, et Filio eft, fed ut totum habeat cum utroque. Et iterum cum de vocatione gentium Dominus loquere-
tur, intra unum divinitatis nomen Spiritum fanctum prædicans, ait Euntes docete omnes gentes,
baptizantes eos in nomine Patris, et Filii, et Spiritus fancti Et iterum cœleftia Corinthiis preca-
tus Apoftolus hæc fubdidit. Gratia Domini noftri
Jefu Chrifti, et charitas Dei, et communicatio
fanct.

fanɗi Spiritus, cum omnibus vobis. Et ut aper‑
tius in hac Trinitate unitatem fubſtantiæ fateamur,
illud etiam nobis eſt intuendum, quomodo Deus,
cum de mundi et hominis creatione diſponeret,
facramentum Trinitatis oſtenderet, dicens. Facia‑
mus hominem ad imaginem, et fimilitudinem, noſ‑
tram. Cum dicit noſtram, oſtendit utique non u‑
nius. Cum vero imaginem et fimilitudinem pro‑
fert, æqualitatem diſtinɗionis perſonarum inſinuat,
ut in eodem opere Trinitatis fit aperta cognitio, in
quo nec pluralitas caffa eſt, nec fimilitudo diſſenti‑
ens, dum et conſequentia fic loquuntur : Et dixit
Deus, et facit, et benedixit Deus. Et neceſſe eſt
ut creationis totius auɗor, Deus unus fit. Quam
fidei rationem antiqua, denique, per Mofen bene‑
diɗio pandit et comprobat, qua benedicere popu‑
lum facramento trinæ invocationis jubetur. Ait
enim Deus ad Mofen Sic benedices populum me‑
um, et ego benedicam illos. Benedicat te Domi‑
nus, et cuſtodiat te. Illuminet Dominus faciem
fuam fupei te, et mifereatur tui. Attollat Domi‑
nus faciem fuam fuper te, et det tibi pacem. Quod
hoc ipfum Propheta David affirmat, dicens: Bene‑
dicat nos Deus, Deus noſter, benedicat nos Deus,
et metuant eum omnes fines terræ. Quam Trini‑
tatis unitatem fupernæ Angelorum virtutes hymno
venerantur, et ter numero, Sanɗus, Sanɗus, Sanc‑
tus Dominus Deus Sabaoth, indefinenti canentes

ore,

ore, in unius faftigium dominationis gloriam ejus
exaltant. Quod ut adhuc apertius fidelium fenfi-
bus inculcetur, cœleftium myfteriorum confcium
producimus Paulum. Ait enim · Divifiones autem donationum funt, idem autem Spiritus : et divifiones miniftrationum funt, idem autem Dominus . et divifiones operationum funt, idem vero
Deus qui operatur omnia in omnibus. Et certe
has divifionum differentias pro qualitate ac merito
participantium, Spiritum fanctum docuit operari,
cum ipfarum gratiarum differentias partiretur, in
ultimis intulit, dicens: Hæc autem omnia operatur unus atque idem Spiritus, dividens propria
unicuique prout vult. Unde nullius ambiguitati
relinquitur locus, quin clareat Spiritum fanctum
et Deum effe, et fuæ voluntatis actorem, qui cuncta
operari, et fecundum propriæ voluntatis arbitrium
divinæ difpenfationis dona largiri, apertiffime demonftratur. Quia ubi voluntaria diftributio præ-
dicatur, non poteft videri conditio fervitutis. In
creatura enim fervitus intelligenda eft, in Trinitate
vero dominatio, ac libertas. Et ut adhuc luce clarius unius divinitatis esse cum Patre, et Filio,
Spiritum sanctum doceamus, Joannis Evange-
listæ testimonio comprobatur, ait namque:
Tres sunt qui testimonium perhibent in coe-
lo, Pater, Verbum, et Spiritus sanctus, et
hi tres unum sunt. Numquid ait tres in diffe-
rentiæ qualitate fejuncti, aut quibuflibet diverfi-
tatum

tatum gradibus longo feparationis intervallo divi-
fi ? Sed tres, inquit, unum funt. Ut autem magis magifque fancti Spiritus cum Patre, et Filio,
una divinitas in creandis rebus omnibus demon-
ftraretur, habes creatorem Spiritum fanctum in
libro Job primo · Spiritus, inquit, divinus eft qui
fecit me, et Spiritus omnipotentis qui docet me.
Et David dicit Emitte Spiritum tuum, et creabun-
tur, et renovabis faciem terræ. Si renovatio, et
creatio, per Spiritum erit, fine dubio et principium
creationis fine fpiritu non fuit. Poft creationem igitur oftendamus, quia vivificat etiam Spiritus fanctus, ficut Pater et Filius Equidem de perfona
Patris refert Apoftolus : Teftor in confpectu Dei,
qui vivificat omnia. Vitam vero dat Chriftus,
Oves, inquit, meæ vocem meam audiunt, et ego
vitam æternam do illis. Vivificamur vero à Spiritu fancto, ipfo dicente Domino : Spiritus eft
qui vivificat. Ecce una vivificatio Patris, et Filii, et Spiritus fancti, aperte monftrata eft. Præ-
fcientiam rerum omnium in Domino effe, et occultorum cognitionem, licèt nemo Chriftianus ig-
noret, tamen ex Danielis libro monftrandum eft.
Deus, inquit, qui occultorum cognitor es, qui
præfcius omnium antequam nafcantur. Hæc eadem
præfcientia in Chrifto eft, ficut refert Evangelifta.
Ab initio autem fciebat Jefus quis effet eum tra-
diturus, vel qui effent non credentes in eum Quod
fit autem occultorum cognitor, ex hoc manifeftum

eft,

eſt, cum obſcura conſilia Judæorum traducens
dicebat: Quid cogitatis nequam in cordibus veſ-
tiis? Similiter præſcire omnia Spiritum ſanctum
ipſe manifeſtavit dicens ad apoſtolos: Cum venerit Spiritus veritatis, docebit vos omnia, & ventura annunciabit vobis. Qui ventura nuntiare
perhibetur, præſcire omnia non dubitatur, quia
ipſe ſcrutatur etiam altitudines Dei, & novit omnia quæ in Deo ſunt: ſicut memorat Paulus dicens. Spiritus enim omnia ſcrutatur, etiam altitudines Dei. Item in eodem loco. Sicut nemo ſcit
hominum quæ ſunt hominis niſi ſpiritus ejus qui in
ipſo eſt: ita nemo ſcit quæ ſunt Dei niſi Spiritus
Dei.

Ad intelligendam vero potentiam Spiritus
ſancti, pauca de terribilibus proferamus. Ven-
diderat poſſeſſionem, ut ſcriptum eſt in Actibus
Apoſtolorum, ſuppreſſa parte pecuniæ, doloſus
diſcipulus, reliquum pro toto ante pedes ponens
Apoſtolorum Offendit Spiritum ſanctum quem
putabat latere. Sed quid ad eum dixit continuo
beatus Petrus: Anania, quare ſatanas replevit
cor tuum, ut mentireris Spiritui Sancto? & infra:
non es mentitus hominibus, ſed Deo Atque ita
percuſſus virtute ejus cui mentiri voluerat, ex-
piravit. Quid hic vult beatus Petrus intelligi
Spiritum Sanctum? Utique clarum eſt, cum dicit: Non es mentitus hominibus, ſed Deo. Mani-

C   feſtum,

feftum eft ergo, quoniam qui mentitur Spiritui
fancto, Deo mentitur. & qui credit in Spiritum
fanctum, credit in Deum. Tale aliquid, imò fortius quiddam, dominus in Evangelio oftendit:
omne peccatum, & blafphemia, remittitur hominibus: qui autem blafphemat in Spiritum
fanctum, non remittetur ei neque in hoc feculo,
neque in futuro. Ecce terribili fententia irremif-
fibile dicit effe peccatum ei qui in Spiritum
fanctum blafphemaverit Compara huic fententiæ
illud quod fcriptum eft in libro Regum Si pec-
cando peccaverit vir in virum, orabunt pro eo ·
fi autem in Dominum peccaverit, quis orabit pro
eo? Si ergo blafphemare in Spiritum fanctum, &
peccare in Deum fimile, id eft inexpiabile crimen
eft, jam quantus fit Spiritus fanctus, unufquifque
cognofcit. Deus, qued ubique fit prefens, im-
pleat omnia, ore difcimus Efaiæ: Ego, inquit,
Deus approximans, & non de longinquo? Si
abfconditus fuerit homo in abfconditis, ergo ego
non videbo eum? nònne cœlum & terram ego
impleo? Quod autem Deus fit ubique, falvator
in evangelio: Ubicunque, ait, fuerint duo vel
tres collecti in nomine meo, ibi & ego fum in
medio eorum. De fpiritu adæquè fancto, quod
adfit ubique, dicit Propheta ex Perfona Dei. Ego
in vobis, & fpiritus meus ftat in medio veftrum
Et Salomon ait Spiritus domini replevit orbem
terrarum, & hoc, quod continet omnia, fcientiam
habet

habet vocis. Item David dicit: Quo ibo à Spiritu tuo, & à facie tua quò fugiam? ſi aſcendero in cœlum, tu illic es; ſi deſcendero in infernum, ades Si ſumpſero pennas meas in directum, et habitavero in extremis maris. Etenim illic manus tua deducet me, & continebit me dextera tua. Habitat Deus in ſanctis ſuis ſecundum promiſſionem, quia dixerat: Habitabo in illis. Quod vero dominus Jeſus dicit in evangelio: Manete in me, & ego in vobis · probat hoc Paulus dicens. An neſcitis quia Jeſus Chriſtus eſt in vobis? Hoc autem totum in Spiritus habitatione adimpletur, ſicut memorat Joannes: Ex hoc, inquit, ſcimus quia in nobis eſt, quia de Spiritu ſuo dedit nobis. Similiter & Paulus: Neſcitis quia templum Dei eſtis, & Spiritus Dei habitat in vobis? Et iterum dicit · Glorificate et portate Deum in corpore veſtro. Quem Deum? Utique Spiritum ſanctum, cujus templum eſſe videmur. Nam quod arguat Pater, arguat Filius, arguat Spiritus ſanctus, ita probatum eſt. In Pſalmo quadrageſimo nono legitur: Peccatori autem dicit Deus. Et infra. Arguam te, et ſtatuam contra faciem tuam. David ſimiliter orans dicit ad Chriſtum: Domine, ne in ira tua arguas me, quia ipſe venturus eſt arguere omnem carnem. Quod vero de Spiritu ſancto ſalvator in evangelio: cum venerit, inquit, Paraclitus, ille arguet mundum de peccato, et de juſtitia, et de judicio. Hoc providens David clamabat Dominum: Quò ibo à Spiritu

tuo,

tuo, et à facie tua quò fugiam? Nam et quòd
bonus fit Pater, bonus Filius, bonus Spiritus
fanctus, fic probatur Dicit Propheta· Bonus es
tu, Domine, et in bonitate tua doce me juſtifica-
tiones tuas. De ſe autem ipſe unigenitus Ego
ſum paſtor bonus. De Spiritu æquè ſancto David
in pſalmo dicit· Spiritus tuus bonus deducet me
in terram rectam. Quis autem illam dignitatem
Spiritus fancti poſſit tacere? Antiqui enim Prophetæ clamabant Hæc dicit Dominus. Hanc
vocem Chriſtus adveniens in ſuam perſonam
revocavit dicens. Ego autem dico vobis. Novi
autem Prophetæ quid clamabant? fic Aga-
bus Propheta in Actibus apoſtolorum: Hæc
dicit Spiritus fanctus. Et Paulus ad Timotheum:
Spiritus, inquit, manifeſte dicit. Quæ vox omnino demonſtrat indifferentiam Trinitatis. Dicit ſe Paulus à Deo Patre & Chriſto vocatum
fuiſſe et miſſum. Paulus, inquit, Apoſtolus, non
ab hominibus, neque per hominem, ſed per Jeſum
Chriſtum, et Dominum patrem. In actibus autem apoſtolorum legitur quod a Spiritu fancto ſit
ſegregatus et miſſus. Sic enim ſcriptum eſt Hæc
dicit Spiritus fanctus Segregate mihi Barnabam,
et Saulem, in opus quo vocavi eos. Et paulo
poſt Ipſi, inquit, miſſi ab Spiritu fancto, deſcen-
derunt Seleuciam. Item in eodem libro· atten-
dite vobis, et univerſo gregi, in quo vos Spiritus
fanctus conſtituit epiſcopos. Ne quis autem Spiri-
　　　　　　　　　　　　　　　　　　　　tum

tum fanctum, quia Paraclitus dictus eft, contemptibile aliquid æftimet. Paraclitus enim advocatus eft, vel pofitus confolator, fecundum Latinam linguam. Quæ appellatio etiam Filio Dei communis eft, ficut dicit Joannes. Hæc, inquit, fcribo vobis, ne peccetis. Sed fi quis peccaverit, Paraclitum habemus apud Patrem, Jefum Chriftum. Nam et ipfe Dominus, cum dicit ad Apoftolos, Alterum Paraclitum mittet vobis Pater. fine dubio, cum dicit alterum Paraclitum, fe quoque Paraclitum manifeftat. Sed neque à Patre hoc nomen Paracliti alienum eft. Beneficentiæ enim nomen eft, non naturæ. Denique ad Corinthios Paulus ita fcribit. Benedictus Deus, et Pater Domini noftri Jefu Chrifti, pater mifericordiarum, et Deus totius confolationis, qui nos confolatur. Et cùm confolator dicitur Pater, confolator dicitur Filius, confolator etiam Spiritus fanctus, una tamen nobis confolatio à Trinitate præftatur, ficut et una remiffio peccatorum, Apoftolo affirmante. Abluti, inquit, eftis, et juftificati, et fanctificati eftis in nomine Domini noftri Jefu Chrifti, et in Spiritu Dei noftri. Poffemus plura adhuc de divinis fcripturis proferre teftimonia, quæ juxta baptifmi facramentum, Trinitatem unius gloriæ, operationis, ac potentiæ, manifeftant. Sed quia ex his plenus eft fapientibus intellectus, multa prætervimus ftudio brevitatis.

Faciam

Faciamus ergo recapitulationem dictorum nos-
tiorum. Si de Patre procedit Spiritus fanctus, fi
liberat, fi Dominus eft, & fanctificat; fi creat cum
Patre & Filio, fi ubique eft, & implet omnia, fi
habitat in electis, fi arguit mundum, fi judicat, fi
bonus & rectus eft, fi de eo clamatur, Hæc dicit
Spiritus fanctus, fi Prophetas conftituit, fi Apoftolos mittit, fi Epifcopos præficit, fi confolator
eft, fi cuncta difpenfat prout vult, fi abluit & juf-
tificat, fi tentatores fuos interficit, fi is qui eum
blafphemaverit, non habet remiffionem, neque in
hoc feculo, neque in futuro, quod utique Deo
proprium eft · Hæc cum ita fint, cui de eo dubitatur quod Deus non fit, cum operum magnitudine
quod eft ipfe manifeftet? Non utique alienum effe
à Patris et Filii majeftate, qui non eft ab opere
virtutum alienus. Fruftra illi nomen divinitatis
negatur, cujus poteftas non poteft abnegari. Fruftra prohibebor eum cum Patre et Filio venerari,
quem exigor cum Patre et Filio confiteri. Si ille
mihi, cum Patre et Filio, confert remiffionem peccatorum, confert fanctificationem, et vitam perpetuam, ingratus fum nimis et impius, fi ei cum
Patre et Filio, non refero gloriam. Aut fi non
cum Patre et Filio colendus, ergo nec confitendus
in baptifmo eft. Si autem omnimodo confitendus
eft fecundum dictum Domini, et traditionem Apoftolorum, ne femiplena fit fides, quis me poterit ab
ejus cultu prohibere? In quem enim credere jubeor,

ei etiam deinde fupplicabo. Adorabo ergo Patrem, adorabo et Filium, adorabo et Spiritum fanctum, una eademque veneratione. Quod fi quis durum hoc putat, audiat quomodo David ad culturam Dei fideles hortatur. Adorate, inquit, fcabellum pedum ejus. Si religionis eft adorare fcabellum pedum ejus, quanto magis religiofum fi ejus Spiritus adoratur? ille utique Spiritus, quem beatus Petrus in tanta fublimitate prædicavit, dicens. Spiritu fancto miffo de cœlis, in quem concupifcunt Angeli profpicere. Si Angeli eum cupiunt afpicere, quanto magis nos homines mortales defpicere non debemus, ne forte et nobis dicatur, ficut dictum eft ad Judæos· Vos femper Spiritui fancto reftitiftis, ficut et patres veftri.

Quod fi hæc tanta et talia non inclinant animum ad venerandum Spiritum fanctum, accipe adhuc aliquid fortius. Sic enim Paulus inftruit Prophetas ecclefiæ in quibus utique, et per quos, Spiritus fanctus loquebatur. Si inquit, omnes prophetaverint, intret autem aliquis infidelis, aut idiota, convincitur ab omnibus, examinatur ab omnibus, occulta quoque cordis ejus manifefta funt: et tunc cadens in faciem adorabit Deum, pronuntians quia vere Deus in vobis eft. Et utique in eis Spiritus fanctus eft qui prophetant. Si ergo infideles cadunt in faciem, et adorant Spiritum fanctum perterriti, et confitentur inviti, quanto magis

fidelibus

fidelibus expedit, ut voluntariè, et ex affectu, adorent Spiritum sanctum? Adoratur autem Spiritus sanctus, non quasi separatim, more gentilium, sicut nec Filius separatim adoratur, quia in dextera Patris est · sed cum adoramus Patrem, credimus nos et Filium, et Spiritum sanctum adorare. quia et cum Filium invocamus, Patrem nos credimus invocare, et cum Patrem rogamus, à Filio nos exaudiri confidimus, sicut ipse Dominus dixit Quicquid petieritis Patrem in nomine meo, ego faciam, ut honorificetur Pater in Filio. Et si Spiritus sanctus adoratur, ille utique adoratur cujus est Spiritus. Illud autem nullus ignorat, quia divinæ majestati nec addi quicquam, nec minui, humanis supplicationibus potest, sed unusquisque secundum propositum voluntatis suæ, aut gloriam sibi acquirit, fideliter venerando, aut confusionem perpetuam, pertinaciter resistendo. Certum est enim, quia contentio et superbia damnat · honorificentia vero fructum devotionis expectat. Quare autem fideles non honorificent integre Trinitatem, ad quam se pertinere confidunt, cujus nomine se renatos, cujus servos se nominari, gloriantur? Nam sicut ad nomen Dei patris homines Dei appellantur, ut Helias homo Dei appellatus est. sic à Christo Christiani nuncupamur, sic etiam ab Spiritu spiritales appellamur. Si igitur vocetur quis homo Dei, et non sit Christianus, nihil est. Qui si Christianus vocetur, et non fuerit spiritalis, nec sibi satis de salute confidat.   Sit

Sit ergo nobis, fecundum falutaris baptifmi confeffionem, fides integra Trinitatis, fit una devotio pietatis, nec more gentilium, poteftatum diverfitates opinemur, aut creaturam quantum ad deitatem in Trinitatem fufpicemur, fed nec Judæorum fcandalo moveamur, qui filium Dei negant, qui Spiritum fanctum non adorant · fed potius perfectam Trinitatem adorantes, et magnificantes, ficut in myfteriis ore noftro dicimus, ita confcientia teneamus Sanctus, Sanctus, Sanctus, Dominus Deus Sabaoth. Ter dicentes Sanctus, unam omnipotentiam confitemur, quia una eft religio, una glorificatio Trinitatis, ut audiamus ab Apoftolo, ficut audierunt Corinthii Gratia Domini noftri Jefu Chrifti, et dilectio Dei, et communicatio Spiritus fancti, cum omnibus vobis.

Hæc eft fides noftra, Evangelicis, et Apoftolicis, traditionibus, et omnium quæ in hoc mundo funt catholicarum ecclefiarum focietate fundata, in qua nos, per gratiam Dei omnipotentis, permanere ufque ad finem vitæ hujus confidimus, et fperamus.

Directa xii kalendarum Majarum, per Januarium Zattarenfem, Villaticum à Cafis medianis, epifcopos Numidiæ, Bonifacio Foratianenfi, Bonifacio Gatianenfi, epifcopis Byzacenis.

No. XV.

No. XV.

Extracts from *Erasmus*'s Letter to *Fischer*.

Christophoro Fischero, Protonotario Apostolico, Erasmus Roterodamus S. D.

Æstate superiore, quum in pervetustâ quâpiam bibliothecâ venarer, (nullis enim in saltibus venatus jucundior) forte in casses meos incidit præda neutiquam vulgaris, *Laurentii Vallæ* in Novum Testamentum Annotationes. &c.

Quòd si quibus non vacat totam *Græcorum* linguam perdiscere, hi tamen *Vallæ* studio non mediocritèr adjuvabuntur, qui mirâ sagacitate Novum omne Testamentum excussit, non pauca obiter annotans, et ex Psalmis, quorum usitata editio à *Græcis* fluxit, non *Hebræis.* Plurimum itaque studiosi debebunt *Laurentio, Laurentius* tibi, per quem publicum accepit, cujusque et judicio bonis ingeniis erit commendatior, et patrocinio contra maledicos instructior.

Parisiis, Anno 1505.   V A L E.

No. XVI.

The Preface to the Bible of COMPLUTUM.

Ad Lectorem.

Ne mireris aut vitio vertas o studiose lector et in hac novi testamenti Greca editione aliter quam in veteri nude tantum littere fine ullis aut spirituum aut tonorum notis impresse publicentur: opere precium visum est hujus tibi rei rationem assignare. Ea enim hujusmodi est Antiquissimos grecos absque hisce fastigiis litterarum scriptitasse notius est: quod ut sit multis argumentis comprobandum. Docent enim id aperte antiqua non pauca exemplaria. ut *Callimachi* poemata nec non et Sibyllina carmina · ac preterea etiam marmorea monumenta vetustissima que rome adhuc visuntur nudis solum characteribus incisa. Ut liquido constet hujusmodi virgularum apicumque suprascriptiones non in illa primeva grece lingue origine fuisse excogitatas: nec ad ejus integritatem usquequaque pertinuisse Cùm igitur universum novum testamentum (preter Evangelium *Matthei*, & epistolas ad Hebreos) grece primum sicut a spiritu sancto dictatum est scriptum esse constet · visum est priscam in eo lingue illius vetustatem majestatemque intactam retinere. ac opus ipsum pretermissis etiam ipsis quibusvis minimis appendiculis

culis excuſſum ad imaginem antiquarum ſcripturarum publicare. Ne rei tam ſancte authoritati ac venerande majeſtati adjectitiis novitiiſque rebus detrimentum afferri videretur accedit quòd (ſi verum fateri volumus) hic ſpirituum tonorumque defectus nullum prorſus impedimentum ad rectam intelligentiam afferre valet his qui aliquantum in Græca eruditione promoverunt. Ceterum ne alicui dubium aliquod poſſit occurrere in qua videlicet ſyllaba accentum oporteat collocari. ſimplex tantum apex in polyſyllabis dictionibus adjectus eſt. et is quidem non tanquam grecus accentus: ſed tanquam notula ſignumque quo dirigi poſſit lector ne in prolatione modulationeve dictionum aliquando labatur. In veteris autem teſtamenti editione Græca cum ea ſolum tranſlatio ſit non originalis textus· non fuit conſilium quicquid ex vulgari ſcribendi modo tollere aut immutare. Et quod non doctis ſolum ſed omnibus in univerſum ſacrarum litterarum ſtudioſis hoc opere conſulendum eſt. appoſite ſunt dictioni cuique litterule Latine ordine alphabeti indicantes que dictio dictioni e regione reſpondeat ne ſit novitiis et nondum adhuc in grecis litteris provectis errandi locus. Rurſus cum nonnulle dictiones grece multiplices ſive equivocas aut alias ambiguas ſignificationes aliquò habere videantur. libuit hoc etiam annotare puncto ſuppoſito litterule latine ſupra dictionem grecam collocare. Et ut prefatiuncule tandem huic modus imponatur: illud lectorem non lateat: non quevis

exemplaria

exemplaria impreſſioni huic archetypa fuiſſe ſed antiquiſſima emendatiſſimaque ac tante preterea vetuſtatis ut fidem eis abiogare nefas videatur. Que ſanctiſſimus in Chriſto Pater et Dominus noſter Leo *decimus* Pontifex maximus huic inſtituto favere cupiens apoſtolica Bibliotheca educta miſit ad Reverendiſſimum Dominum Cardinalem Hiſpanie: de cujus authoritate et mandato hoc opus imprimi fecimus. Vos autem litterarum ſtudioſi hoc divinum opus noviter excuſſum alacii animo ſuſcipite. et ſi Chriſti Opt. Max ſectatores videii vultis et eſſe nil jam ieſtat quod cauſemini quominus ſacram ſcripturam adeatis. Non mendoſa exemplaria · non ſuſpecte tranſlationes. non inopia textus originalis ſolùm animus et propenſio veſtia expectatui. Que ſi non defuerit: fiet piocul dubio ut litterarum divinarum ſuavitatem deguſtantes ieliqua ſtudia omnia contemnaris. Valete et omnia boni conſulite.

No. XVII.

Et quoniam videmui omne baptiſma ſpiritale *trifeiiam* diviſiſſe, veniamus etiam ad probationem narrationis piopoſitæ, ne videamur proprio ſenſu, et temere hoc fcciſſe. Ait enim *Joannes* de Domino noſtro in Epiſtola ſua nos docens, Hic eſt qui venit per aquam et ianguinem *Jeſus Chriſtus.* Non in aqua tantum, ſed in aqua et ſanguine. Et

Spiritus

Spiritus eft qui teftimonium perhibet, quia Spiritus eft veritas. Quia tres teftimonium perhibent, fpiritus, et aqua, et fanguis Et ifti tres in u-
num funt Ut ex illis colligamus, et aquam præftare
fpiritum folitum, et fanguinem proprium hominibus præftare Spiritum folitum, et ipfum quoque
Spiritum præftare Spiritum folitum Nam cum
effundatur aqua ficuti et fanguis, Spiritus etiam
effufus fit a Domino fuper omnes qui crediderunt,
utique et aqua, et proprio nihilominus fanguine,
tunc deinde et Spiritu fancto, poffunt homines bap-
tizari.

(Towards the end of the Treatife) Ex quibus univerfis oftenditur,—*Spiritu* ablui animas. Porro
per *aquam* lavacri, corpora. *Sanguine,* quoque,
feftinantius perveniri, per compendium, ad falutis
præmia.

      (Tractatus ignoti Auctoris, inter *Cypriani*
        Opera, falfo illi afcripta, p. 21, Edit.
        Oxon.)

No. XVIII.

Note, in the margin of the Complutenfian *Edition
of the New Teftament, referring to the fifth Chapter of the firft Epiftle of St.* John, *verfes* 7, *and* 8.

Sanctus *Thomas* in expofitione fecunde decretalis
                                   de

de fumma trinitate et fide catholica tractans iftum paffum contra abbatem *Joachim* viz Ties funt qui teftimonium dant in celo Patei · Verbum: Lt fpiritus fanctus . dicit ad litteiam veiba fequentia. " Et ad infinuandam unitatem trium per-
" fonarum fubditur Et hii tres unum funt. Quod
" quidem dicitur piopter effentie unitatem. Sed
" hoc *Joachim* perveife tiahere volens ad unita-
" tem charitatis et confenfus inducebat confe-
" quentem auctoiitatem. Nam fubditur ibidem :
" tres funt qui teftimonium dant in terra Spiritus :
" aqua. et fanguis. Et in quibufdam libris ad-
" ditur Et hi ties unum funt. Sed hoc in veiis
" exemplaribus non habetur : fed dicitur effe ap ·
" pofitum ab heieticis Ariianis ad pervertendum
" intellectum fanum auctoiitatis premiffe de uni ·
" tate effentie trium peifonaium." Hec beatus *Thomas* ubi fupia.

No. XIX.

A TABLE *of the MSS (accoiding to the account of* F. LE LONG) *made ufe of by* ROBERT STEPHENS *in his folio edition of the New Teftament.* 1550.

ɑ —— The, *Alcala* or *Complutenfian* edition ; containing all the New Teftament.

β —— The four Gofpels, and Acts of the Apoftles.

γ —— The

γ —— The four Gofpels, the King's MS No. 2867.

δ —— The New Teftament, excepting the Revelation, the King's MS No. 2871.

ε —— The New Teftament, excepting the Revelation, the King's MS. No 3425.

ϛ —— The four Gofpels.

ζ —— The four Gofpels, the Epiftles of St. *Paul*, St. *James*, St. *Peter*, and the firft of St. *John*, the King's MS No. 2242.

η —— The four Gofpels, the King's MS. No. 2361.

θ —— The New Teftament, excepting the Revelation.

ι —— The Acts and the Epiftles of the Apoftles, the King's MS. No. 2878.

ια —— The Acts and the Epiftles of the Apoftles.

ιβ —— The four Gofpels.

ιγ —— The Acts and the Epiftles of the Apoftles, except the third of St *John* and that of St. *Jude*.

ιδ —— The Gofpels of St. *Matthew*, St. *Luke*, and St. *John*.

ιε —— Seven Epiftles of St. *Paul*, beginning with the firft to the *Corinthians*, the King's MS.

ιϛ —— The Gofpels of St. *Luke* and St. *John*.

[*Emlyn's* Works, vol. II. *Lond.* edit. A. D. 1746, p. 283—4]

No. XX.

No. XX.

EXTRACT *from the words of* ERASMUS, *where he speaks of the* CODEX BRITANNICUS, *vol. X, p. 353*—Ed. LUGD. BATAV. A. D. 1706.

Veruntamen, ne quid diffimulem, repertus eft apud *Anglos Græcus* codex unus, in quo habetur quod in vulgatis deeft. Scriptum eft enim hunc ad modum, Οτὶ τρεις εισιν οι μαρτυρουντες εν τω κρανω Πατηρ, λογος, και Πνευμα, και ουτοι οι τρεις εν εισιν. Και τρεις εισιν μαρτυρουντες εν τη γη, πνευμα, υδωρ, και αιμα· ει την μαρτυριαν των ανθρωπων &c.—Quanquam haud fcio an cafu factum fit, ut hoc loco non repetatur, quod eft in Græcis noftris, και οι τρεις εις το εν εισιν. Ex hoc igitur codice Britannico repofuimus, quod in noftris dicebatur deeffe: ne cui fit caufa calumniandi —Quanquam & hunc fufpicor ad Latinorum codices fuiffe caftigatum.

No. XXI.

Ratio veræ Theologiæ, per Erafmum.—(Edit. *Le Clerc*, 1704, *vol. v. p.* 74—115.)

Quod apud *Joannem* capite duodecimo *Pharifæi* deftinant & *Lazarum* interficere: typum habet,

D quod

quod improbi non folùm oderunt *Chriftum* ipfum, fed eos quoque per quos *Chrifti* nomen illuftratur. Adnotandus eft apud eumdem circulus, in quo ferè fe volvit, ubique & focietatem & fœdus *Chriftianum* commendans : præfertim capite duodecimo, & decimo tertio, fe declarat idem effe cum Patre adeo ut qui Filium norit, norit & Patrem : qui Filium fpernat, fpernat & Patrem : nec feparatur ab hac communione Spiritus fanctus. Sic enim legis in Epiftola : *Tres funt qui teftimonium dant in cælo, Pater, Sermo, & Spiritus . atque hi tres unum funt.* In idem confortium trahit fuos, quos palmites appellat : obfecrans, ut quemadmodum ipfe idem erat cum Patre, ita & illi idem effent fecum. Impertit iifdem communem Patris fuumque Spiritum, omnia conciliantem.

XXII.

Hieron Opera, per *Erafmum*, Edit. *Paris.* vol. iv, A. D. 1546, p. 42, D.

Atque ut, confundentes *Arium*, unam eamdemque decimus Trinitatis effe fubftantiam, et unam in tribus perfonis fatemur Deum : ita impietatem *Sabellii* declinantes, tres perfonas expreffas fub proprietate diftinguimus.—Pater femper Pater eft, Filius femper Filius eft, Spiritus fanctus femper Spiritus fanctus eft Itaque fubftantia *unum funt.* Perfonis, ac nominibus diftinguuntur.

EXPLA-

EXPLANATIO FIDEI,—Ad *Cyrillum*: *Edit*. ERASMI, *vol. iv, p*. 43, K.

Nobis, igitur, unus Pater, et unus Filius verus Deus, et unus Spiritus fanctus verus Deus. ET HI TRES UNUM SUNT, una divinitas, et potentia, et regnum. Sunt autem *tres perfonæ*, non duæ, non una.

Auguft. in Epift. *Johan*. Cap. 5. Vol. 3. Edit. *Paris*. A. D. 1680, p. 896.

Et quid eft finis *Chriftus*? Quia *Chriftus* Deus, et finis præcepti caritas, et Deus caritas; quia *Pater, et Filius, et Spiritus fanctus, unum funt.*

AUGUSTINUS contra *Maximinum, Arianum*, Lib. 2. (Vol. VIII. p. 698.)

Tres enim perfonæ funt Pater, et Filius, et Spiritus fanctus: ET HI TRES (quia unius fubftantiæ funt) UNUM SUNT. Et fummè unum funt, ubi nulla naturarum, nulla eft diverfitas voluntatum.—HI, ergo, TRES QUI UNUM SUNT propter ineffabilem conjunctionem Deitatis, quâ ineffabilitèr copulantur, unus Deus eft.

No. XXIII.

GRATISSIMUM fane mihi fuiffet, vir plur. reverende,

ende, fi liteias Tuas ad GIBBONEM legere potuiffem,
quo melius ea Tecum communic rem, quæ præcipue fcire Tua intereit Libi s autem *Anglicanis*
plerumque ferò ad nos venentibus, harc quoque
difcuffionem eructam BEROLINI nuftra quæfivi.
Sec ut a lplomirus Tibi officium meum probem;
quæ ad lucem difquifitionibus Tuis affundendam
valere opinor, breviter ea commemorabo.

Locum 1 *Joan.* v. 7, diligentiffime delineavi,
ita ut literæ literis, lineæ lineis, accuratiffime
refponueant, cumque infra, de fimilitudine inter
Codicem Ravianum et editionem *Complutenfem* fermo
fit faciendus, et ex hac eundem locum depictum
cernis in fchedula hifce literis adjecta. Quod,
quidem, ad antiquitatem Codicis RAVIANI attinet,
vereor ut fufficiat, fi meam tantùm fententiam
Tecum communicare velim. Sunt enim tam
multa in *Germania* recentiffimis temporibus, hac
de ie, a viiis eruditiffimis difputata, ut meum non
fit inter criticos tantos tantas componere lites.
Malo igitui notatu digniffima, quantum in Epiftola, quæ in libri molem excrefcere non debet, fieri
poteft, afferre, et tum penes Te arbitrium efto.

Codex *Ravianus* duobus conftat voluminibus,
in membiana nitidiffime confcriptis. Nec fcribæ,
nec patriæ, nec æræ, ufpiam fit mentio. A capite
ad calcem cujufvis libri biblici (five evangelii five
epiftolæ) linea lineam excipit, nulla adjecta nota
capitum

capitum, aut commatum ςίχων, ρημάτων, &c —
Nullus invenitur accentus, fpiritus, &c —FRI-
DERICUS GUILELMUS, Elector *Brand* emit codicem
ducentis imperialibus à *Chriftiano Ravio*, qui per aliquod tempus in oriente vitam degerat, et pòft pro-
fefforis munere *Upfaliæ*, & denique *Francofurti*, cis
Viadrum functus eft. *Ravius* affirmat, fè hunc-
ce codicem, multis cum aliis (qui cum hoc bibli-
othecam Regis ornant) ex Oriente fecum afpor-
taffe, et non defuere, qui ei vetuſtatem quinque,
imò decem, feculorum tribuerent La *Croze* primus fuit, inter omnes, qui A D. 1696, Berolinum
profectus, codice infpecto palam afferavit ·
" *falfarii cujufdam froude pro antiquo venditum effe,*
" *manu verò recenti ex Editione* POLYGLOTTA COM-
" PLUTENSI *fuiffe defcriptum Qui, ait, codicem*
" *editum* Complutenfem *vidit, is vidit et manufcrip-*
" *tum Codicem noftrum, ne demtis quidem mendis ty-*
" *pographorum , quas fcriba indoctus ita fideliter ex-*
" *preffit, ut omnino conftet, hominem illiteratum ab eru-*
" *dito aliquo nebulone ei fraudi perficiendæ fuiffe præ-*
" *fectum.*" Et in hac quidem fententia permanfit
La Crozius, ex quo ipfe bibliotheca Regis credita
eft, id quod è *Thefauro epiftol. La Crozii* (Tom 1.
p. 63 Tom. III, 1 feqq.) fatis conftat.

Per longum temporis fpatium, multi (ne dicam
omnes) Critici inter *Germanos*, et *Batavos*, *La
Crozii* fententia freti, flocci fecere codicem noſ

tium,

trum; nec *Wetſtenius* eum dignum exiſtimavit qui valeret ad confirmandam lectionem aliquam variantem. Nec eſſe videbatur, cur *La Crozio* diffiderent. Bibliothecæ enim Regiæ præerat, habebat igitur copiam, pro lubitu, ſcrutandi;—vir erat eruditiſſimus, fidei *Nicænæ* addictus. Non defuere, tamen, qui *La Crozio* aſſentire dubitarent, id potiſſimum urgentes, eum nullo argumento ſententiam ſuam confirmaſſe, nec unicum unquam in medium protu tiſleſphalma typographicum, quod è *Polyglottis Compl.* in codicem *Ravianum* irrepſerit.

Novitas externa negari omnino non poteſt. Membrana admodum alba eſt; et ei adhuc calx, ſive creta, adhæret. Verum enim vero vix, ac ne vix quidem, exir de *fraudem* evinci poſſe, exiſtimo. Cicta, enim, quæ adhuc in membrana cernitur, ſai m a tempore, quo *Ravius* exemplar vendidit, uſque ad noſtram ætatem ſupereſt. Quid ni quod per ſeculum unum factum eſt, per duo, aut tria, ante hæc, fieri potuiſſet? Et dixerit forſan codicis *Raviani* fautor: ante *Ravium* illum non adeo multorum manibus eſſe verſatum, id quod ſufficiat ad ſplendorem novitatis ei ſervandam. Sun in bibliotheca Regis alii MSS (v. c *Suetonii*, 1472 ſcripti) qui majorem etiam præ ſe ferunt novitatis ſpeciem. Atramentum, quod a *La Cro-*

zio

zio albicans vocatur, jam non nisi *tenuotum* est, et vetustatis speciem habet Magnum quidem apparet discrimen inter atramentum, quod naturâ albicat, et quod vetustatis vi evanuit, sed quis nostrum hodie dignoscere potest, utrum atramentum codicis nostri, quod nunc serie annorum paliuisse videtur, tempore *La Crozii* eandem indolem habuerit, an nunc demum contraxerit? *Literæ* Codicis *Raviani* non congruunt MSS antiquioribus, contrà simillimæ sunt typis in Polyglottis *Complutensibus* Illud statim apparet: hoc vero in dubium vocari posset Magna omninò deprehenditur similitudo inter figuram literarum Codicis *Raviani*, et Polyglottorum *Complutensium* (si ab indole calamo pictarum et typis impressarum discesseris) nec tamen tanta, ut dici queat ad harum imitationem illas esse expressas. Quid? quod typi, qui *Alcalæ*, a Cardinali *Ximenio* parabantur, procul dubio ad exemplar MSS *Græcorum* (præcipue forsitan *Rhodii*) fusi sunt Quod si itaque Cod *Ravianus* congruat typis *Complutensibus*, nil probaret hæc similitudo, cur enim non respondeat figura literarum unius MS *Græci* literis alterius, et cur igitur non congruat *Ravianus* Codex *Rhodio*, vel alio archetypo, ad cujus similitudinem typi *Complutenses* fusi esse possunt? Id tamen manifestum est, ductum literarum Codicis *Raviani* non attingere secula ante xv; nec id silentio præcereundum puto, primas paginas magis

anxiè

anxiè effe delineatas, in fequentibus vero agiliorem, expeditioremque manum apparere : ex quo forfan colligi poffet opus effe hominis ducendarum literarum non adeo gnari.

Quod *La Crozius* fimpliciter dicit, fcribam indoctum etiam mendas typograhicas expreffiffe, ut omnino conftet, &c.—id quidem nimis feftinanter ab illo dictum eft. Codex Ravianus a textu *Complutenfium* INNUMERIS LOCIS difcrepat. In folo Evangelio *Matthæi*, præter ea quæ abfque dubio lapfus fcribentis funt, 50 lectiones variantes inveniuntur, quibus Codex *Ravianus* ab editione *Complutenfi* difcedit, quarum notatu digniffimæ funt. *Matth* 11 · 13, Editio *Complutenfis* legit απο-λειται *Ravianus* contrà αποκλειψαι. XV. 22 *Complutenfis* εκραυγασεν αυτω *Ravianus* εκραξεν οπισω αυτε XVI: *Complutenfs* ωφελειται, *Ravianus* ωφεληθησεται —XVII: 2, *Complute ifis* ως το φως *Ravianus* ως χιων XXIII: 8, *Complutenfis* κατηγητης *Ravianus* διδασκαλος—Cap. ix 30, *Ravianus* poft ανεωχθησαν αυτων addit παραχρημα—XI. 21, poft ςποδω addit *Ravianus* καθημεναι— xiii 4, poft τα πετεινα *Ravianus* addit τε ερανε —I *Joan* V: 10, *Complutenfis* legit θεω *Ravianus* υιω—*Judæ*, 22, *Complutenfis* ελεειτε διαρρινομενοι, *Ravianus* ελεγχετε διακρινομενες. Sufficiant hæc. fatis, enim, fuperque, demonftrant fcribam non literarum *Græcarum* rudem fuiffe.

Nec id flocci faciendum eft, omnes iftos va-

variantes

riantes lectiones uno vel altero MS confirmari, id
quod noftris temporibus poft *Millii*, *Wetßenii*, ali-
orumque recenfiones textus *Græci*, nihil probaret,
fed ante centum, et quod excurrit, annos haud fa-
cile a falfario quovis perfici poterat.

Attamen qui omnem lapidem movere vellet, ei
omnes loci, quibus codex *Ravianus* a *Complutenfi*
difcedit, diligenter colligendi effent, ut inde perf-
piceret an variantes lectiones ex *editionibus princi-*
pibus, quarum XIX forte conferendi copia fuiffet
falfario, hauriri potuerint Qui fententiæ *La*
Crozii favent, id inter alia potiffimum urgent, 1.
Joan. v 4, in codice *Raviani* deeffe verba και αυτη
—τον κοσμον, quæ in Polygl *Complutenfi* integram,
et quidem unicam lineam complent. '' En'' (ait
auctor quidam in *Collectionibus Halenfibus ad promo-*
vendam eruditionem theologicam, quas *Semlerus* edidit)
'' fcriba tranfilit lineam, neceffe igitur eft, ut
'' nec plura, nec pauciora, omitteret, quam quæ
'' in *una* lineola comprehenduntur ?''—Fateor
mihi ipfi hoc argumentum validiffimum vifum
fuiffe. Ex quo vero curiofius textum examinavi,
ftatim deprehendi ομοιοτελευτα induxiffe fcribam.
Bis enim in eodem commate occurrit κοσμον , et
cafu factum effe poteft, ut quæ a κοσμον priori ad
κοσμον fecundum fequuntur, in editione *Complutenfi*
lineolam compleant. Et in epiftola *Judæ*, v. 15,
omifit fcriba codicis *Raviani* fex verba (περι παντων
των εργων αβεβειας αυτων) quæ in textu *Complutenfi*

non

non una lineola comprehenduntur, sed aperte *homoioteleutis* seductus, omisit quæ duo ista αυτων interiarent.

Lectiones, quæ singulares vocantur, codici *Raviano* cum Polyglottis *Complutensibus* communes esse innumeras, vix est quod memorem. Nihil vero exinde colligendum esse mihi quidem videtur, nisi quod codex noster eidem familiæ sit annumerandus, cui is, ex quo *Complutenses* editores potissimum textum suum hauserint. Majus faciunt momentum mendæ typographorum, quæ in Polyglottis *Complutensibus* leguntur, quæque suspicantur, ex his in codicem nostrum esse transcriptas. Ita, videlicet, in *Raviano*, æque ac in editione *Complutensi*, exaratum est: *Matt* XXII. 19, προυηνεγκαν—*Galat* III. 19, διαταγεισα—*Act.* XXV: 19, δυσειδαιμονιας—I *Joan* I · 6, ψευδωμεθα—I. *Joan.* II: 27, αρισμα διδασκη—Cap III: 2, ομοιοι—*Apocal.* II. 17, λευον, &c.

Quid? quod in rebus minutissimis nonnunquam mirabilis consensus servatur inter MS nostrum, et editionem impressam; ambo, exempli gratia, I. *Joan.* II: 22, ειμη — Cap III: διατουτο— *Apocal.* II: 2, ημη junctim exhibent —*Act* VII. 20, 22, 29, seq ubi *Complutensia* Μωσης, et Μουσης, legendo alternant, et Codex *Ravianus* iisdem vicibus ponit, et omittit, το υ, et quæ ejusmodi sunt reliqua'

reliqua !—Nec tamen hic elabendi rima codicis *Raviani* defenſoribus deeſt. Dicere enim poſſent : ſine dubio editores *Complutenſes* quendam MS (fortaſſe *Rhodium*) fideliter deſcribendam curarunt, et poſt variantes lectiones è MSS aliis collectas, quas e re ſua arbitrabantur, inſeruerunt, parum attenti ad lapſus librarii, quo utebantur, non ſolúm repetierat, ſed et hic illic incurius auxerat. (ex. *Millius* in proleg § 1091 ſeqq.) Id ſaltem manifeſtum eſt, perverſarum lectionum, quæ plerumque ſphalmata typographica nuncupantúr, nonnullas editorum potius, ſive incuriæ, ſive imperitiæ, quam typographo eſſe tribuendas, quum eædem in Lexico repetantur ; ſic circa αφειδησαν, *Rom.* iv. (pro quo Codex *Ravianus* exhibet αφεθησαν) 1 *Cor.* iv. 11, γομυιτευομεν (quod et codex *Ravianus* legit) in lexico quoque chorda oberrant eadem.

Quæ cum ita ſint, haud abſonum foret, ſi cui placeret, *codicem noſtrum apographum eſſe,* NON *e* *Complutenſibus, ſed ex* ALIO MS, *quem editores* Complutenſes *potiſſimùm ſecuti ſint, concinnatum.*

Cupidiſſimus ſum literas Tuas ad *Gibbonem* legendi, et me tibi devinctiſſimum reddes, novæ editionis exemplar mecum communicando. Poſt *Wetſtenium,* enim, in *Germania* tot Critici, præcipue *Semlerus, Michaelis,* et MoſQuæ *Matthei* (qui decem omnino codices primum examinavit) aliique,

que, γνησιοτη-ἁ lectionis 1 *Joann* v: 7, oppug-
nârunt,—ut jam statione decessisse videantur dicti
illius propugnatores.

Vale. Scribo *Berolini*, xxv Martii,

MDCCLXXXV

J. F. ZOELLNER.

No. XXIV.

GENNADII *Patriarchæ* CONSTANTINOP. *Expositio
pro Concilio* FLORENT. *Cap.* 1 *Sect* v. (*Vide
Max. Bibl. Patr. Edit.* LUGDUNI, *A. D.* 1677.
Vol xxvi, *p.* 566.)

Accedat, igitur, veritatis præco, et confessor
magnus, cælebris *Athanasius*, ut mecum eadem tes-
tificetur Hic, enim, in confessione suæ fidei,
cujus principium, " Quicunque vult salvus esse,
" ante omnia opus est, ut teneat Catholicam fi-
" dem," sic inquit *Spiritus sanctus, a Patre, et
Filio, non factus, nec creatus, nec genitus, sed procedens*——Cum in hunc locum pervenerim, su-
biit mihi vehementèr flere, et in vocem pro-
rumpere cum lacrymis, et ejulatu, et eos deplo-
rare, qui sponte sua adversus lucem oculos occlu-
dunt, et veritati oppugnant, nec solum veritati
contradicunt, verùm etiam sanctos eccleiæ doctores aspernantur, neque aspernantur solùm, sed
etiam injuria afficiunt. Quamnam defensionem,

vel

vel commiserationem invenient, qui hæc faciunt ?
O tuam patientiam, CHRISTE *Rex* quomodo blaf-
phemantium ora non comburuntur ATHANA-
SIUM *dicere non verentur ebrium fuisse, et vino op-*
pletum, quando hæc scripsit. Verè plenus erat
spiritualis poculi, sapientiæ, et gratæ ex Spiritus
sancti fonte scaturientis, non ut hi, miserabiles,
dicunt. Propitius sit illis Dominus, ac nobis.
Tollatur ab eis hæc imprudentia, nobisque contingat sub Athanasii pedibus consistere !

F I N I S.

E R R A T A.

For " MSS"	page 9,	line 4,	Read *MS*
— " correct"	— 18	— 8	—— *collect*
— " little more"	— 38	— 28	—— *somewhat less*
— " them"	— 180	— 28	—— *those MSS*
— " prophane"	— 329	— 25	—— *profane.*
After " parts"	— 55	— 30	Add *of*
— " to"	— 94	— 8	—— *some, at least, of*
— " Remigius"	— 218	— 17	—— BEDE
— " 337"	— 240	— 13	—— *Be that, however,* *as it may, the*
— " from"	— 263	— 10	—— *nearly*
— " and"	— 296	— 19	—— *when*
— " verse"	— ——	— 21	—— *they*
In page	— 19	— 9	Dele *it.*

INDEX.

Lightning Source UK Ltd.
Milton Keynes UK
UKHW032144061218
333598UK00006B/280/P